Rhetoric, Politics and Society

Series Editors

Alan Finlayson
University of East Anglia
United Kingdom

James Martin
Goldsmiths, University of London
United Kingdom

Kendall Phillips
University of Syracuse
USA

Rhetoric lies at the intersection of a variety of disciplinary approaches and methods, drawing upon the study of language, history, culture and philosophy to understand the persuasive aspects of communication in all its modes: spoken, written, argued, depicted and performed. This series presents the best international research in rhetoric that develops and exemplifies the multifaceted and cross-disciplinary exploration of practices of persuasion and communication. It seeks to publish texts that openly explore and expand rhetorical knowledge and enquiry, be it in the form of historical scholarship, theoretical analysis or contemporary cultural and political critique. The editors welcome proposals for monographs that explore contemporary rhetorical forms, rhetorical theories and thinkers, and rhetorical themes inside and across disciplinary boundaries. For informal enquiries, questions, as well as submitting proposals, please contact the editors: Alan Finlayson: a.finlayson@uea.ac.uk James Martin: j.martin@gold.ac.uk Kendall Phillips: kphillip@syr.edu

More information about this series at
http://www.springer.com/series/14497

Kim Hong Nguyen
Editor

Rhetoric in Neoliberalism

Editor
Kim Hong Nguyen
University of Waterloo
Canada

Rhetoric, Politics and Society
ISBN 978-3-319-39849-5   ISBN 978-3-319-39850-1 (eBook)
DOI 10.1007/978-3-319-39850-1

Library of Congress Control Number: 2016957369

© The Editor(s) (if applicable) and The Author(s) 2017
This work is subject to copyright. All rights are solely and exclusively licensed by the Publisher, whether the whole or part of the material is concerned, specifically the rights of translation, reprinting, reuse of illustrations, recitation, broadcasting, reproduction on microfilms or in any other physical way, and transmission or information storage and retrieval, electronic adaptation, computer software, or by similar or dissimilar methodology now known or hereafter developed.
The use of general descriptive names, registered names, trademarks, service marks, etc. in this publication does not imply, even in the absence of a specific statement, that such names are exempt from the relevant protective laws and regulations and therefore free for general use. The publisher, the authors and the editors are safe to assume that the advice and information in this book are believed to be true and accurate at the date of publication. Neither the publisher nor the authors or the editors give a warranty, express or implied, with respect to the material contained herein or for any errors or omissions that may have been made.

Cover illustration: © age fotostock / Alamy Stock Photo

Printed on acid-free paper

This Palgrave Macmillan imprint is published by Springer Nature
The registered company is Springer International Publishing AG
The registered company address is: Gewerbestrasse 11, 6330 Cham, Switzerland

To my parents whose love and care for my being has been hegemonically framed by neoliberalism but will always exceed it.

Acknowledgments

There is talk of a decline in philoxenia or love of strangers. But, the folks, some of whom did not know me until this project, illustrate otherwise. I want to begin by thanking Gerald Voorhees, who was the first to listen to the idea, learn and advise on its progress, and contributed significantly to the intellectual rigor and process of the project. In the spirit of scholarly exchange and to check my own editorship, I asked several colleagues to review the abstracts and essays for the volume or otherwise sought their expertise: Cathy Chaput, Frankie Condon, Rob Danisch, Bill Herman, Shana MacDonald, Jennifer Simpson, Brad Vivian, Gerald Voorhees, and Vershawn Young. They helped me make tough choices, advise the authors, think critically about various aspects of our scholarly enterprise and the genre of anthologies, and shared their knowledge and experience in editing. As a good neoliberal subject, I would have wanted to speed up the writing and publishing process to add another line to my CV. They helped me stay focused on the quality of this project. A first-time sole editorship would not have been possible without their honest guidance and thoughtful work. Thank you.

Of course, it should go without saying, but worth more than the mention here that I am thankful to my professors who have helped me get here: my undergraduate advisors who to this day still care about my success and overall well-being, E. James Baesler and Thomas Socha; my dissertation director and advisor whose lessons about argument, rhetoric, and the role of the intellectual continue to shape my work, Bruce E. Gronbeck; my dissertation committee whose lectures and scholarship guide my thinking: David Depew, Barbara Biesecker, Gail Boldt, and David Hingstman.

Finally, I want to thank my parents, Hung and Dam; my siblings, Ann, Hoi, Hiep, Phuong, Tho, Thuy, Kieu, Hien, Hoa, Han, and Huynh; and my daughter, Quinn. They all provided me with ways of reasoning, thinking, and being about the world that my American education struggles to comprehend. May this project be defined by that struggle.

Contents

1 Rhetoric in Neoliberalism   1
Kim Hong Nguyen

2 Accountable to Whom? The Rhetorical Circulation of Neoliberal Discourse and Its Ambient Effects on Higher Education   15
Phillip Goodwin, Katrina Miller, and Catherine Chaput

3 Warren Buffett's Celebrity, Epideictic Ethos, and Neoliberal Humanitarianism   39
Mark Meister and Carrie Anne Platt

4 Rhetorical Agency in a Neoliberal Age: Foucault, Power, Agency, and Ethos   63
Robert Danisch

5 The Capable American: Ethos, Pathos, and the Governance of Education   87
Samuel M. Jay

6 Constitutive Rhetoric in the Age of Neoliberalism   109
David W. Seitz and Amanda Berardi Tennant

7	Branding Citizens: The Logic(s) of a Few Bad Apples Jennifer Wingard	135
8	The Psychotic Discourse of 9/11 Truth Jodi Dean	157
9	Computational Culture and the New Platonism in Neoliberal Rhetoric Gerald Voorhees	189

Afterword 209
Bradford Vivian

References 221

Index 225

Rhetoric in Neoliberalism

Kim Hong Nguyen

There is a growing concern in the discipline of rhetorical studies about the credibility and public relevance of speech. Kathleen Hall Jamieson (1988) documents the decline in television coverage and newspaper reprinting of political speeches and the significant reduction in traditional forms of deliberation in favor of public discourse that is conversational and organized by personal narrative. Sharon Crowley and Debra Hawhee (2009) argue that the modern view of rhetoric as a form of manipulation is a key indication of the diminishing credibility of speech. Crowley and Hawhee and Jamieson all contrast this modern view of public speech to that of ancient Greco rhetorical values of copia, rhetorical invention, and altruistic citizenship in order to show that modern public speech has become increasingly functional and efficient, aimed at communicating as clearly as possible with the least number of words. Walter Ong (1982) describes how literate culture abstracts knowledge from the context in which and by whom it is produced, leading to neutral and abridged discursive formats like lists, statistics, facts, and how-to manuals. Bradford Vivian (2006) attributes the privileging of quotes that function as sound bites and other economical communicative practices to neoliberalism as a structural enterprise for media and cultural industries and as an ideology that promotes

K. Hong Nguyen (✉)
Speech Communication, University of Waterloo, Waterloo, ON, Canada

efficiency. Megan Foley (2012) argues that the circulation of sound bites is not indicative of a decline but rather demonstrates audience attachment to public speech in another truncated form. Whether economization is a symptom of speech's decline or rise, discourse in the contemporary era must be evaluated using new interpretative heuristics and ways of knowing to understand its value, effect, and magnitude.

Each of the essay writers in this volume contend with contemporary discourse's efficacy and effectiveness by contextualizing and analyzing rhetoric in light of neoliberal governmentality and hegemony. The chapters in this collection illustrate that anxiety about speech in its modern forms takes place within a politically fractious scene of self-interested agents: words, phrases, and beats are copyrighted and protected by intellectual property law for entrepreneurs and corporations, further diminishing the "cultural commons" (McLeod 2001). American Tea Party candidates often speak without regard to history, facts, and other commonly agreed upon notions of truth. The documentary *The Corporation* (2003) discusses a landmark case that involved silencing two Fox News journalists exposing the health risks in consuming milk produced by Monsanto. The Bush administration was not held accountable for lying about weapons of mass destruction in Iraq and other crucial details that brought about the post-9/11 War on Terror and on Iraq. Occupy Wall Street protests struggled to carve out a space for vocalizing dissent against corporate stakeholders in debt creation and governmental bailouts. Justice for Trayvon Martin, Afghan civilians, and for so many others is on the horizon in our permanent state of exception. It is common parlance to both watch and dismiss advertisements, talk shows, and even the news and governmental discourse as tools of misinformation and propaganda. An "irony bribe," as Dana Cloud (2010) puts it in relation to reality television, describes how audiences employ their skills at media literacy about authenticity and conventional narratives to accept the fiction of reality television. Jodi Dean analyzes this phenomenon about the proliferation of all sorts of discourse as communicative capitalism: "Facts, theories, judgments, opinions, fantasies, jokes, lies—they all circulate indiscriminately" (2014, 153). While the believability of discourse might be a concern as old as Plato's cave, neoliberalism has fundamentally changed cultural literacy putting the individual ego and self-interest (and not the public good or collective or communal interest) at the center of sense-making and at the center of justice.

Once theorized as an economic policy, neoliberalism has pervaded almost all spheres of our cultural landscape. In neoliberalism, workers equipped with smartphones, elevator pitches, and business cards are obliged to be flexible to meet the increasing demands of the workplace. Sheryl Sandberg's Lean In Movement and professional advice that reconceives work as monetizing one's passion naturalize the commitment to work as a private endeavor. With the prospect of having to self-manage and provide for themselves, students are compelled to think about their education as preparation for the world of business and profit, take on unpaid internships for lines on their CVs, and build friendships with those who fortify their networking potential. Parents are pressured to make choices about children's diet, activities, and home environment to maximize language acquisition and to ensure their children's future success. Toys from Baby Einstein and Leap Frog, parenting magazines and memoirs like *Battle Hymn of a Tiger Mom*, and the rise of intensive mothering are indicative of the ever-conscious production of the neoliberal child-subject.

While CEOs and business entrepreneurs of new start-up ventures are celebrated as modern heroes saving companies from the recession's downward spiral and making a profit-making business from nothing, the cultural values of neoliberalism have material impact. Public funds have been both reduced and shifted toward subsidizing and increasing corporate ventures and profits. The public good both conceptually and materially has diminished over time. Recent news stories testify to the effects of neoliberalism on subjects. Shanesha Taylor went on the Today Show to explain her "moment of desperation" for leaving her two children in her car while she went to an interview in Scottsdale, Arizona (Kim 2014). Angel Henderson of Acworth, Georgia was arrested after she left her two children in a locked bedroom so that she could go to work (Shaw 2014). Moritz Erhardt, a 21-year-old intern with a history of epilepsy, died after working all night for several nights in a row at Bank of America's investment banking division in London (Kennedy 2013). Concerns over population growth in Japan increase as young generations claim to care more about work and friends (Buerk 2011; Haworth 2013). Movie star Gabrielle Union summed up her fertility struggle: "The penance for being a career woman is barrenness" ("Gabrielle Union" 2015). Intense demands on one's health, family, and community are reasoned as normalized consequences of professional advancement and progress.

As a political rationality that advances competition as its primary guiding principle and the "free market" as less expensive, less restrictive, and more efficient than the public sector, neoliberalism emphasizes the individual responsibility, privatization, and deregulation as good sources for decision-making and judgment. Pierre Dardot and Christian Laval define neoliberalism as "the set of discourses, practices, and apparatuses that determine a new mode of government of human beings in accordance with the universal principle of competition" (2013, 4). Neoliberalism is premised upon capital as essential to the biopolitical production of life and thus, the acceptance and adoption of capitalism's values, tenets, and logics permeate political, juridical, legal, social, and cultural realms of life. Dardot and Laval go on to explain that neoliberalism is markedly different from capitalism: "Neoliberalism is the *rationality of contemporary capitalism*—a capitalism freed of its archaic references and fully acknowledged as a historical construct and general norm of existence" (italics in original 4). Capitalism as an economic system of power and the vocabulary that names its entailments are so embedded and diffused in modern everyday life that publicly naming capitalism and its practices, differentiating the proletarian from the bourgeoisie can seem like unproductive and pessimistic modes of self-presentation, regulation, and adjustment. At one level, there is an acknowledged ignorance that encourages subjects to do the work of capitalism without being thoughtful, overthinking, or critically engaging that work. At another level, there is a pernicious disavowal of intent that enables biopolitical production of life to become the primary alibi for the drive of capital. As Wendy Brown astutely explains, "[N]eoliberalism can become dominant as governmentality without being dominant as ideology" (2005, 49). Neoliberalism produces a subject that participates in ways of thinking and acting that are in accordance to capitalist structures without having to evaluate how their thinking and actions compete or contradict other ideologies they may have.

Michel Foucault called the neoliberal subject, *homo economicus*, to delineate how subjects are expected to perceive, think, and act using economized/economizing logics and rationalities in neoliberalism. As he once argued in 1979, "*Homo economicus* is an entrepreneur, an entrepreneur of himself" (Foucault 2008, 226). The subject of economic interest or, *homo economicus*, is encouraged to calculate and balance their decisions and actions in relation to the maintenance and advancement of their self-interest and self-governance. As Lois McNay explains, "The autonomous citizen is s/he who manages these diverse networks—work, household, pension, insurance, private property—in the most responsible and prudent fashion vis-à-vis the avoidance of risk and the maximization of their own happiness" (2009, 61). "Sharing" enterprises like monetizing housing, vehicles, and other properties when not in use, locating strategies that not only maintain one's job but also advance one's prospect of promotion, using social media during off-work hours for further staging the professional self, and marketing all aspects of one's life as a lifestyle brand on blog sites (e.g. Gwyneth Paltrow's Goop and Blake Lively's Preserve)—all of these once-scrupulous or self-absorbed practices are now-conventional and acceptable habits of everyday life in neoliberalism. An entrepreneur of every aspect of his or her life, the subject of neoliberalism is encouraged to generate "a relationship of the subject to him- or herself as 'human capital' to be infinitely increased—that is, a value to be ever further valorized" (Dardot and Laval 2013, 15).

This conception of the neoliberal subject is distinct from the subject of right theorized by Jean-Jacques Rousseau and others. Through allegiance to the sovereign or state, the subject of right gained privileges, such as protection of person and property and movement within sovereign borders, by relinquishing natural freedoms that benefited solely his or her own self-interest. In return, the subject of right is expected to support sovereign, governmental, or communal interests, whose interference and role aimed to ensure equal liberties for all. Rousseau writes, "What man loses by the social contract is his natural freedom and an unlimited right to everything that tempts him and that he can get; what he gains is civil freedom and the proprietorship of everything he possesses" (1978, 56). In recognizing that the sovereign seeks to satisfy equally the needs of all subjects, the subject of right "respects not so much what belongs to others as what does not belong to oneself" (Rousseau 1978, 57). While the subject of right conducted him or herself in mutually coexistence with the sovereign and state, the subject of interest represents, according to Foucault, "an essential, fundamental, and major incapacity of the sovereign" (2008, 292). In other words, the economic subject is compelled to think and act in accordance to his or her own self-interest. Self-interest in neoliberalism functions productively to encourage subjects to adapt, modify, and improve themselves. Such self-improvement and self-government operates to the benefit of all to the degree that neoliberalism has created the conditions of possibility for each subject to live up to his or her own potential and "for the interplay of their rivalry to satisfy the collective interest" (Dardot and Laval 2013, 47). This "collective interest" is satisfied by way of individual pursuit of the economized capacity made possible through neoliberalism. To wit, whereas a subject of right accepts that their right to resources "is always subordinate to the community's right to all" (Rousseau 1978, 58), the subject of interest can not only act patriotically by virtue of their economic participation and pursuit in securing their own self-interest but also that right to do so is now the primary condition for the survival of neoliberal governmentality. As President George W. Bush called upon Americans in his first speech following the 9/11 attacks, "I ask your continued participation and confidence in the American economy" (President Bush 2001, np).

This conception of the neoliberal subject is different from the subject of capitalism theorized by Adam Smith,[1] Friedrich Hayek, Milton Friedman, and others. While the differences between their philosophies of economics are worth exploring, the subject of capitalism creates an external product, improves the process of production, and shows mastery of skill in the creation of that external product. This adaptation and improvement of the product in accordance to surrounding market conditions by the subject of capitalism is part of the means of production and is largely contained to the realm of the factory or workplace. Whereas the subject of capitalism might consult books and websites on their craft and area of expertise, the subject of neoliberalism might consult blog sites, such as Lifehacker. com, and apps, like Evernote, that make more efficient and simplify their lifestyle for enhanced mood, well-being, and productivity. Tips on how to better fit more leisure time in a day and get deeper rest at night, whether tycoons work on weekends and prefer yoga for exercise, and the shopping habits and brand loyalties of celebrities and other popular figures make intelligible "the good life" for that which the economic subject is expected to strive. Governed by neoliberal rationality, the subject learns to maximize his/her self as a worker, as the very product that is to be produced, improved upon, and championed.

The subject of capitalism is taken up by rhetorical critics Deidre McCloskey, James Aune, and others. In these studies, the market is represented as a closed, independent system outside of political and social relations. McCloskey's project known as the rhetoric of economics sought to analyze how rhetoric was instrumental in producing economic philosophy and knowledge. Like McCloskey, Aune (2001) uses rhetorical criticism to analyze economics, but with the difference that Marxism informs and motivates his critique. According to Catherine Chaput and Joshua Hanan, "Because both [McCloskey and Aune] understand rhetoric as a representational expression of a more primordial economic reality, power negotiation becomes confined to discovering the language that correctly describes economics as an a-priori condition" (2014, 2). These studies presuppose the economy as a separate, a priori domain of life that influences the ways in which rhetoric is understood, made, and taken up. Trapped in a logic of influence, discourse in McCloskey's and Aune's understanding is both analyzed and judged in relation to a narrow notion of agency as political communication. In Aune's Marxist work, power is conceived as a repressive force, and the subject's agency is understood as correcting false consciousness through demystification and increased knowledge of capitalist structures. Thus, although the subject of capitalism is obliged to work for another's profit, he or she can realize their full potential and agency against capitalism via tactics of resistance to economic oppression. Chaput and Hanan argue that this mode of critique is also related to a common (and incomplete) interpretation of Foucault's understanding of discourse and power: That the role of discourse is hermeneutic and limited to improving our scholarly task at producing knowledge about power relations (2014, 4).

In contrast, understanding power as productive, rhetorical studies of neoliberalism examine how the very understanding of the economy as a distinct, a priori sphere itself is a kind of discourse and discursive move. Thus, rhetoric is not seen as a mere interpretative tool through which meaning-making is achieved, but rather as the very mode and organizing principle that circulates power relations, valuations, and logics. This crucial difference is missed, according to Ronald Greene, when rhetorical scholars focus on discursive forms without regard to the changes in capitalist production, including the role of affective and biopolitical labor. Techne in neoliberalism is arrived at through economic taxis and through learning the ways in which economic taxonomies structure and orient human relations, knowledge, and power (Chaput and Hanan 2014). Arguing that rhetorical agency is communicative labor, Greene contends, "[T]he persuasive, aesthetic, and deliberative characteristics of communication… reside in the matrix of biopolitical production" (2004, 201). Rhetoric as circulation untangles subjects from rigid models of rhetorical agency that privilege commodity production and participation in civic speech, and shifts our attention as both critics and subjects toward communicative labor: "a form of life-affirming constitutive power that embodies creativity and cooperation" (Greene 2004, 201). Communicative labor helps rhetorical scholars better attend to how all subjects—not just the orators behind podia and microphones or the writers whose handwriting is transformed to typescript—participate in the production of power relations, regardless of whether their rhetorical acts are recorded and duplicated for newspaper headlines or spectatorship, and regardless of whether their rhetorical performances (intend to) impact political or economic relations.

Greene's notion of communicative labor extends the concept of affective labor described by Michael Hardt and Antonio Negri as "labor that produces or manipulates affects such as a feeling of ease, well-being, satisfaction, excitement, or passion" (2004, 108). They explain, "Affective labor is biopolitical production in that it directly produces social relationships and forms of life" (110). They rightly point out that this affective labor often falls primarily on the shoulders of women and minorities in service industries who are expected to do the work of relationship making, rapport producing, and reputation enhancing. Analyzing affective labor attends to the ways in which marginalized subjects are positioned and enabled to do the heavy lifting (both metaphorically and literally) of circulating power relations and amplifies how rhetorical agency cannot be simplified along the subordination/resistance binary or in connection to the realms of politics and economics.

However, Greene's communicative labor furthers Hardt and Negri's notion of affective labor. Decision-making processes are negotiated, communities are constituted, and logics are organized through rhetoric and communication practices. Traditional rhetorical scholars have reduced rhetoric (and rhetorical force) to the domain of public address in order to show how power subjugates and creates subjective compliance. In doing so, they not only discount agency but also ignore their disciplinary and intellectual connections within communication studies, which would invite consideration of interpersonal interactions, haptics, and other modes of communicative engagement. Communicative labor as a model of rhetorical agency discourages rhetorical scholars from uncritically continuing to examine the discourses of presidents, prime ministers, fascists, and social movement leaders as comprising the rhetorical canon. To locate how rhetoric gains salience between subjects in neoliberalism, Chaput (2010) advises tracking rhetorical circulation and force through repetition. While rhetorical studies is uniquely equipped to analyze neoliberalism as the rationality of modern-day capitalism, the study of rhetoric in its more quotidian forms and among marginalized subjects is long overdue but necessary in order to understand how rhetoric organizes everyday life in the neoliberal era.

This collection of essays takes these (and more) insights on materialist rhetoric as its point of departure in order to sketch out the changing contours of rhetorical theory and practice in the neoliberal era. Many scholars in the volume presume or explicitly take their cue from Foucault and other Foucauldian scholars in rhetorical studies, whose theorizations of neoliberal governmentality examine how modern subjects are no longer coerced but nevertheless compelled to take on values and logics that promote their own self-management and regulation. Rhetoric has not simply adapted to neoliberalism; rather, neoliberalism has irrevocably reshaped and continues to reshape cultural practices, discursive forms and styles, norms, and conceptions of agency. New and reconfigured vocabularies and languages, logics and rationalities, strategies and tactics have emerged in order to facilitate and challenge neoliberalism's penetration into various spaces. Television commercials and print advertisements tell stories of romance and seduction in abbreviated forms, language is shortened on Twitter and Facebook, speech instructors reduce speeches to minimal lengths of time for classrooms maxed out at an ever-increasing capacity, course assignments require writing that simulates the conciseness of the editorial form in lieu of the typical research paper—these are symptomatic of not just a significant change in literacy and interpretation about discourse but also a major shift at the intersection between discourse, the subject, and power.

This book examines the contemporary rhetorical production of *homo economicus* and the various ways in which neoliberalism has become a way of thinking, orienting, and organizing all aspects of life around economized metrics of individualized and individuated success. The essays that compose this collection consider questions that have long concerned our field with particular emphasis on our cultural milieu. We ask: How are we persuaded to act toward our own economic ends? What are the rhetorical argumentative styles, logics, practices, norms, and conceptions of agency that enable subjects to thrive and resist in a neoliberal era? What are the various rhetorical strategies that neoliberal subjects employ in order to make do, reinforce, and resist economic, social, and political competition? How can rhetorics constitute the desire for equality and justice among unequal populations during neoliberalism? How does rhetoric obscure, maintain, or challenge the ways in which democracy, various institutions, and aspects of our everyday life are recreated in accordance to economic logics and calculative reasoning toward profit?

While neoliberalism primarily has been discussed primarily in relation to economic policy, political philosophy and practices of governance, and linguistic changes reflecting neoliberal values, the essays within the collection explore rhetorical practices, discursive strategies, and cultural logics that make up neoliberalism. The education industry is central to producing subjects capable of adapting to a social and political order based on competition. Transparency and accountability are popularized values in neoliberalism that corporations and organizations use to promote an honest, democratic, and responsible image. This begs Hardt and Negri to ask "Accountable to Whom?" (2004, 290), a question that is also the title of Phillip Goodwin, Katrina Miller, and Catherine Chaput's analysis of university discourses and practices. They inaugurate our conversation with the term, ambient rhetoric, to describe how the environment of higher education is "felt" via a discourse that has no specific addressee, but nevertheless functions as a form of argumentation that shapes the way the subject's body and sensory modes feel and align with discourse. Using a cartographic methodology, Goodwin, Miller, and Chaput consider two case studies from California State University and State University of New York that show how universities participate in the circulation of neoliberal rhetoric through an array of strategies and practices that privilege the biopolitical health of the university over student and faculty concerns. Their essay demonstrates how a rhetorical circulation approach enables scholars and critics to problematize discourses that are not addressed to nor made accountable to anyone.

Blending aspects of rhetorical circulation and neoliberal epideictic, Mark Meister and Carrie Anne Platt ask how the ethos of a philanthropic figure helps prop up neoliberalism as a just system. They describe how Warren Buffett's personal thrifty practices and role as an investor mitigates his social and political advocacy for increased taxes for the wealthy. Their understanding of epideictic ethos captures how ethos is constructed in ways beyond the control of the speaker. At stake in neoliberal rhetoric, according to Meister and Platt, is the capacity to construct ethos. Building upon his work that suggests that Foucault's use of rhetoric and understanding of discourse operative in governmentality is epideictic, evokes a feeling of can-do-ness, and exaggerates the freedom of self-determination (2006), Robert Danisch also argues that ethos is central to the production and circulation of rhetoric. Danisch argues that the care of the self opens up the possibility for recognizing the difference between social imperatives and one's own conduct, which could be used to create new logics, practices, and patterns of conduct. To demonstrate how desire for self-care can function as the basis for relationality in neoliberalism, he examines what we might call a distributed network structure described by Hardt and Negri (2004, 86): Occupy Wall Street protests as a democratic organization with a decentralized hierarchical structure and communicative procedures.

While Danisch's analysis of Occupy Wall Street tethers Foucault's theory of power with a classical notion of the subject to delineate rhetorical agency, Samuel Jay introduces the notion of a "rhetoric of capacity" to highlight how neoliberal governance aims to create opportunities for economic subjects. In his analysis of the K-12 educational policy and discourses of the Obama administration, Race to the Top, Jay shows how the Obama administration used classical Aristotelian proofs, which situated Race to the Top within a history and grid of intelligibility of austere educational reform. Jay points to how instruction in neoliberal citizenship begins early, made possible by measurements of education quality that produce subjects that might maximize their "capacity." David Seitz and Amanda Tennant propose that Ranciere's political theory help account for the constitutive power of rhetoric to make and organize audiences that are subject to individualistic values in neoliberalism. They analyze the mediated attention around revitalization efforts of Braddock, Pennsylvania, and in particular, "the new Braddock worker" in order to consider how communicative practices premised on the notion of Ranciere's "count" illustrate "true democratic moments and change."

Recognizing how the "juridico-political order in neoliberalism is not independent of but belongs to the relations of production" (Dardot and Laval 2013, 10), Jennifer Wingard's application of rhetorical assemblage bears similarities to the rhetorical circulation model. In contrast to the enduring concept of ideograph, which describes how language repeats and circulates ideological and hegemonic values in political discourse (McGee 1980), a brand is Wingard's term for how language operates in all kinds of discourse in neoliberalism (Wingard 2013). She focuses on one particular brand for her analysis, "bad apple," which is a rhetorical figure through which neoliberal governmentality can "make live and let die" (Foucault 1997, 254) by assigning blame to individuals for violence that is both legal and exceptional. Wingard suggests that in the cases of George Zimmerman and Lt. Robert Bales, branding bodies as "bad apples" mobilize a neoliberal ethos that attributes violent action as individual choice, while protecting the state-sanctioned practices that enable violence.

Whereas Wingard follows Foucault's notion of power to make sense of transparency and exposing racism and the police state, Dean uses Lacanian psychoanalysis to argue that the production of violence (9/11) is staged for itself: a production of power for a new order. Psychotic discourse, Dean argues, promotes, and positions subjects as questioning truth-seekers unable to repress the fiction that makes the symbolic order work efficiently, effectively, and affectively. In communicative capitalism or how discourse that circulates and appears to be equal with all others gains value against other discourses, she suggests that new media and networked communications can be central to creating a new grid of intelligibility for subjects to learn about themselves, each other, to build community.

Finally, Gerald Voorhees argues that rhetorical circulation, value, and judgment in our contemporary milieu is made possible by a New Platonism, whereby subjects are encouraged to interpret and judge discourses that articulate an already circulating truth. Voorhees shows that computational culture functions as neoliberalism's "pretense" or heuristic that neoliberal values of quantification, economization, and maximization can be achieved.

This edited collection should illustrate a range of conceptual inquiries and insights the field of rhetorical theory and criticism can make about neoliberalism. Hopefully, this project shows the strength and significance of rhetorical studies to provide language and analytical structures about how discourse circulates in neoliberalism. These essays in rhetorical studies demonstrate a paradigm shift away from the sovereign, autonomous subject as the rational locus of discursive control and dissemination and toward the production of discourse as central to power's limits and possibilities in the creation of subjectivities, including the economic subject of neoliberalism. This paradigm shift points to the ways in which rhetorical studies is best equipped with recognizing, analyzing, and contending with neoliberalism as the rationality of contemporary capitalism.

Note

1. Although Adam Smith is often dubbed the father of modern capitalism and credited for illuminating the virtues of self-interest and the invisible hand of the market, David Depew (2011) shows how contemporary readings of Smith run against the historical grain of Smith's republicanism.

References

Achbar, Mark, Jennifer Abbot, and Joel Bakan, directors. 2003. *The Corporation*. Vancouver, BC: Big Picture Productions. Film.

Aune, James Arnt. 2001. *Selling the Free Market: The Rhetoric of Economic Correctness*. New York: Guilford Press.

Buerk, Roland. 2011. Japan singletons hit record high. *BBC,* November 28. http://www.bbc.com/news/world-asia-15915118. Accessed 8 Feb 2016.
Brown, Wendy. 2005. *Edgework: Critical Essays on Knowledge and Politics.* Princeton, NJ: Princeton University Press.
Cloud, Dana. 2010. The Irony Bribe and Reality Television: Investment and Detachment in The Bachelor. *Critical Studies in Media Communication* 27(5): 413–437. doi:10.1080/15295030903583572.
Chaput, Catherine. 2010. Rhetorical Circulation in Late Capitalism: Neoliberalism and the Overdetermination of Affective Energy. *Philosophy and Rhetoric* 43: 1–25. doi:10.1353/par.0.0047.
Chaput, Catherine, and Joshua S. Hanan. 2014. Economic Rhetoric as Taxis. *Journal of Cultural Economy* 8: 42–61. doi:10.1080/17530350.2014.942349.
Crowley, Sharon, and Debra Hawhee. 2009. *Ancient Rhetorics for Contemporary Students.* New York: Pearson Education.
Danisch, Robert. 2006. Power and the Celebration of the Self: Michel Foucault's Epideictic Rhetoric. *Southern Communication Journal* 71: 291–307. doi:10.1080/10417940600846078.
Dardot, Pierre, and Christian Laval. 2013. *The New Way of the World: On Neoliberal Society,* trans. Gregory Elliot. Brooklyn, OH: Verso.
Dean, Jodi. 2014. Communicative Capitalism: This Is What Democracy Looks Like. In *Communication and the Economy: History, Value and Agency,* eds. Joshua S. Hanan, and Mark Hayward, 147–164. New York: Peter Lang.
Depew, David. 2011. Adam Smith and Edmund Buke: Texts in Context. *POROI: An Interdisciplinary Journal of Rhetorical Analysis and Invention* 7(1): Article 4. doi:10.13008/2151-2957.1082.
Foley, Megan. 2012. Sound Bites: Rethinking the Circulation of Speech from Fragment to Fetish. *Rhetoric & Public Affairs* 15: 613–622. doi:10.1353/rap.2012.0052.
Foucault, Michel. 2008. *The Birth of Biopolitics: Lectures at the Collège de France, 1978–1979,* ed. Michel Senellart, trans. Graham Burchell. New York: Palgrave Macmillan.
———. 1997. *'Society Must Be Defended': Lectures at the College de France, 1975–1976.* New York: Picador.
Gabrielle Union. 2015. Penance for being a career woman is barrenness. *Toronto Sun,* September 15. http://www.torontosun.com/2015/09/15/gabrielle-union-penance-for-being-a-career-woman-is-barrenness. Accessed 8 Feb 2016.
Greene, Ronald Walter. 2004. Rhetoric and Capitalism: Rhetorical Agency as Communicative Labor. *Philosophy and Rhetoric* 37: 188–206. http://works.bepress.com/ronaldwaltergreene/10.
Hardt, Michael, and Antonio Negri. 2004. *Multitude: War and Democracy in the Age of Empire.* New York: The Penguin Press.

Haworth, Abigail. 2013. Why have young people in Japan stopped having sex? *The Guardian*, October 20. http://www.theguardian.com/world/2013/oct/20/young-people-japan-stopped-having-sex. Accessed 8 Feb 2016.

Jamieson, Kathleen Hall. 1988. *Eloquence in an Electronic Age: The Transformation of Political Speechmaking*. New York: Oxford University Press.

Kennedy, Maev. 2013. Bank intern Moritz Erhardt died from epileptic seizure, inquest told. *The Guardian*, November 22. http://www.theguardian.com/business/2013/nov/22/moritz-erhardt-merrill-lynch-intern-dead-inquest. Accessed 8 Feb 2016.

Kim, Eun Kyung. 2014. Shanesha Taylor opens up about leaving kids in car: It was a 'moment of desperation.' *The Grio*, July 25. http://thegrio.com/2014/07/25/shanesha-taylor-opens-up-about-leaving-kids-in-car-it-was-a-moment-of-desperation/. Accessed 8 Feb 2016.

McLeod, Kembrew. 2001. *Owning Culture: Authorship, Ownership, and Intellectual Property Law*. New York: Peter Lang.

McGee, Michael Calvin. 1980. The 'ideograph': A link between rhetoric and ideology. *Quarterly Journal of Speech* 66: 1–16. doi:10.1080/00335638009383499.

NcNay, Lois. 2009. Self as Enterprise: Dilemmas of Control and Resistance in Foucault's 'The Birth of Biopolitics.' *Theory Culture Society* 26: 55–77. doi:10.1177/0263276409347697.

Ong, Walter. 1982. *Orality and Literacy: The Technologizing of the Word*. London: Routledge.

President Bush Addresses the Nation. 2001. *WashingtonPost.com*, September 20. http://www.washingtonpost.com/wp-srv/nation/specials/attacked/transcripts/bushaddress_092001.html. Accessed 12 Feb 2016.

Rousseau, Jean-Jacques. 1978. *On the Social Contract: With Geneva Manuscript and Poltiical Economy*, ed. Roger Masters, trans. Judith Masters. Boston, MA: Bedford/St. Martin's.

Shaw, Michelle E. 2014. Acworth toddlers left home alone, mother arrested. *AJC*, January 10. http://www.ajc.com/news/news/acworth-toddlers-left-home-alone-mother-arrested/nchFm/. Accessed 8 Feb 2016.

Vivian, Bradford. 2006. Neoliberal Epideictic: Rhetorical Form and Commemorative Politics on September 11, 2002. *Quarterly Journal of Speech* 92: 1–26. doi:10.1080/00335630600687107.

Wingard, Jennifer. 2013. *Branded Bodies, Rhetoric, and the Neoliberal Nation-State*. Lanham, MD: Lexington Books.

Accountable to Whom? The Rhetorical Circulation of Neoliberal Discourse and Its Ambient Effects on Higher Education

Phillip Goodwin, Katrina Miller, and Catherine Chaput

Although criticism of the corporate university is at least a century old, its current variation focuses on the myriad ways that higher education aligns university practices with the logic of neoliberalism: the privatization of knowledge (Slaughter and Rhoades 2004), the casualization of academic labor (Bosquet 2008), the consumerization of education (Williams 2006, 2008), and, more recently, the student loan bubble (Goodnight et al. 2015).[1] These scholars paint a vivid picture of the university as a site of both profit-making and subject formation, using rhetorical investigations to underscore the university's economic interestedness and examine the constitutive role of its education. Because this critique relies on a politics of representation in which individual identities are fully formed, clearly attuned to their interests, and in visible struggle with other identity groups, it positions rhetoric as a tool to leverage educational power brokers. This alliance between rhetoric and democratic processes is second nature to many rhetoricians, and yet it has been complicated by those who view individual identity as unstable, interests as informed by unconscious motives, and the discursive terrain as uncontainable. Positioning oneself with this latter perspective requires, says Ronald Walter Greene, that we replace our long-held belief that rhetoric's power lies in its ability

---

P. Goodwin • K. Miller • C. Chaput (✉)
Department of English, University of Nevada Reno, Reno, NV, USA

to represent the world and our interests in that world with attention to how rhetorical practices distribute different elements "into a functioning network of power" (1998, 22). His alternative method, one indebted to a Foucauldian biopolitical analysis, asks critics to chart the circulation of rhetoric among divergent spaces that collectively govern individual and group practices.

Tracing this rhetorical circulation offers an important first step toward understanding the way neoliberalism operates within everyday practices and yet it necessitates a second step, one that explains how these different sites—institutional as well as informal and historical as well as contemporary—operate according to a diffuse biopolitical governing force. For, as Michel Foucault contends, the political economy of neoliberalism works hand in glove with biopolitics to maintain "power's hold over life" (2007, 239). In language reminiscent of Raymond Williams, he characterizes American neoliberalism as "a whole way of being and thinking" (Foucault 2008, 218); it is, he says, "a general style of thought, analysis, and imagination" (Foucault 2008, 219). Given Foucault's broad description of neoliberalism, it should not be surprising that he views biopolitics—its primary mode of power—as "an omnipresent government, a government which nothing escapes" (2008, 296). So conceived, the political economic terrain of neoliberalism requires an apparatus that regulates freely determined behavior in an ever-present but unobtrusive manner. It does so, in part, through the circulation of neoliberal commonplaces that have achieved the coveted status of common sense and thus have earned a golden pass: they need no author or credible source to certify their truth-value. This theory of biopolitics has important implications for rhetoric as it expands the persuasive function from deliberative address to everyday discourse, challenging rhetoricians to explain how neoliberal power exerts significant instrumentality with no apparent authorial subject to hold accountable.

Viewed from this perspective, neoliberalism and its biopolitical operations have insinuated themselves into what Thomas Rickert (2013) characterizes as an ambient rhetoric. The key feature of such rhetoric is its pervasive and generally camouflaged status. Ambient rhetoric bleeds into everyday life habits and, Rickert says, dissolves the Burkean separation between actively rhetorical behavior and purportedly passive actions. As he explains it, ambient rhetoric "gives rise to a discourse and withdraws from that discourse" (Rickert 2013, 63). This mode of rhetoric has no identifiable speaker and no specific audience; instead, it permeates an environment so that individuals absorb its messages much like we breathe air—instinctively and unconsciously. A widespread recognition of this rhetorical form exists both in and out of the field. Take, for example, Judith Butler's (2006) *Precarious Life,* a book dedicated to theorizing the regulation of what does and does not appear in the public sphere. Her final chapter illustrates the power of ambient rhetoric through a personal anecdote about the contemporary university. The story begins with Butler attending a meeting in which a university press director recalls a separate meeting with the University President at which the humanities were declared irrelevant. As the director spoke, it was unclear to Butler who asserted this reality; nevertheless, she says, it was presented as "a view to take seriously" (2006, 129). What, Butler wonders, is the rhetorical form of this call for accountability that has no authorial subject and replaces the object of its address with impersonal statistical data?

Our answer is that an ambient biopower serves as neoliberalism's primary rhetorical form. Biopolitics, perpetuated through everyday structures, thrives on a form of rhetorical address like the one described by Butler who explains that "although I did not know whose voice this person was speaking, whether it was his own or not, I did feel that I was being addressed" (2006, 129). Two things stand out in her description: first, there is no clear author for this form of rhetoric; and, second, it addresses its audience vis-à-vis the body and its sensory capacity. It is a form of argumentation one *feels* rather than logically derives. There is no identifiable rhetorical situation or argument to interrogate; instead, there are feelings aligned with claims that saturate environments. As contemporary neoliberalism increasingly functions through environments replete with such affective values, it becomes imperative to decipher its rhetorical modality.

Using Greene's (1998) cartographic methodology and a sensibility toward such ambient rhetoric, this chapter explores how the felt environment of education shifts from social justice to market considerations. The chapter proceeds in two parts: first, we track the rhetorical circulation of educational discourse through its historical formation and, second, we analyze the rhetorical form of this ambient rhetoric through two case studies. The history we outline is culled from deliberations about federally funded educational initiatives interwoven with popular discourse manifested in newspapers, magazines, and best-selling economic literature. The evolution of this conversation reveals a transition in the underlying warrant for education policies from the national social good to international market competition and a transformation of the recipients of this intervention from individuals with social needs to statistical populations with market needs—a hallmark of Foucauldian biopolitics. The case studies are drawn from the California State University (CSU) and the State University of New York (SUNY) systems of higher education as the two largest and most emulated models of higher education.[2] CSU's Mandatory Early Start Program (MESP) and SUNY's Strategic Plan, each of which launched in 2010, represent crucial neoliberal cases as both use impersonal statistics to assess and regulate student populations; both have been opposed by counterpublics that rely on the personalized value structures of specific faculty and student audiences; and, both reveal the limitations of resisting neoliberal assessment with traditional argumentation strategies. We end by advocating a rhetorical structure more capable of engaging the neoliberal terrain of higher education.

Educational Accountability: From the Great Society to the Neoliberal Marketplace

To track the reticulate nature of the assessment and accountability environment of higher education, we begin by exploring primary and secondary initiatives and their upward push on university practices. The 1965 Elementary and Secondary Education Act (ESEA) offers a useful starting point. This act, as President Johnson put it during the signing ceremony, represents "a major new commitment of the federal government to the quality and equality of education for all children" (1965). Commentary from the time suggests ESEA passed because of the autonomy it provided state and local school agencies to determine how best to use the funds, assuaging fears of government-controlled education. Most of the money was distributed in the form of grants directly to school districts serving students from low-income households ("The Head of the Class" 1965; "The Big Federal Move" 1965). ESEA not only preserved the rights of state and local agencies but, consonant with other post-World War II policies, used federal tax dollars to serve a Keynesian agenda of government spending as well as a social justice initiative intended to alleviate poverty. The overwhelming bi-partisan support for the bill—it passed the Senate 75-20 and the House 263-153—indicates that most members of Congress agreed that social welfare begets social justice and that government could indeed manufacture the Great Society through carefully placed resources (GovTrack n.d.).

For the next decade, belief in the importance of government spending to supplement private investment and promote economic mobility continued to be the motivating force behind policies of greater federal involvement in education. Republicans and Democrats alike embraced the idea of designing and funding educational policies to bolster the weakest members of society. Indeed, President Nixon followed Johnson's education agenda quite closely. While proposing the establishment of the National Institute of Education (NIE) Nixon coupled his arguments for implementing new measures of assessment, accountability, and research into student learning with calls to close the gap between poor students and their counterparts. NIE's purpose, Nixon said in an address to Congress, is "to begin the serious systematic search for new knowledge needed to make educational opportunity truly equal" (Nixon 1970). The oft repeated message in his address was that the federal government should "take the lead" in developing educational research in order to narrow the achievement gap (Nixon 1970). From Nixon's perspective, the goal of educational assessment was to provide research that would enable the government to better supplement the least successful schools in order to alleviate the economic consequences of low educational achievement. Both Johnson and Nixon, in no uncertain terms, asserted education as a vehicle for social mobility and economic equality.

Coming into office on the heels of roughly 40 years of such social welfare initiatives, President Reagan fundamentally shattered the commonplace belief that poor school performance stems from a lack of funding. Although he used the same underlying assumption as earlier legislation—these policies promote the social good—Reagan redefined the social good according to market principles and promoted the belief that any program interfering with free market competition hinders social justice. With wide endorsement of this neoliberal philosophy, Reagan deviated significantly from previous policies. The Omnibus Reconciliation Act of 1981, for example, affected over 250 programs through large-scale budget cuts to domestic spending and consolidated 77 categorical aid programs into block grants (Peters 1981; Darling-Hammond and Marks 1983). He justified dismantling grant and welfare programs by claiming that a decreased federal role in social policy would increase competition, which he linked with personal autonomy, efficiency, and the social good. Reagan summarized these efforts in his 1982 State of the Union Address in which he boasts that with "a single stroke we will be accomplishing a realignment that will end cumbersome administration and spiraling costs at the federal level while we ensure these programs will be more responsive to both the people they're meant to help and the people who pay for them" (Reagan 1982). Federal resources, because they are freely donated, decrease the incentive to put them to effectiveness use; if, however, such funding was not automatic but competitive, then the desire for those dollars would increase and educators would be driven to improve the quality of education. Thus, for Reagan, competition for scarce resources always improves the government dole.

Reagan built credibility for this marketization of social justice by attacking the ineffectiveness of government led social policies. A common theme found in many speeches during Reagan's early presidency was the failure of social welfare to adequately address the needs of those they were intended to help.[3] At a fundraising dinner in 1983, for instance, Reagan blamed Johnson's administration for the failing economy and high inflation; as he concluded, the "expansion of government programs that took place under the aegis of the Great Society coincided with an end to economic progress for America's poor" (Reagan 1983). In this rhetorical *coup d'état* Reagan derides the Great Society's desire to plan the alleviation of economic inequality, declaring, on the contrary, that the elimination of such state programming is the true act of social justice. The assertion of Johnson's failure essentially cleared a path for advancing market principles as an effective alternative to explicit social welfare initiatives—a neoliberal sentiment that was fast accruing support.

Among the more important popular treatises on neoliberalism was Milton Friedman's bestselling *Free to Choose* and its accompanying TV series, both of which came out in 1980 and transformed Friedman into a household name. Friedman advocated deregulating the private sector, dismantling welfare programs, and introducing market structures in all aspects of public life. The role of government, he taught, is to create conditions that promote voluntary exchange and thus allow individuals to act according to incentives and businesses to promote efficiency through competition (1980, 33–37). Consonant with his larger argument, Friedman called for bringing the market to bear on public schools. For him, education is no different than industry: "the difference is not between schooling and other activities, but between arrangements under which the consumer is free to choose and arrangements under which the producer is in the saddle" (Friedman 1980, 156). Friedman contends that in a bureaucracy, such as one finds in the growing federal government, power shifts from individuals to interest groups or, in the case of education, from teachers to administrators. Such bureaucratization denies parents control over the "kind of schooling their children receive" because "power has instead gravitated to professional educators" (Friedman 1980, 151–152). In short, bureaucracy creates an imbalance in the relationship between producers and consumers and, therefore, reduces individual freedom. Reagan's first education reform, the Education Consolidation and Improvement Act (ECIA), embedded in the sweeping Omnibus Act, revised the federal role in education in precisely the way Friedman suggested. The ECIA consolidated funds earmarked for direct student services (from tutoring to desegregation) into block grants or bundled resources with no mandate that the money be used for its original purpose and little oversight as to how the funds addressed underserved student populations.

The administration explained and justified these new policies toward schools using a neoliberal discourse that inescapably parallels Friedman. For instance, Secretary of Education Terrence Bell often addressed the benefit of deregulated block grants with a free-to-choose argument that opposed the efficiency of individual choice to the bureaucracy of government planning. If implemented properly, said Bell, competitive market structures and incentive practices more effectively accomplish the social justice goals of educational equality than categorical and direct aid. A *New York Times* article summarizing this idea cites Bell explaining that "we need block grants to give states more latitude, so specific requirements in Federal programs can be harmonized with local programs. That will make money go farther, and benefit many children" (1981, qtd. in Bennetts).[4] The problem of federal policy for Bell, who ventriloquizes Friedman, is that it proposes to alleviate poverty from the top down rather than allowing local constituencies to compete for money using their own creative initiatives.

With federal money solidly reconstituted as block grants, Reagan's second Secretary of Education, William Bennett, focused on school vouchers—another of Friedman's proposals. As Friedman characterized it, wealthy Americans, among whom he included himself, have more choices because "we can send our children to private schools… or we can choose where to live on the basis of the quality of the public school system" (1985, 157–158). According to this framework, social justice stems from providing more choices rather than more resources. Bennett echoed these sentiments in a speech delivered at the National Press Club in November 1985. He said that "unfortunately, the majority of Americans do not have freedom to make a choice. Some do. The affluent have a voucher. It is known as the ability to buy the school of their choice by buying the neighborhood of their choice" (1985, 455).[5] Bennett's comments reinforced the neoliberal narrative that the education market, driven by parental choice, not only produces better results but does so efficiently and without much government oversight.

Besides a timely synergy with Friedman and other neoliberal advocates, Reagan's administration also produced its own motivating forces with the *A Nation at Risk* report. Published by the National Commission on Excellence in Education, *A Nation at Risk* warned that a "tide of mediocrity" in American education threatened our standing in an increasingly global economy (United States 1984, 5). Filled with apocalyptic language, the report used falling scores on standardized tests, like the College Board's widely-used SAT and National Assessment of Educational Progress (NAEP), to argue that American students were falling behind their counterparts from other industrialized nations. It promoted the same market principles of competition and choice espoused by Friedman, but it also linked educational success with the nation's ability to thrive in the global economy. In its assessment, Americans

> live among determined, well-educated, and strongly motivated competitors. We compete with them for international standing and markets, not only with products but also with the ideas of our laboratories and neighborhood workshops. America's position in the world may once have been reasonably secure with only a few exceptionally well-trained men and women. It is no longer. (United States 1984, 6)

The report's intent to "examine the quality of education in the United States" and to make "practical recommendations for educational improvement" was simultaneously enlarged by its global lens and narrowed by its focus on workplace training for the new economic horizon. In this way, the report serves as the crucial linchpin that connects funding to curricular changes.

By framing education as foundational to economic competitiveness, the report tautologically locates education's *raison d'etre* as the training of a globally competitive workforce. Not only does it promote workforce instruction for school-aged children, the report takes a further step by suggesting that the current workforce must be retrained. Those presently employed, it says, "will need further education and retraining if they—and we as a Nation—are to thrive and prosper" (United States 1984, 17). According to this logic, training adult workers takes priority over educating the nation's poorest and most under-resourced populations. Public education must have only one master and that is the global marketplace. Not surprisingly, Friedman underscores this point, stating that schools should be responsive to market forces and not be used for "promoting social mobility, racial integration, and other objectives only distantly related to their fundamental task" (1980, 155). The fundamental task for education implied by Friedman and explicit in *A Nation at Risk* is to produce workers able to function productively and competitively in a market economy and not to engineer a more progressive citizenry.

As government oversight moved from funding economically needy students in effort to alleviate poverty to training students with the most job-market potential, the culture of testing and assessment also readjusted. At the forefront of this movement, Governor Lamar Alexander of Tennessee collaborated with others to produce *Time for Results: The Governors' 1991 Report on Education*. Published in 1986 by the National Governors Association, this report outlined a five-year plan for educational accountability and issued recommendations from its Task Force on Parent Involvement and Choice. Reading almost as if it came out of *Free to Choose*, the Task Force concluded that

> the public school system controls both the production and consumption of education. The system tells the students what they will learn, at what speed and what quality. Students and their parents have little to say about it. A more responsive system would incorporate what students and their parents say they need with the education services necessary to meet those needs. (The National 1986, 67)

The Task Force did call for greater school choice, but it primarily focused on such things as incentives for schools that align curriculum with workforce demand and experiment with business collaborations (84–86). By making education accountable to the market, these reforms introduced a biopolitical regulating structure tethered the fluctuations of neoliberalism.

In this market environment, standardized test scores increasingly became the surrogate for professional expertise. Greater importance was placed on NAEP tests as their purpose changed from providing a single snapshot of what students know to gathering comparative data on students within and among different states. In addition to NAEP, a host of other assessments became a permanent part of the educational calendar. Scores on these tests became the vehicle for policy makers to enforce their new workforce curricula at the same time that they allowed a consumerized public to measure the purported quality of their educational product. Moreover, the increased reliance on testing to measure achievement and ensure accountability led to policies that linked funding to student performance on standardized tests. For instance, the 1988 reauthorization of ECIA, also known as the Hawkins-Stafford Amendments, tied Chapter I funding (money earmarked for underserved populations) to standardized test scores. The amendments increased funding by $500 million but required schools to demonstrate improved test scores. If schools did not improve scores within a year, they were ineligible for additional funds and if they did not improve scores after two years, they were targeted for government intervention. Thus, the new plan incentivized teaching to the test through the threat of losing funding, a warning that later acquired teeth with President George W. Bush's No Child Left behind legislation.[6]

These K-12 initiatives and their neoliberal agendas implicate higher education through a trickle up effect that has become an inescapable part of tertiary education's ambient environment. As early as 1983, Educational Testing Service (ETS) published a report that attempted to align high school with college curricula and emphasized technical skills with computers because of their increasing workplace importance (College Board 1983). A few years later, The Task Force on College Quality, headed by then governor of Missouri John Ashcroft, called for implementing tests like those in K-12 to assess student learning and determine the effectiveness of academic programs (The National 1986, 155). In 2006, the Department of Education's *A Test of Leadership*, better known as the Spellings Report after Secretary of Education Margaret Spellings, placed higher education under the same economic lens as K-12 education. With a tone reminiscent of *A Nation at Risk*, the report asserts that the USA's ability to educate citizens at advanced levels has been eclipsed by other advanced nations and argues for a recommitment to the "core public purpose" of higher education. Just as higher education exerts its weight on earlier educational levels, there is also a bottom-up influence. Both avenues and their complex intersections with other discourses should be kept in mind as we investigate the ambient rhetoric of higher education. For it is precisely this tightly interlaced history that disappears into the everyday discourse of traditional college-aged students who have lived their entire educational lives under the influence of No Child Left Behind, naturalizing neoliberalism within the goals of higher education. To illustrate this pervasiveness, we explore two cases wherein the market statistics of biopolitics supersede well-crafted rhetorical arguments, suggesting that the neoliberal environment maintains an attendant rhetorical form.

The Neoliberal Milieu: From CSU's Mandatory Early Start to SUNY's Seamless Transfer

The CSU system, which recently implemented new remediation mandates, illustrates how the neoliberal milieu contains both structural and rhetorical implications. In October 2008, the CSU held a system-wide conference on remediation that emphasized the need for early intervention. Then, in a January 2009 report to the CSU Board of Trustees Committee on Educational Policy, Executive Vice Chancellor Gary W. Reichard asserted that students need to "achieve proficiency as early as possible after they begin their studies in the CSU" (2009). A few months later, the Board of Trustees passed a resolution directing the Chancellor to begin early remediation across all 23 campuses, despite faculty opposition. Finally, in the spring of 2010, Chancellor Charles Reed issued Executive Order 1048 that mandated a previously voluntary summer remediation project called Early Start (CSU "Early Start FAQ" 2011). Under E.O. 1048, all students who have yet to demonstrate proficiency through the English Placement Test and Entrance Level Mathematics exam or the high school Early Start Assessment Program must enroll in remedial instruction during the summer prior to their first fall term.[7] The system-wide policy requires unconditional reciprocity among all campuses, but allows students to choose from a number of different iterations of the MESP—week-long intensive workshops, two-week self-paced online courses, or traditional six-week summer courses—at any CSU campus or California community college. The destination institution must grant reciprocal credit regardless of which remedial apparatus or which campus the student chooses.

Several faculty organizations voiced concerns about the standardization of previously varied and locally designed developmental programs. For instance, the CSU Academic Senate passed a resolution in opposition to the supplanting of "diverse campus approaches" for helping students "achieve proficiency either prior to, or during, their first year" with required Early Start "as a pre-condition for enrollment at any CSU campus" (1). The CSU English Council, an independent professional organization affiliated with the California Association of Teachers and the National Council of Teachers of English (NCTE), also created a position statement that urged the Chancellor "to abandon simplistic notions of proficiency determined by a score on a single test, as well as the obsession with where and when students receive particular types of educational experiences" (CSU English). Faculty opposition questioned the premises for mandatory early remediation (the perceived deficiency of the current programs and unacceptably high remediation rates) as well as the purported benefits of the summer remediation requirement (decreasing time to graduation, increasing degree completion, and reducing educational costs). It further emphasized that voluntary versions of early start, used at over two-third of CSU campuses, were attaining a high rate of success. Indeed, more than 85 percent of students in the system completed their remedial coursework before the end of their first year (Naqvi 2014, 3). These protests had no perceivable impact on the CSU policy, and their failure, it seems, stems in part from the mismatch of two rhetorical forms. The faculty offered a deliberative discourse based on the educational needs of individual students and professional expertise in meeting those needs that was virtually unintelligible to an administration that proposed its initiatives using a biopolitical discourse that privileged administrative ease, statistical merit, and market success.

In this unequal dialogue, institutional timelines and other statistical metrics trump instructional expertise. For example, MESP assesses satisfactory progress at the starting line rather than the finish line of a university education; this shift, never explicitly defended, enables CSU to characterize effective programs as suddenly unsatisfactory. Just as Judith Butler searched in vain for a responsible agent declaring the liberal arts irrelevant, there exists a deep educational lacuna for the need to remediate prior to entering the university. Given that the vast majority of students were being successfully remediated, there was no educational warrant for this intervention. This apparent contradiction does not matter, however, because the impetus for these mandatory changes emerges from the need to align the university's biopolitical metrics with its neoliberal agenda. Under neoliberalism, as we saw with K-12 initiates, campuses compete for federal funding as well as for students by producing better assessment outcomes. Whereas opponents of the MESP measure success qualitatively through the experience of individual students who learn, retain, and transfer their skill sets to other courses, the administration measures success quantitatively: a small percentage of remedial students entering universities; a low ratio of general education to major courses; and, ultimately, a short time to graduation with as few credit hours as possible. Marketable numbers take precedence over professional advice about the quality of education, foregrounding the administration of homogeneous student populations while individual learning experience fades into the background. As Chancellor Reed makes clear in a memo accompanying E.O. 1048, MESP is "designed to facilitate a student's graduation through changes in policies" (2010). Administrative policy replaces professional expertise as the means of facilitating student graduation and renders arguments about local educational particularities beside the point.

Impervious to professional challenge, these policy changes govern the student population and thus, counterintuitively, are not reducible to a cost–benefit analysis. Unlike disciplinary power, which focuses on adjusting particular individuals, biopower focuses on policies that regulate a population's biometrics. A healthy university, evidenced by the statistics of its population, is not only marketable to private investment and potential students; it is also the means by which a university avoids resistance to its centralized authority. Statistical averages serve as the object of intervention and not the students because the goal shifts from individual conformity to statistical well-being. Those who conceive of the contemporary university as primarily beholden to an economic bottom line, as does legal analyst Jameel Naqvi (2014, 2), fundamentally misunderstand neoliberalism, which aligns populations according to constantly fluctuating marketplace needs regardless of cost. Economic arguments often cut both ways and deflect from the real purpose of biopolitics, which Foucault argues is to adjust and maintain population demographics that match its governance needs. Under neoliberalism, the cost to educate a given individual or to fund a particular program can be extremely high without raising any concern as long as the vital statistics of the overall university remain within an acceptable range.

As neoliberalism, driven by marketability and competition, replaces professional agency with statistical accountability, it bolsters a rhetorical structure that obscures the individual in favor of the population. Whether discussing student experiences or its price tag, the new discourse replaces personal narratives with numerical averages. It does not matter, as the Council suggests, that MESP will alter the experience of college students who require remediation (CSU English 2009, 1). It is further irrelevant that students who are required to enroll in early remediation during the summer face an "undo financial burden...which could lead to resentment, hardship, and disenrollment" (CSU English 2009, 1). The Board of Trustees and Chancellor do not employ or engage individualized accounts. Instead, they construct remedial students as an aggregation in need of correction. Because the population, as Foucault emphasizes, is not the collection of individual subjects but "a set of elements in which we can note constants and regularities," it neither tells nor responds to individual stories, no matter how compelling (2007, 74). The arguments of CSU's administration are less attuned to the considerations of particular students and more resonant with market considerations; thus, they abandon the narrative form that privileges individual experience in favor of the suasive power of biopolitical regulation through statistical averages. Put another way, the MESP program is an example of how neoliberalism is made operative in the CSU system through diffuse power structures (and their ambient rhetoric) that relies on an inconspicuous biopolitical apparatus to move students through their college careers in a manner that turns education into a system of commodity production rather than a process of human transformation.

An even more sweeping instance of system-level administrative authority imposing a mandate and stripping professional educators of local autonomy occurred in the same year within the SUNY system. *The Power of SUNY*, released in 2010, is a strategic plan designed to more fully connect public universities with the economic vitality of the state. Dubbing our current moment "the entrepreneurial century," the strategic plan includes a number of interrelated initiatives intended to cultivate an "entrepreneurial mindset" that shapes market practices, creates additional jobs, and locates the economic engine of New York State in its universities (SUNY 2010). The plan incorporates university campuses into a state-wide network of resources, faculty, and students available for the research and development activities of its private business partners.[8] SUNY Chancellor Nancy Zimphor calls this networked apparatus SUNY's "systemness" and endorses policies that purport to move students quickly and efficiently from universities into careers—a process she refers to as the "seamless education pipeline" (2012a, b). From the perspective of this strategic plan, education is nothing more than the armature for producing workers aligned with the emergent needs of the neoliberal marketplace. Because the best university systems have the fewest breaks in this overall structure, the plan imposes a universal organization that seals potential cracks in the pipeline. Policies like Seamless Transfer and Open SUNY—

the two initiatives central to our study—push programs to meet evolving workplace demands, standardize general education requirements, and mandate that all but the most frivolous elective credits transfer between campuses.

Mirroring the CSU remediation debate, faculty unions, university governing bodies, and professional organizations resisted the system-wide restructuring. Many of those opposing SUNY's new mission asserted faculty independence in curricular decisions as essential to the quality of student education and instrumental to the needs of an institution's specific student population. The SUNY Council of Writing (SUNY CoW) used this standpoint to criticize both Seamless Transfer and Open SUNY. Seamless Transfer participates in "systemness" by standardizing transfer requirements across campuses while Open SUNY, the system's online instruction, offers credit-bearing courses from all 64 schools that must be accepted by any SUNY campus. The SUNY CoW resolution argues that the online platform and enormous enrollment projections of Open SUNY courses run counter to the best practices of professional writing instruction. It further maintains that there has been no peer-reviewed research to suggest these platforms are pedagogically effective for writing intensive courses. The resolution appeals to professional expertise and argues that close, interactive work with students is a central aspect of writing pedagogy (SUNY Council 2013). Again, however, these arguments seem to fall on deaf ears, suggesting not only a new structure of higher education but also an entirely new method of rhetorical exchange within and about that system.

Without explicitly stating it, the strategic plan presupposes a neoliberal rationale for SUNY's reorientation toward economic needs and, in doing so, supplants earlier educational rationales from social progress to democratic training. Chancellor Zimphor's description of "systemness" as a way to increase productivity by controlling costs, broadening student access, increasing degree completion, and preparing students for careers invokes a market agency that prioritize production and output over professional and pedagogical concerns (2012a, b). This focus on outcomes replaces individualized student learning with marketable degrees and a host of statistical measurements. In this way, marketability functions as the ultimate goal of this university system, one that must compete as an educational commodity by constantly improving its own biopolitical metrics through such statistical indices as shortened time to degree, higher graduation numbers, and thriving corporate partnerships. Within this new environment, the individual and the professional simply do not have the argumentative weight they once did. Consequently, when oppositional organizations invoke the lack of peer-reviewed research supporting these changes or cite recommendations from disciplinary experts about the need for limited class size, they assert a futile claim to professional authority.

Ultimately, SUNY faculty lost authority to big data assessment, which enables the system to track progress toward system-level outcomes aligned with its neoliberal mission. Funneling accountability toward biopolitical discourse, big data values numerical outcomes over pedagogical processes and redefines the rules of argumentation in higher education. Under this system of assessment and accountability, each school is required to define its campus-level outcomes within the framework of SUNY's new mission (SUNY "SUNY Excels"). Moreover, these campus outcomes must be measurable by *The Power of SUNY's* metrics: patents issued, private investments made, new jobs created, percentage of students enrolled in online courses, time to graduation, and number of graduates with a STEM degree, among other indices. This method of biopolitical assessment embeds the new economic mission of SUNY into the programming of individual institutions and redefines student and faculty populations, degree programs, and campus resources as the means by which the university achieves its market agenda. As big data analysis—itself the result of digital technologies that came to fruition within the neoliberal era—usurps professional agents, it also redefines meaningful discourse within numerical averages, statistical variance, and mathematical probabilities. SUNY CoW's calls for sound pedagogical practices tailored to each classroom have little resonance within this new field of assessment. Expert faculty members who can recognize the individual needs of students and address them through close, interpersonal instruction cannot be measured by large-scale data gathering. Indeed, the individual simply disappears from this mathematical rubric because, as we have said, under the pervasive field of neoliberalism students and faculty are no longer individuals, but populations to be regulated.

SUNY's new strategic plan and the responses from professional organizations illustrate an increasing problem of address in the neoliberal university. The institutionalization of neoliberal practices through big data assessment aligned with the needs of marketability makes it difficult for counter-voices to intervene in policy decisions. Such decisions are determined by the biopolitical health of the university—its measurable numbers—and not by faculty experts or by the individual experiences of students. The conditions that create these policy decisions and the complex relationships between the business world and the state to which SUNY has attached itself do not correlate to the traditional means of argument—stable identity structures, interests related to those identities, and power authorities willing to engage on-the-ground disputes. As both the CSU and SUNY cases illustrate, arguments that do not fall within the scope of neoliberal assessment outcomes do not resonate with administrative governing bodies. In such an environment, biopolitical rhetoric prevails over the more experientially grounded arguments of those of us who live, work, and stake our intellectual lives within the institutions of higher education. To compete for a voice in the neoliberal university means that we must rethink our discursive strategies. To that end, we conclude with a short exploration of short-term and long-term strategies.

Reconstituting Ambient Rhetoric from Neoliberalism to the Common

Our discussion of changing federal policy as well as our exploration of the current climate of higher education offers a skeptical view of biopolitics as an apparatus that works on behalf of neoliberalism. Nonetheless, there is no reason that biopolitics cannot be used for other agendas. As we have explained it, biopolitics functions as the discursive modality for communicating in a world dominated by an unspoken ambient faith in the global marketplace. Because the market works in dynamic relationship to a host of institutional and everyday practices, rhetoric's deliberative triangulation (speaker, audience, and subject) evolves within, rather than preexists, this complex circulation of energies, ideas, systems, and possibilities. For Rickert, this "emergent coadaptation" (2013, 104) positions rhetoric within an ongoing and mostly inaudible process that orients, modulates, and determines the beliefs and behaviors of human beings and the institutions they forge rather than as an outside apparatus for negotiating those processes. Rhetorical influence, from this perspective, circulates disinterestedly and is therefore constantly open to redirection. No doubt, the work of reconstructing an ambient environment is not insignificant—after all, the current landscape of neoliberal education was crafted over the last 35 years or more. Yet it is, we believe, rhetorical work worth doing.

To begin this process, critiques of neoliberalism should appropriate its mode of biopolitical address. In many ways, this is a simple call for Burkean identification, which asserts that "you can persuade a man only insofar as you can talk his language by speech, gesture, tonality, order, image, attitude, idea, *identifying* your ways with his" (1969, 55). As we illustrated in our case studies, those organizations that opposed the California and New York mandates failed to speak the language of neoliberalism and, consequently, did not compel their administrative audiences. If they had employed statistics, mathematical models, and algorithms of future probabilities to promote their educational agendas, they may have forced the administration to discuss their concerns. More than cosmetic, this discursive accommodation signals a host of attitudes and ideas within the broader neoliberal culture that may enable greater communication between professionals and administrations. Against our pedagogical instincts, we also believe critics should avoid disputes about the value of pegging education to the global marketplace. Neoliberal models have succeeded in part by focusing their message and refusing to participate in their opponent's educational frame. Critics spread themselves thin and water down their arguments by attempting to address professional problems beyond their expertise. Instead, they should focus on specific objections, informed by their expert knowledge but structured within the privileged mode of biopolitics. This short-term adjustment will facilitate greater communication, which may lead to long-term modifications, but it likely will not dramatically alter the neoliberal structure of higher education. To begin chipping away at that larger complex requires a widespread investment in reshaping the ambient environment.

The ambient environment of neoliberalism has replaced the collective professional expertise with the authority of market statistics and reconstituted the student as individual consumer. In this way, it has privatized the project of producing an educated citizenry. We suggest a long-term strategy to revalorize the collective agenda vis-à-vis divergent forms of communicative labor. To be clear, this does not mean a return to identity politics or digging our heels into professional identities; rather, we advocate underscoring the commonality of public spaces, experiences, and properties. Michael Hardt and Antonio Negri popularized the notion of the common as an oppositional strategy opposed to the global power of empire, or what we have been calling neoliberalism (2000, 2004). From their perspective, the multitude—what Foucault calls "the people" (2007, 43)—works outside officially sanctioned apparatuses in order to produce a decentralized power capable of mobilizing the surplus energies of everyday people. Like the networked history we outlined—one that interlaced federal policy with popular media, economic doctrine, and cultural myth-making—we need to forge a multiperspectival form of communication that unites people without relegating their connection to a point on the grid of identity. As Hardt and Negri assert, "*it takes a network to fight a network*" (2004, 58). The common, which designates the collective and cooperative labor of production that undergirds the entire neoliberal order, offers a rhetorical spin on global economic interconnectivity. The common, according to political theorist Jodi Dean, highlights "creativity, thought, knowledge and communication as themselves always plural, open, and productive" rather than professionally bound and determined (2012, 134–135). Radically inclusive, the common promotes discourse that is neither professional nor individual but organized toward the collective future.

From this perspective, the task is not negotiating specific political problems but working toward a manifestation of the common. The first step in this reconception is to understand the site of agency not as the individual or an identifiable group but as a networked common. Take, for example, the student loan debt crisis. Like so many other touchstones of education, the federal student loan system first emerged on a broad scale in 1965 with President Johnson. Rather than loan students the money to attend universities, the federal government guaranteed the loans of private banks and other organizations. Deeply embedded in the ideological and institutional networks of neoliberalism, student loans emphasize individual responsibility, privatization, and market competition. Banks, however, only invest in these markets to the extent that they produce increased profits and this means rising interest rates. Universities, which are also in market competition, must constantly improve their product vis-à-vis biopolitical metrics and a flashy infrastructure—state-of-the-art fitness centers, dormitories, and entertainment facilities as well as classrooms, laboratories, and campus landscapes. This ratchets up the tuition costs which become exponentially increased through high-interest loan repayments. This crisis cannot be adequately addressed through identity politics that pit students against banks and emphasize the need for transparency as though clear information will solve the diversity of problems threaded through the practice of borrowing money to finance the ballooning costs of education. It is our contention that such a neoliberal problematic will only be solved by a networked community that understands itself and the future from a common, rather than an individual, perspective. The more we promote this networked common, the more possible it is that our ambient rhetorical environment will also change.

Notes

1. See, for instance, Henry Pritchett's (1905) *Atlantic Monthly* article titled "Shall the University Become a Business Corporation?" as well as Thorstein Veblen's (1918) indictment of the corporate university, *The Higher Learning in America: A Memorandum on the Conduct of Universities by Business Men*.
2. SUNY is the largest system of higher education in the nation. It is comprised of 64 institutions including community colleges, four-year colleges, research universities, academic medical centers, as well as agricultural and technical institutes. It enrolls more than 460,000 students and employs more than 34,000 faculty members. Its west coast counterpart, CSU consists of 23 campuses that serve as the primary means for attaining bachelor's and master's degrees within the state of California. CSU enrolls 447,000 students and employs over 23,000 faculty members with an annual budget is more than $5 billion.
3. This is an example of what A.O. Hirschman (1991) calls the perversity thesis. See his *The Rhetoric of Reaction* for an explanation of the thesis as well as James Aune's (2001) use of it in *Selling the Free Market*.
4. In many instances, deregulation of direct-aid redistributed resources away from poorer districts into wealthier districts; or, if resources did arrive at the appropriate school districts, they were often used to benefit students least in need of aid. See Anne Henderson (1986) as well as Richard Jung and Michael Tashjian (1983).
5. This line of argument gathered significant strength in the popular media. For instance, Pear (1985) cites Bennett (1985) as saying "our most affluent families do exercise choice, by buying a home in the neighborhood of their choice, or by sending their children to a private school. The poor do not now have that kind of choice" (qtd. in Pear 1985).
6. The No Child Left Behind Act enforces accountability through testing. Under the law, all students in grades 3 through 8 are tested yearly in reading and math. Schools that fail to make adequate yearly progress toward student proficiency are sanctioned. For example, schools that are marked as "needing improvement" must offer students the option of transferring to another public or charter school in the district; if, after two years, the school has not improved it must make Title I funds available to supplemental education services like private tutoring; after four years, the school must make corrective actions like replacing staff and implementing new curricula; and after five years, school districts must restructure schools, which "may include reopening the school as a charter school, replacing all or most of the school's staff or turning over school operations either to the state or to a private education company" ("NCLB Parents Guide" 9).

7. California high school students may earn an exemption from the tests through a college readiness exam that includes 15 multiple choice items in both mathematics and English language arts plus a 45 minute essay (Educational Testing Service 4).
8. For example, initiatives like SUNY-INC, START-UP NY, and SUNY Works outsource university resources to private business. SUNY-INC and START-UP NY encourage businesses to locate in New York by offering tax breaks, campus space, and the option to commercialize faculty research. SUNY Works further incentivizes partnership with private business by outsourcing students through increased co-ops and internships. The SUNY Works website explains that the benefits of these programs include a "year-round supply of motivated and capable students" who "can meet short term needs" and whose "wage requirements are modest."

References

Aune, James Arnt. 2001. *Selling the Free Market*. New York: Guilford Press.
Bennett, William J. 1985. Educators in America: The Three R's. *Vital Speeches of the Day* 51(15): 453–456.
Bennetts, Leslie. 1981. Federal Government Role in Education Is at Issue. *The New York Times*, July 25. Accessed 9 Jul 2014.
Burke, Kenneth. 1969. *A Rhetoric of Motives*. Berkeley, CA: The University of California Press.
Butler, Judith. 2006. *Precarious Life: The Powers of Mourning and Violence*. New York: Verso.
Bosquet, Marc. 2008. *How the University Works: Higher Education and the Low-Wage Nation*. New York: New York University Press.
California State University. 2011. Early Start FAQ. *CSUSuccess.org*. Accessed 27 Oct 2014.
California State University Academic Senate. 2009. Opposition to Implementation of Mandatory Early Start Programs. May 7–8.
California State University English Council. 2009. CSU English Council Position Statement: Mandatory Early Start. CSU English Council. Accessed 27 Oct 2014.
College Board. 1983. *Academic Preparation for College: What Students Need to Know and Be Able to Do*. New York: College Board.
Darling-Hammond, Linda, and Ellen L. Marks. 1983. *The New Federalism in Education: State Responses to the 1981 Education Consolidation and Improvement Act*. Santa Monica, CA: The Rand Corporation.
Dean, Jodi. 2012. *The Communist Horizon*. New York: Verso.

Educational Testing Service. 2014. *The California State University English Placement Test (EPT) and Entry Level Mathematics Examination (ELM) 2014 Information Bulletin.* Princeton, NJ: Educational Testing Service.

Foucault, Michel. 2007. *Security, Territory, Population,* ed. Michel Senellart, trans. Graham Burchell. New York: Palgrave.

———. 2008. *The Birth of Biopolitics,* ed. Michel Senellart, trans. Graham Burchell. New York: Palgrave

Friedman, Milton. 1980. *Free to Choose: A Personal Statement.* New York: Harcourt Brace Jovanovich.

Goodnight, G. Thomas, David Hingstman, and Sandy Green. 2015. The Student Debt Bubble: Neoliberalism, The University, and Income Inequality. *The Journal of Cultural Economy* 8: 75–100.

GovTrack. n.d. To Pass H.R. 2362, The 1965 Elementary and Secondary Education Act. GovTrack. https://www.govtrack.us/congress/votes/89-1965/s48. Accessed 9 Dec 2014.

Greene, Ronald Walter.1998. Another Materialist Rhetoric. *Critical Studies in Mass Communication* 15(1): 21–41.

Hardt, Michael, and Antonio Negri. 2000. *Empire.* Cambridge, MA: Harvard University Press.

———. 2004. *Multitude: War and Democracy in the Age of Empire.* Cambridge, MA: Harvard University Press.

Henderson, Anne T. 1986. Chapter 2: For Better or Worse? *Phi Delta Kappan* 67(8): 597–602.

Hirschman, Albert O. 1991. *The Rhetoric of Reaction.* Cambridge, MA: Harvard University Press.

Johnson, Lyndon B. 1965. Johnson's Remarks on Signing the Elementary and Secondary Education Act. LBJ Presidential Library. Accessed 24 Jul 2014.

Joint Statement on the Education Summit with the Nation's Governors in Charlottesville, Virginia. 1989. George Bush Presidential Library and Museum. Accessed 12 Jul 2014.

Jung, Richard, and Michael Tashijan. 1983. Big Districts and the Block Grant: First-Year Fiscal Impacts. *Phi Delta Kappan* 65(3): 199–203.

Naqvi, Jameel. 2014. Initial Review of CSU's Early Start Program. In *California Legislative Analyst's Office.* Sacramento, CA: Legal Analyst's Office Publications.

Nixon, Richard M. 1970. Special Message to the Congress on Education Reform. The American Presidency Project. Accessed 5 Aug 2014.

Pear, Robert. 1985. Reagan Proposes Vouchers to Give Poor a Choice of Schools. *New York Times,* November 14. Accessed 6 Jul 2014.

Peters, Jean. 1981. Reconciliation 1982: What Happened? *PS* 14(4): 732–736.

Pritchett, Henry. 1905. Shall the University Become a Business Corporation? *Atlantic Monthly,* September, 289–299.

Reagan, Ronald. 1982. Address Before a Joint Session of the Congress Reporting on the State of the Union. Ronald Reagan Presidential Library and Museum. Accessed 19 Jul 2014.

———. 1983. Remarks at a Fundraising Dinner Honoring Former Representative John M. Ashbrook in Ashland, Ohio. Ronald Reagan Presidential Library and Museum. Accessed 16 Aug 2014.

Reichard, Gary W. 2009. Proficiency in English and Mathematics. Presentation to the Committee on Educational Policy at the CSU Board of Trustees Meeting, Long Beach, CA, January 27–28.

Reed, Charles B. 2010. Early State Program—Executive Order No. 1048. Memo to the CSU Presidents. June 11.

Rickert, Thomas. 2013. *Ambient Rhetoric: The Attunements of Rhetorical Being*. Pittsburgh, PA: University of Pittsburgh Press.

Slaughter, Sheila, and Gary Rhoades. 2004. *Academic Capitalism and the New Economy: Markets, State, and Higher Education*. Baltimore, MD: John Hopkins University Press.

State University of New York. 2010. *The Power of SUNY: Strategic Plan 2010 & Beyond*. SUNY. Accessed 14 Jul 2014.

State University of New York. n.d. *SUNY Excels*. SUNY. Accessed 12 Sept 2014.

SUNY Council on Writing. 2013. Resolution on Massive Open Online Courses and the Teaching of Writing. *SUNY Council on Writing*. July 21. Accessed 9 Sept 2014.

The Big Federal Move into Education. 1965. *Time* 85(18): 54–59.

The Head of the Class. 1965. *Time* 86(16): 70–79.

The National Governors' Association. 1986. *Time for Results: The Governors' 1991 report on Education*. Washington, DC: The National Governors' Association, Center for Policy Research and Analysis.

United States. Department of Education. 2006. *A Test of Leadership: Charting the Future of U.S. Higher Education*. Washington, DC: U.S. Department of Education.

United States. The National Commission on Excellence in Education. 1984. *A Nation at Risk: The Full Account*. Cambridge, MA: USA Research.

Veblen, Thorstein. 1965 (1918). *The Higher Learning in America: A Memorandum on the Conduct of Universities by Business Men*. New York: A.M. Kelley.

Williams, Jeffrey. 2006. The Pedagogy of Debt. *College Literature* 33(4): 155–169.

———. 2008. Teach the University! *Pedagogy* 8(1): 25–42.

Zimphor, Nancy L. 2012a. Getting Down to Business. SUNY. January. Accessed 12 Sept 2014.

———. 2012b. 'Systemness' Keeps College Affordable, Productive, Accessible. The Nelson A. Rockefeller Institute of Government. January. Accessed 14 Sept 2014.

Warren Buffett's Celebrity, Epideictic Ethos, and Neoliberal Humanitarianism

Mark Meister and Carrie Anne Platt

On August 14, 2011, billionaire celebrity and Berkshire Hathaway chairman and chief executive Warren Buffett took to the op-ed pages of the *New York Times* to issue a call for raising taxes on high-income earners. In a guest editorial titled "Stop Coddling the Super-Rich," Buffett used his own wealth and his own celebrity status to make a case for addressing the inequity of current income taxation. At only 17.4 percent of his taxable income, Buffett's rate was significantly lower than the other 20 people in his office, who had an average tax rate of 36 percent. Buffett went on to argue that one of the simplest and most effective means for reducing the growing US deficit was for Congress to address this inequity:

> But for those making more than $1 million—there were 236,883 such households in 2009—I would raise rates immediately on taxable income in excess of $1 million, including, of course, dividends and capital gains. And for those who make $10 million or more—there were 8,274 in 2009—I

M. Meister (✉) • C.A. Platt
Department of Communication, North Dakota State University, Fargo, ND, USA

would suggest an additional increase in rate. My friends and I have been coddled long enough by a billionaire-friendly Congress. It's time for our government to get serious about shared sacrifice. (Buffett 2011)

This opinion piece was not the first time that Buffett had called for an increase in taxes paid by the richest Americans. He has often used the fact that he pays a lower tax rate than his longtime secretary, Debbie Bosanek, as an example of what is wrong with the system. He also restated his case a year later, calling for a minimum 30 percent tax on top earners (Buffett 2012). But, it is surprising when we consider the strong performance of Berkshire Hathaway during this same recession (Newman 2008), which demonstrated why Buffett is popularly known as the "Oracle of Omaha" and renowned for his shrewd business sense. His focus on corporate stability and financial austerity ran counter to the logic of investing in subprime mortgages and enabled both Buffett and his investment company to emerge from the recession relatively unscathed. Buffett is a speaker, investor, and celebrity, who has shown, time and time again, that he knows what he is talking about when it comes to wealth and he has the rhetorical assets of celebrity status and friends reflective of his financial and luminary reputation (Korczynski 2005).

But, as we argue in this chapter, Buffett's rhetorical agency cannot be fully understood without considering how the discursive formation that celebrates and constructs him as a particularly astute investor also limit his ability to advocate for government intervention in the economic sphere. This case study expands the concept of epideictic ethos by referencing Buffett's super-rich, ultra-celebrity, and mass-mediated embodiment of neoliberalism. As Noam Chomsky argues in his critique of neoliberalism (1999), the media and popular culture are essential to preservation of the economic status quo. The proliferation of private interests, free market enterprise, and corporate exceptionalism extolls the virtues of the wealthy few. Neoliberalism, according to Robert McChesney (2001), bolsters antigovernment discourse by celebrating capitalism as a totalizing imperative for what is in the best interest for all. McChesney argues that neoliberalism "posits that society works best when business runs things and there is little possibility of government 'interference' with business as possible…[i]n short, neoliberal democracy is one where the political sector controls little and debates even less" (6). According to novelist and social critic Walter Kirn (2004), "It's Buffett the symbol that matters now, Buffett the folk hero, Buffett the communicator…as a charismatic, reassuring, quotable prototype of the honest capitalist...capable of influencing elections, galvanizing rock-concert-size crowds, and in general defining how we Americans feel about the system that underlies our wealth." (160) Buffett symbolizes both wealth earned and the self-restraint to retain it, exemplifying neoliberalism and justifying a system that keeps wealth among the wealthy. In short, Buffett's celebrity dictates his neoliberal ethic. Celebrity status is fundamental to the free-market version of capitalism that Buffett may critique, but ultimately cannot distance himself from. Buffett's celebrity and his wealth prioritizes his legitimacy as a "big citizen" capable of engaging the contradictions enveloped in celebrity-driven philanthropy (Rojeck 2013).

Buffett, the celebrity philanthropist, is seemingly uncomfortable with the ironies of neoliberalism. In spite of his celebrity status as one of the world's most successful investors, his public support of President Obama and the Clinton Foundation, and the endorsement of his tax reform ideas by several economists (Huang 2012; Hungerford 2011), Buffett's attempts at persuasion have had little to no influence on US tax policy. His idea (popularly referred to as "The Buffett Rule" by the White House) of setting higher minimum tax rates for the wealthy (The National Economic Council 2012) met strong opposition by Congress in 2011 (Rubin 2012). And this was not the first nor the last time Buffett attempted to shape the American tax code. According to *Forbes* contributor Jerry Bowyer (2012), Buffett periodically proposes tax hikes; "Every year he say the rich pay too little, and less than the middle class. Every year conservative think tanks and pundits go to work tearing the reasoning to pieces, and every year Mr. Buffett ignores their reasoning." The consistent opposition to Buffett's proposed tax hikes to the rich may be the natural result of the neoliberal rhetoric that infuses current economic policy, where the market is seen as a rational force that needs no—and indeed suffers from—government regulation. As the economy continues to recover from the recession of 2008, policymakers are reluctant to make changes that might prompt the wealthy to invest less or hire fewer workers for their enterprises. But Buffett and his "rule" for taxing the rich cannot insulate him from the neoliberal praxes that constitute his accumulation of wealth, his dogged-determination in retaining it, and his humanitarian efforts for giving his wealth away through his highly praised philanthropic activities. Celebrity-driven philanthropy, notes Barker (2011, 146), "played an integral role in financing the neoliberal revolution… Ford, Rockefeller, and Carnegie also worked to promote neoliberalism, and did so through a subtle process of co-opting what would otherwise have been its progressive dissenters…the benevolent rhetoric of humanitarianism puts a sparkle on charitable aid givers, while aggressive corporate behavior in poor countries largely goes unheeded." We argue that Buffett's celebrity philanthropy rhetorically bolsters his ethos epideictically. We explain Buffett's celebrity philanthropy in rhetorical terms by extending Dale Sullivan's (1993b) conception of epideictic ethos as a plausible construct by which neoliberalism insulates itself from social criticism and welcomes media praise.

We start by outlining traditional understandings of the rhetorical situation and epideictic ethos in order to call attention to their limits for understanding rhetorical agency in an age where the ethos of public figures is constructed by both the media and the figure him or herself. We then argue for an expanded version of epideictic ethos that considers the role of discursive formations, or what Catherine Chaput (2010) has termed "rhetorical circulations." We illustrate the value of this approach through a case study of Buffett the symbol, focusing on how Buffett has been constructed as a public figure through the mediated representations of press coverage and biographies, illustrating how Buffett's wealth and celebrity contributes to the epideictic ethos that ends up constraining his rhetorical agency. In what follows, we trace the evolution of epideictic rhetoric from a classic rhetorical genre to a contemporary ideological heuristic capable of rhetorical-critical critiques on issues vital to the public sphere. A shift in thinking about epideictic rhetoric as a faculty of the speaker to epideictic encounters that foreground the audience affords insight into the interplay between what a speaker praises and the values held by an audience. The functioning of speaker praise and audience values opens a space in epideictic moments where ideology and ethos interact. It is in this space where we can see how prevalent neoliberal ideas can powerfully shape the ethos of a trusted economic oracle—specifically when it comes to the topics on which he appears credible, and the decisions he seems worthy of making. Laura Rittenhouse, author of *Buffett Bites: The Essential Investors Guide to Warren Buffett's Shareholder Letters*, exemplifies how powerful ideal neoliberal values are manifested via ethos, describing him as a capitalist who is not a materialist. A virtuous tycoon with tremendous drive and insecurity; deposit and enticement. Buffett effectively manages a rhetorical ethos of the under-consumer, or as Kirn (2004) once called him the "anti-Trump", affecting his ability to take issue with neoliberal ideas and policy.

Expanding Our Understanding of Epideictic Ethos to Celebrity Studies

Before considering epideictic ethos, we must understand how scholarly approaches to epideictic rhetoric have changed. "Epideictic genres continue to mutate, evolve, and disappear, but the need to ground social mores, political institutions, and communities through epideictic continues to endure," notes Lauer (2015, 4). The epideictic form constitutes both tradition and revelation; an identification with the temporal and with the potential, as well as the conservative and progressive.

Aristotle presented epideictic as a type of speech that promotes civic virtue through stylized displays of praising or blaming that facilitate public political dialogue (Hauser 1999). Epideictic rhetoric shapes both practical and aesthetic identifications in its engagement with democracy and civic virtue (Beale 1978). Unlike deliberative or forensics speeches, epideictic rhetoric facilitates audience interest by appropriating common values (Condit 1985), extolling praise (Chase 1961) or blame (Sullivan 1994), facilitating civic understanding (Agnew 2008), urging a course of action (Crable and Vibbert 1983), capturing political favor (Harpine 2004), and performing ceremonial rituals (Adams 2006).

For Aristotle, the speaker was most central to these rhetorical processes. As he put it, virtue is a faculty (*Rhetoric*, ix.), and so is epideictic speech that praises virtues. The epideictic speaker is most concerned with *dynamis*; unlike encomium (which "deals with achievements," and is pronounced "upon those who have achieved something"), praise—the central *telos* of epideictic speech—"is language that sets forth greatness of virtue; hence it is necessary to show that a man's actions are virtuous" (ibid.). Accordingly, Aristotle's *Rhetoric* concerns itself primarily with the means through which a speaker can promote and show virtue, through subtle changes in phrasing (ix. 36), or amplification (ix. 37), which he situates as epideictic rhetoric's counterpart to examples and enthymemes in forensic and deliberative rhetoric, respectively.

Aristotle recognizes the importance of the audience to epideictic rhetoric, but offers few practical implications for how audiences impact epideictic speech ("We ought also to consider in whose presence we praise, for, as Socrates aid, it is not difficult to praise Athenians among Athenians"—ix.30). This focus on speaker, notes Pratt (2012), is problematic because the audience, as described by Aristotle, becomes transfixed by the speaker's ability rather than the subject matter of the speech. Cynthia Miecznikowski

Sheard (1996) argues that understanding epideictic rhetoric "hinges on an audience that receives it as the inspired discourse or ritual celebration" (776). The emphasis on the audience as the key facilitator of meaning creation is an important theme in more recent rhetorical scholarship on epideictic rhetoric. Oravec's (1976) description of epideictic's educational function exemplifies this theme. Accordingly, epideictic rhetoric is the "connection between the principle and the manifestation of the principle..." (166) that is arguably impacted by the use of narrative and other literary and rhetorical devices that extoll moral action (Poulakos 1987), community pride (Miller 1993), authoritative legacy (Carter 1991), and civic pedagogy (Sullivan 1993a).

Evolving from its grounding in classical rhetorical theory, epideictic rhetoric constitutes the sacred and the secular, emphasizes both the ceremonial and the rational, bolsters both praise and blame, reinforces adherence to commonly held values, and magnifies the vice of the censured. It has been described by rhetorical scholars as both "frivolous oratorical flights" and as vital to "teaching public morality" (Hauser 1999, 14). In all, the didactic function of epideictic, note Perelman and Olbrechts-Tyteca (1969), requires critical focus on the dynamic interplay between speaker and audience; a lively process that meshes *phronesis, telos, philoi, techné,* and *dynamis*. And also, arguably, to our understanding of neoliberal rhetoric. Contemporary rhetorical critics explain the epideictic-neoliberal consequences by examining its relationship to collective memory (Bostdorff 2011), public witnessing (Vivian 2012), ecology and global warming (Singer 2010), and commemorative politics (Vivian 2006). Lauer suggests that epideictic's temporal orientation "enables speakers and audiences to compare different states of being...epideictic discourse can juxtapose the 'is' and the 'really is'" (2015, 13). The revelation of the "really is" by epideictic rhetoric arguably facilitates a process of revelation through its aesthetic practices, relevancy to common values, and cohesion with community (Danisch 2006). In all, neoliberal economics and politics are arguably constituted via epideictic rhetoric because of it reveals formulaic, familiar, and foreseeable social and cultural conditions. The epideictic speaker often speaks the "common language" of a homogeneous audience who seemingly all celebrate shared or blame divergent peoples, values, politics, and events in support of or in opposition to traditional conservative politics. Epideictic rhetoric arguably reveals the "hidden values and assumptions" (Lauer 2015, 13) of what really are the neoliberal values that make "various communities cohere" (Danisch 2006, 293).

In a rhetorical space characterized by such divergence, what common language is revealed? Bradford Vivian (2006) argues that instances of epideictic rhetoric are defined by their subsuming of reason and other foundations for careful deliberation under the patina of emotion and values such as patriotism, due to the latter being better suited to the sensationalism and spectacle of corporate media culture. As Vivian states: "The symbolic rituals of mass mediated spectacles offer an affective idiom that appears to engender a common civic identity from public displays of sentiment during an era of widespread political polarities, conflicting moral paradigms, and heterogeneous cultural traditions" (15). Dana Cloud (2003) refers to the identification that results from neoliberal sentiment as an "affective public," one that fails at deliberation because of its basis in emotion rather than reason.

The classic interplay between speaker and audience extends epideictic rhetoric into a modern arrangement between the commercial and the consumer. The contemporary version of epideictic rhetoric privileges neoliberal ideals through a powerful discourse of benevolence (Vivian 2006; Cloud 2003) especially by celebrity capitalists such as Buffett. Humanitarianism, charity, and altruism meld with corporate interventions that engage consumers more with celebrity promotional culture than with thoughtful public discourse (Barker 2011). An emphasis on audience changes the relationship between the speaker of epideictic rhetoric, and the context in which such a speech is given. Epideictic rhetoric, argue Perelman and Olbrechts-Tyteca (1969), shapes a "common language" that integrates shared cultural beliefs and cultural traditions of both speaker and audience. If the purpose of epideictic speech "is to increase the intensity of adherence to values held in common by the audience and the speaker" (52), then audiences—the values, norms, beliefs, and opinions they hold—shape the epideictic moment as much as the speaker does.

Sullivan (1993b) discusses this interplay between audience, speaker, and context in epideictic rhetoric, calling attention to the role of *ethos* in such moments, and arguing that ethos is developed both prior to and during their encounter with the speaker, with audience members considering the reputation of the speaker prior to the epideictic appeal. In epideictic encounters, the *ethos* of a speaker, in other words, can be shaped by the norms, values, and preconceptions held by an audience as much as it is by the rhetorical choices of a speaker. Sullivan posits, "[e]pideictic speakers make allusions to historical events or works and thereby themselves with the tradition...[They] are able...to make broad generalizations because they express sentiments already held by the audience" (123). Identification between the speaker and audience bolsters the prospects for a successful epideictic encounter, described by Sullivan as, "one in which the rhetor, as a mature member of the culture, creates an aesthetic vision of orthodox... leading to imitation...epideictic instructs the auditors and invites them to participate in a celebration of tradition, creating a sense of communion" (118). The simultaneous process of understanding and accepting each other's rhetorical vision manifests the epideictic appeal as dependent on matching meanings of reputation, authority, and goodwill. Arguably, then, ethos in epideictic moments is conceived not as a persuasive strategy that results in compliance by an audience, but constituted through an ideological interplay between rhetorical act and audience, the result of a process in which the speaker's trustworthiness, goodwill, and authority are as much constituted by her audience as the audience is constituted by the rhetorical act (Charland 1987).

Buffett's Celebrity Humanitarianism as Epideictic Ethos

This constant recreation of ethos may be one reason that biographers and journalists consistently remind us of Buffett's modest and ordinary lifestyle. We know where he lives, what he eats, and what he reads. And all are modestly ordinary. Biographers Roger Lowenstein (1995) and Alice Schroeder (2009) both point out that Buffett still lives on Farnam Street in Omaha—in the house he purchased in 1958 for $31,500. Schroeder documents how Buffett described the house: "While the largest house on the block it had an unpretentious and charming air, with dormers set into the sloping shingled roof and an eyebrow window" (192). Schroeder describes Buffett's favorite meal as the modest fare of steak, hash browns, and a Coke. Buffett does not have a chauffeur, and according to Matthews (2009) he "often picks up visitors at the airport himself, [and] goes into the office seven days a week" (32). Buffett has a low regard for Wall Street financial research, preferring to depend on his own assessment of financial news. Lowenstein (1995) writes that Buffett reads newspapers every morning upon rising at 4:30 am, including the *Wall Street Journal*, the *Financial Times*, the *New York Times*, *USA Today*, and the *Omaha World-Herald*.

Buffett's celebrity humanitarianism, especially as constructed by his numerous biographers and flattering media profiles, fosters epideictic moments saturated with precise references to his character; a character grounded in the neoliberal ideals of individualism, capitalism, and competition. Buffett's neoliberalism is arguably "packed" with epideictic stock; a result of his celebrity wealth and philanthropy that constitutes his epideictic ethos through reputation, vision, authority, goodwill, and consubstantiality (Sullivan 1993a, b). Although Buffett's celebrity is constituted through neoliberal discourse, his identity as a neoliberal is frequently obscured through rhetorical strategies that de-emphasize his status as one of the wealthiest men in the world. This obfuscation, intentional or not, can be seen in constructions of Buffett as a simple man with simple tastes, a theme which dominates the mediated representations of his success. Biographers and media writers all describe Buffett's legendary simplicity. According to journalist Rick Newman (2008), at least 50 biographies (2007–2013) focus on Buffett's notorious thrift. Newman notes: "He has made more money than just about anyone, but appears to have no use for it" (27). Some have called him the reluctant billionaire with a desire for wealth attainment but not the luxuries of wealth (Schroeder 2009).

Our goal is to demonstrate how the discursive formations that surround and constitute Buffett as a public figure are infused with a neoliberal ideology that affirms private competition over government regulation of the market. We also wish to highlight how Buffett himself contributes to a neoliberal ethos, both through the image he has cultivated for public consumption and through the tenets of investing he espouses to his followers.

Buffett's Reputation: Celebrity Wealth and Friends

In broad terms, celebrity status often follows mega-wealth attainment, particularly in our present era of mass and instant media where celebrity investors and CEOs are prevalent for their social influence, the friends they keep, their apparent sincerity, as well as the riches they bank. Buffett's "initial ethos," or his reputation, is one he shares with other ultra-rich. For Buffett, celebrity status followed wealth attainment, in much the same way as Hayward et al. (2004) define the CEO celebrity as a mediated phenomenon that occurs when journalists report, broadcast, or transmit corporate profits as caused by its leaders' actions. In simple terms, what is often reported by the media are the profound selling techniques, powers, or skills of the celebrity CEO and/or investor. Buffett's celebrity status reflects social and media interest on skilled "rainmakers," a term that author Ford Harding (2006) uses for those profoundly talented sellers. According to Harding, describing top sellers and profiteers as "rainmakers" avoids directly referencing them as "sellers" and thus averts their social power, network, and assets as exclusively profit-driven. Buffett's celebrity status, notes Schroeder (2009), contributes to what she calls Buffett's "snowball," a metaphor that describes Buffett's focus on selling and compounding the profits from sales, a fixation that began in childhood. Schroeder writes:

> It is the winter of Warren's ninth year. Outside in the yard, he and his little sister, Bertie, are playing in the snow. Warren is catching snowflakes…he starts to pack them into a ball. As the snowball grows bigger, he places it on the ground…He gives it a push, and it picks up more snow. He pushes the snowball across the lawn, piling snow on snow. Soon he reaches the edge of the yard. After a moment of hesitation, he heads off, rolling the snowball through the neighborhood…And from there, Warren continues onward, casting his eye on a whole world of snow. (n.p.)

Schroeder's vignette constructs Buffett's capitalistic virtues as mythic qualities reflecting determination, wonder, and accumulation that often characterize successful sellers. As Korczynski (2005) argues, selling is fundamental in capitalistic social relations. Selling promotes the enchanting myth of customer sovereignty that facilitates opportunities for the seller to influence consumer needs. The enchanting myth of customer sovereignty, notes Korczynski, extends Marx's critique that the capitalist is interested not so much in the consumer per se but in obtaining the consumer's money, and to do so, "the process of enchantment can be usefully thought of as the creation of pleasurable dreams and fantasies around an array of time, space, self-image, social relations and material products" (74). Dreams and fantasies of commodity accumulation are often entrenched through the rhetorical construction of empathy and consumers are keen to how these sales techniques privilege the seller and thus potentially halting the sale. To facilitate the sale, the seller combines fantasy-commodity accumulation with consumer sovereignty which "relates to the playing out of a feeling of individual automony and has a sense of independence…tied to it" (75). In rhetorical terms, the seller's ethos attracts audience attention, and together each facilitates the rhetorical vision Korczynski and Ott (2004) call, the "enchanting myth of consumer sovereignty" (590). For Buffett and other celebrity CEOs and investors, journalists and consumers celebrate their wealth and vending skills; their reputation and fame manifests itself in public image.

Just how significant is Buffett's celebrity status, his reputation are reflective of his epideictic ethos. Among Buffett's friends are Bill and Melinda Gates, Bono, David Beckham, Paul McCartney, LeBron James, Jay-Z, Ndamukong Suh, and Bill and Hillary Clinton. Buffett is regularly interviewed and reported about by mainstream media, TV business reports, and investment blogs. This press coverage echoes the neoliberal ethos emphasizing the value of the free market, celebrating private charity, and lauding individual frugality. As of November 30, 2015, CNBC's *Warren Buffett Watch Blog* documents his preference for Hillary Clinton as the 45th U.S. President, his *Forbes* 400 Lifetime Achievement Award for Philanthropy (where during the ceremony he was serenaded by U2's Bono), his close friendship with Bill Gates, his opinions about "hot" stocks and economic forecasts, and his simple and thrifty lifestyle that arguably provide evidence of how the mass media contours Buffett's epideictic ethos for public consumption.

Buffett's Vision: Value-Investing and Thrift

With little exception, biographies and media coverage of Buffett frame him as the reluctant billionaire who finds more pleasure in being thrifty than in being wealthy. When Buffett began his financial career in the mid-1950s, he would often travel from Omaha to attend meetings in swanky New York City clubs and restaurants wearing tennis shoes and open-collared shirts with the sleeves rolled up. His austere presence seemed out-of-place in the glass and marbled towers of Wall Street. Buffett's "awe-shucks" attire, notes biographer Jay Steele (1999), was the topic of gossip among Wall Street elites in the 1960s, and upon visiting New York City in 1968, Buffett promised his wife Susie that he would wear a suit for upcoming business meetings. Buffett did wear a suit, but according to Steele, he still looked scruffy and un-kept. When a reporter asked about his style of dress, Buffett quipped: "I buy expensive suits. They just look cheap on me" (6). This quote is just one example of the folksy and frugal ethos that Buffett has cultivated for himself, an ethos that also manifests itself in the "value-investing" financial philosophy that informs Buffett's approach to the market.

Value-investing is a financial mind-set concerned with acquiring and maintaining wealth over the long-term rather than engaging in risky investments that hint at short-term gains. The financial mind-set of value-investing operates as a psychological and rhetorical construct that guides not only his financial investments but also his ethos. For Buffett, wealth is based on thrift, a concept defined in the *Millionaire Next Door: The Surprising Secrets of America's Wealthy*, as involving the slow process of becoming successful by saving money instead of spending it, budgeting down to the last cent, investing carefully and prodigiously, seeking out good advice when necessary, and spending a tremendous amount of time on money matters. In other words, Buffett and his followers reject the temptations of instantaneous short-term greed for long-term wealth. This focus on thrift affirms the idea that good individual choices are the route to financial success, a major tenet of neoliberal economic policy. In short, Buffett and his fellow value-investors are depicted by the media as different and indifferent to what we typically associate with wealth in modern times—the fast-paced and speculative realities of Wall Street. For example, Buffett's shareholders point to the technology market collapse of 2000–2002 as evidence of Buffett's brilliance of value-investing. While the technology stocks tumbled in 2001, Buffett's Berkshire Hathaway investors profited (Kirn 2004). During the market tumbles of 2007–2009, Buffett advised Americans to be patient and to ignore investing fads, manias, and to adhere to sound financial principles for the long term (McArdle 2009). *Fortune* editor and recent Buffett biographer Carol J. Loomis (2013) documented the following quip as evidence of Buffett's commitment to value-investing: "I [Berkshire Hathaway] simply attempt to be fearful when others are greedy and greedy only when others are fearful… Our favorite holding period is forever" (278).

BUFFETT'S AUTHORITY: RIDICULE WALL STREET

Sullivan (1993a, b) notes that the epideictic rhetor "has the ability to see connections, to interpret reality convincingly" (120). In this vein, the epideictic rhetor is often perceived as a "seer, a prophet with supernatural vision" (120). The third component of epideictic ethos, authority, as an image of orthodoxy created through the rhetor's use of generalities that reflect the culture's consciousness of reality, wisdom, and prudence. Buffett does this by ridiculing Wall Street's "get rich" schemes.

Buffett's authority is strengthened by his consistent ridicule of Wall Street while championing the "common" investor's long-term fortitude. Buffett's vision is antithetical and skeptical of Wall Street, and in constructing this epideictic ethos and presence, his contrarian authority seems more clairvoyant than prophetic. Buffett writes: "We have 'professional' investors, those who manage many billions who...instead of focusing on what businesses will do in the years ahead...now focus on what they expect other money managers to do in the days ahead. For them, stocks are merely tokens in a game, like the thimble and flatiron in Monopoly" (1995, 81). In fact, Buffett's value-investing strategy is based on avoiding what he calls "the institutional imperative" (95). This imperative prioritizes the corporation and not the investor, and as such, "rationality frequently wilts when the institutional imperative comes into play" (95). Buffett points to the raise and collapse of the "junk bond" market of the 1990s as an example of how championing the corporation over the investor is foolish.

The junk bond phenomenon and collapse "resulted from a managerial failing and the tendency of executives to mindlessly imitate the behavior of their peers, no matter how foolish it may be to do so. In their lending, many bankers played follow-the-leader with lemming-like zeal; and they are experiencing lemming-like fate" (1995, 97). To counter-act the workings and fads of the Wall Street elites, Buffett describes his strategy of value investing as "lethargy bordering on sloth remains the cornerstone of our investment style" (97). Buffett's ridicule for Wall Street is seemingly based on its irrational preoccupation with time. Wall Street's "get rich fast" is not only irrational but according to Buffett, follows adrenalin and not commitment, temperance, and patience. Far too often, "as the adrenalin of deal-makers surge...debt became something to be refinanced rather than repaid...such an attitude is clearly delusional" (106). Schroeder (2009) describes why Buffett labels bankers as promoters rather than investors. Bankers should perform a gate-keeping role and guard investors against the promoter's propensity to indulge in excess. Accordingly,

> promoters, after all, have throughout time exercised the same judgment and restraint in accepting money that alcoholics have exercised in accepting liquor. At a minimum, therefore, the banker's conduct should rise to that of a responsible bartender who, when necessary, refuses to profit from the next drink to avoid sending a drunk out on the highway. (Lowenstein 1995, 412)

Likewise, Buffett points to the major folly of investment and banking promoters desire to buy stocks at bargain prices. These "bargain-hunters" seem to get so caught up in making a great deal as to promote their investment authority and prowess that they forget or reject Buffett's standard authority when deciding to buy a stock: "It's far better to buy a wonderful company at a fair price than a fair company at a wonderful price" (1995, 94). Moreover, Buffett's advice to all investors is to be skeptical of Wall Street forecasts and calculations:

> to invest successfully, you need not understand beta, efficient markets, modern portfolio theory, option pricing, or emerging markets. You may, in fact, be better of knowing nothing of these. That, of course, is not the prevailing view at most business schools, whose finance curriculum tends to be dominated by such subjects. In my view, though, investment students need only two well-taught courses—How to Value a Business, and How to Think About Market Prices." (93)

BUFFETT'S GOODWILL: CELEBRITY "WARREN WATCH"

Epideictic ethos not only is facilitated by reputation, vision, and authority but also includes a fourth rhetorical construct, the presentation of good reasons. As Sullivan (1993b) posits, "the epideictic speaker or writer is also engaged in teaching, in passing on traditionally accepted values, and it is in the role of a teacher that he or she must provide good reasons" (125). Buffett's philanthropy highlights his austerity and identification with people who attain wealth, not for luxury or power but for sharing it.

Omaha World-Herald reporter Steve Jordon is assigned by his editors to report on all things "Buffett." Each Sunday, the *Omaha World-Herald* documents Buffett's appearances, his financial prognostications, and his growing reputation as a philanthropist in a section called "Warren Watch." For example, in June 2010, Jordon reported on a dinner hosted by Buffett and Bill Gates. The dinner included billionaires Oprah Winfrey, George Soros, Ted Turner, among others, and its purpose was to discuss how each should pledge their riches to change society. Beyond describing the commonalities each of these billionaires share, Jordon's article also distinguishes Buffett's ethos beyond Oprah's, George's, and Ted's. Jordon includes in the report Buffett's recent appearance at the Sing Sing Prison graduation ceremony that seemingly provided further significance to Buffett's donation of $1.93 billion to the Bill & Melinda Gates

Foundation. In the weekly "Warren Watch" section, readers are quick to learn, if not repeatedly reminded, that Buffett is the "billionaire next door." Buffett is, as one faithful Berkshire annual meeting attendee noted, "is one of us helping us" (Matthews 2009, 121).

According to McArdle (2009), annual meeting attendees ask a central question regarding potential investments: What would Warren do? He answers in plain-spoken wisdom. "Don't speculate. Don't risk money you cannot afford to lose. Don't try to get rich quick. Don't panic when the price drops. If there are no good buys, don't buy anything. Above all, ignore what other people are saying" (31). McArdle observed that the "annual pilgrimage" to Omaha by Berkshire-Hathaway investors runs "against the grain of dominant culture. Only here in Omaha, for one weekend a year, are they a majority. The meeting, with its quasi-ritual speeches, canonical stories and jokes, and the fellowship of other value investors, helps to brace them against a society that almost actively rejects their austere financial philosophy" (30–31). The number and fervor of investors embarking on this pilgrimage also illustrates the obligation that Buffett faces to live up to, and continually recreate, his own ethos.

Buffett cherishes the relationship he has cultivated with his investors and followers, and according to Lowenstein (1995), his philanthropy is an extension of this relationship. Buffett acts without affluence and according to Kirn (2004), his "bread and butter philosophy is homemade and patiently churned" (107). In describing the relationship he nurtures with his followers, Buffett notes, "that I'm as polished as I need to be to work for those I work for" (1995, 194). It is no surprise that what Buffett cares about most when he buys a company is character (Matthews 2009). Every member of the Berkshire "family" knows Buffett's proclivity for character and as reported by Matthews, Buffett once instructed his managers to consider character:

> We can afford to lose money—even a lot of money. We cannot afford to lose reputation—even a shred of reputation. Let's be sure that everything we do in business can be reported on the front page of a national newspaper in an article written by an unfriendly but intelligent reporter (115).

For Buffett, *his* character and *his* reputation are the pillars of his philanthropy. Wealth provides the "good reasons" for why, in his opinion, he does not pay enough taxes (Buffett 2011). He sympathizes for the poor and middle class and "while most Americans struggle to make ends meet, we mega-rich continue to get our extraordinary tax breaks...these and other blessings are showered upon us by legislators in Washington who feel compelled to protect us... It's nice to have friends in high places" (Buffett 2011). For those who seemingly do not have friends in "high places," Buffett fills the void. His philanthropic relationship with the fellow billionaire Bill Gates demonstrates his concern for people and issues not "coddled." In fact, Buffett's wealth, according to Schroder, is the conduit that ironically identifies him most as a *folk hero* primarily and then as a successful investor.

BUFFETT'S CONSUBSTANTIALITY: BUFFETT'S WIT

The fifth construct of epideictic ethos is the creation of consubstantiality. Sullivan (1993b) notes that "the audience must think of the rhetor as one of their own, preeminent among them, no doubt, but still on who belongs to them" (126). The communion created with the audience, is perhaps, Buffett's most powerful rhetorical transcendence. "Buffett Watchers" get "caught up in a celebration" (128) of his vision of reality—a manifestation that Buffett actively orchestrates and cultivates in the biographies written about him. Buffett biographers, especially Lowenstein (1995) and Schroeder (2009), document his life experiences with ordinary "folks" who all share his moral affinity for thrift. In doing so, Buffett's biographers provide testimony to Buffett's epideictic ethos and his unique version of austerity based on wealth and social consciousness.

According to Newman (2008), at least 50 authors have written about Buffett, and these biographies and inquires all emphasize Buffett's wit. For example, Schroeder (2009) discusses how Buffett became apt with "wisecracks, quips, and word-play" (78) as a way to rebel against his resigned upbringing. Accordingly, Buffett often uses common language that is stern with pat wisecracks:

> Charlie [Munger, Berkshire Hathaway's Vice Chairman] and I frequently get approached about acquisitions that don't come close to meeting our tests: I've found that if you advertise an interest in buying collies, a lot of people will call hoping to sell you their cocker spaniels. A line from a country song

expresses our feeling about new ventures, turnarounds or auction-like sales: "When the phone don't ring, you'll know it's me." (Buffett 1995, 154)

Buffett is direct in offering financial advice to corporate America, and not afraid to say what he thinks about spontaneous investing and his own investing mistakes. "Mountains of junk bonds were sold by those who didn't care to those who didn't think" (1995, 102). Nor is he afraid to be honest about his personal mistakes, his pat wisecracks can be self-deprecating: "In another context, a friend once asked me: 'If you're so rich, why aren't you smart?' After reviewing my sorry performance with USAir, you may conclude he had a point" (114).

As chairman of Berkshire-Hathaway, Buffett cultivates a direct relationship with stockholders embodied by his serious and wisecracking words. This approach is straightforward, common, funny, and practical. He seems most pleased with his approachable demeanor—as long as he is approached about business dealings and investing:

> When you...receive a communication from us, it will come from the fellow you are paying to run the business. Your Chairman [Buffett] has a firm belief that owners are entitled to hear directly from the CEO as to what is going on and how he evaluates the business, currently and prospectively. (1995, 27)

For Buffett, "talking business" means frank dialogue. In fact, biographers Schroeder (2009) and Lowenstein (1995) both document Buffett's distaste for "small talk."

IMPLICATIONS AND CONCLUSION

Buffett's unique exigency consists of a lot of wealth and a lot of celebrity status. He grasps the attention of the media's market as easily as he masters the financial market. Buffett's immense wealth and status raises an important question for rhetorical critics interested in the study of neoliberalism: Why has Warren Buffett, one of the wealthiest and most influential men in the USA, who is constantly celebrated for his financial acumen, failed repeatedly at his rhetorical task of changing economic policy? Or put simply, why hasn't Buffett successfully invested his celebrity capital into public policy that, in his words, "stops coddling the super-rich?"

Buffett's chances for persuasion are certainly limited by the rhetoric of neoliberalism, but seemingly opportunities for changing the neoliberal view are possible within its free market spirit. Given that he commands a reputation as the "the billionaire next door" who effectively manages a rhetorical ethos of "the under-consumer," Buffett's ineffective attempts at shaping public economic policy void of neoliberal ideals is not surprising. Buffett's notoriety as philanthropist, or as the "billionaire next door, or as the "anti-Trump" are all "trumped" by his celebrity wealth and his status. In short, Buffett's "awe shucks" wisdom on value-investing watched on CNBC and read in *Forbes*, his homage to Omaha, his impressive philanthropic record, and his brokering of Gillette and Heinz corporate purchases all frame and prioritize an epideictic ethos that effectively highlights his commitment to selling and other neoliberal practices. Buffett's celebrity is the result of his overwhelming commitment to acquiring and maintaining wealth and capital. He is celebrated for his ethos that is constituted by his proclivity toward selling.

Celebrity capitalists like Buffett rely on the influence and growth of the mass media—newspaper, magazine, television, biographies, autobiographies, the Internet, and cinema and pop music—to facilitate cultural influence on consumer consciousness (Giles 2009). In fact, one of the surest ways to become famous in America is to become super-rich, identified by *Forbes* magazine as a billionaire, thus becoming a celebrity within and outside business. Super-rich Americans who have made seemingly important contributions to life and commerce in the world include Buffett and many of his celebrity-capitalist friends: Bill Gates, Ralph Lauren, Martha Stewart, and Steve Wynn (Leslie 2011). This version of the rhetorical situation prioritizes wealth and celebrity as foundational rather than affect.

Chaput (2010) challenges the classic or "affect" approach to epideictic rhetoric, arguing that it makes assumptions about rhetorical situations that no longer hold true in a discursive space dominated by neoliberalism, because "affect functions separately from emotion and cannot be understood in terms of the reason-emotion divide" (3). Chaput's insistence on expanding the scope of the rhetorical situation, and its consequent effect on rhetorical agency in a neoliberal context, is most relevant to the case of Buffett's rhetorical failure in influencing equitable tax policy. Using Foucault's theory of biopolitics as a means for understanding how the discourse of neoliberalism flows throughout society and constitutes neoliberal subjects, Chaput argues that we must

...reshape the internal dynamics of rhetoric, abandoning the understanding of such dynamics in terms of situations—particular moments that demand discursive intervention in order to propel change—and instead conceptualizing them in terms of a milieu of dispersed transhistorical and transsituational moments. This ontological shift takes us from the rhetorical situation as temporally and spatially fixed site of exigency, constraints, and discourse to rhetorical circulation as a fluidity of everyday practices, affects, and uncertainties. (5–6)

As Chaput notes, this new understanding of the rhetorical situation challenges conventional understandings of rhetorical agency, which rely on a "liberal logic of one-to-one influence or cause and effect" (10) and assume that both individuals and their audiences are fully formed, unified subjects that exist prior to any given interaction, "ignoring the fact that rhetoric constructs and deconstructs" identities (10).

Through the lens of rhetorical circulations—and in contrast to more clearly defined rhetorical situations—rhetoric is seen as "an allusive component" that flows throughout many discursive spaces to "connect the differently situated moments comprising its organic whole" and constitute the subjects involved in any particular discussion (12–13). Thus, the multiple discourses that constitute Buffett's identity culminate in his celebrity-wealth and humanitarian status.

Buffett's media-constructed celebrity ethos celebrates wealth as equally rural and urban, regulatory and free market, and frugal and rich, reinforcing a neoliberal ideology that perpetuates the myth of wealth being possible for anyone willing to work hard enough to achieve it. Residing in thrifty Omaha and disciplined in value-investing, Buffett's celebrity is bolstered by laudatory biographical stories of his self-restraint and self-regulation. These stories shape an ethos that both enables and constrains Buffett, providing him with rhetorical agency in matters of private investment but limiting his ability to advocate for economic policies that run counter to neoliberal ideology. In other words, when Buffett says the rich need to pay more taxes, his rhetorical agency is limited by his epideictic ethos: that is, his reputation, vision, authority, goodwill, and identification with his audience as one of the world's shrewdest investors and financiers.

The mediated celebration of Buffett's celebrity supplements a cultural fascination with his legacy of philanthropy. Loomis (2013) recently noted that his commitment of billions to the Bill and Melinda Gates Foundation is a genuine extension of his authentic desire to provide aid support for the world's most unfortunate. For Buffett, wealth provides access to a level of global servitude that the realm of geo-politics cannot match. Wrapped in his wealth and secured in his celebratory spectacle of neoliberalism, Buffett, Bill and Melinda Gates, George Soros, and few others are functioning as the pinnacle neoliberal ambassadors, proving to the world that governments are no match for neoliberal ideals. When Buffett famously calls for more taxes on the ultra-rich, his plea is no doubt genuine. His wealth, his celebrity, and his neoliberal ideals are no match for any government's calls for austerity. Government-sponsored austerity measures are met with much public resistance. At the height of the global recession, from 2007 to 2012, austerity measures were imposed worldwide and public outcry followed. At roughly the same time, Buffett announced that he was giving all of his wealth away. He called for tax increases. He maintained his commitment to value investing, and while homes foreclosed and investment firms were bailed out, Buffett's holdings increased three-fold.

So what is it about Buffett the neoliberal celebrity who paradoxically calls for higher taxes, care for the poor, while living simply, and bound to thrift and austerity so passionately, that he is committed to giving his vast fortunes away? For rhetorical critics, the implications of Buffett's epideictic ethos offer insight into three inter-related neoliberal complexities. First, neoliberalism insulates wealth and the wealthy from popular critical examination because media and politics champion individual wealth attainment over social and cultural prosperity. Besides monetary wealth, those few, like Buffett, who possess symbolic capital that constitutes an epideictic ethos (reputation, vision, authority, goodwill, and identification) shrouded in the virtues of the "self-made" are, no doubt, invested with assets that rhetorically affiliate humanitarianism as a neoliberal virtue. Second, Buffett's epideictic ethos arguably resonates with wealthy elites who engage in what is popularly termed as social responsibility or humanitarianism. Epideictic ethos invites judgments of authenticity, but when corporations and governments make similar attempts, critical opinions often point to the agencies' inauthentic motives. Third, neoliberals who are ultra-rich and who gain celebrity status through philanthropy need the media and foster it in the creation of celebrity status. The manifestations of wealth and virtue are sustained in a mediated spectacle that offers no critical assessment of how ethos, wealth, and philanthropy-widen class and economic status. As this chapter illustrates, epideictic notions of ethos are particularly powerful when affiliated with celebrity status.

In all, Buffett's celebrity-based epideictic ethos and his neoliberal brand of "humanitarianism" represent, contrary to his cultivated image, a threat to democracy worldwide. "This manipulation of the body politic by the *culture industry*," notes Barker (2011, 157), "is not a new phenomenon. What's different is that the agents of neoliberalism are now able to employ more sophisticated forms of propaganda in their cynical abuse of public sentiment." Our analysis cannot fully support Barker's claim regarding neoliberal propaganda, but it does, we believe, illustrate the profound influence of neoliberalism within the rich rhetorical construction of Warren Buffett's celebrity-wealth-epideictic ethos.

References

Adams, John C. 2006. Epideictic and Its Cultured Reception: In Memory of Firefighters. In *Rhetorics of Display*, ed. L.J. Prelli, 293–310. Columbia, SC: University of South Carolina Press.

Agnew, Lois. 2008. "The Day Belongs to the Students": Expanding Epideictic's Civic Function. *Rhetoric Review* 27(2): 147–164.

Barker, Michael. 2011. Celebrity Philanthropy: In the Service of Corporate Propaganda. In *The Propaganda Society: Promotional Culture and Politics in Global Context*, ed. G. Sussman, 145–158. New York: Peter Lang Publishing.

Beale, Walter H. 1978. Rhetorical Performative Discourse: A New Theory of Epideictic. *Philosophy and Rhetoric* 11(4): 221–246.

Bostdorff, Denise M. 2011. Epideictic Rhetoric in the Service of War: George W. Bush on Iraq and the 60th Anniversary of the Victory over Japan. *Communication Monographs* 78(3): 296–323.

Bowyer, Jerry. 2012. When Warren Went Left: The Ideological Seduction of Warren Buffett. *Forbes*. Accessed 12 Nov 2014. http://www.forbes.com/sites/jerrybowyer/2012/11/29/when-warren-went-left-the-ideological-seduction-of-warren-buffett/

Buffett, Warren E. 2011. Stop Coddling the Super-Rich. *New York Times*, August 14. Accessed 14 Nov 2014. http://www.nytimes.com/2011/08/15/opinion/stop-coddling-the-super-rich.html

———. 2012. A Minimum Tax for the Wealthy. *New York Times*, November 25. Accessed 20 Nov 2014. http://www.nytimes.com/2012/11/26/opinion/buffett-a-minimum-tax-for-the-wealthy.html

Buffett, Warren E., and Lawrence A. Cunningham. 1995. *The Essays of Warren Buffett: Lessons for Corporate America* Durham, NC: Carolina Academic Press.

Carter, Michael F. 1991. The Ritual Function of Epideictic Rhetoric: The Case of Socrates' Funeral Oration. *Rhetorica* 9(3): 209–232.

Chaput, C. 2010. Rhetorical Circulation in Late Capitalism: Neoliberalism and the Overdetermination of Affective Energy.*Philosophy and Rhetoric*. 43(1): 1–25.

Charland, Maurice. 1987. Constitutive Rhetoric: The Case of the *Peuple Québécois*. *Quarterly Journal of Speech* 73(2): 133–150.

Chase, J. Richard. 1961. The Classical Conception of Epideictic. *Quarterly Journal of Speech* 47(3): 293–300.
Chomsky, Noam. 1999. *Profit Over People: Neoliberalism and Global Order.* New York: Seven Stories.
Cloud, D. 2003. Therapy, Silence, and War: Consolation and the End of Deliberation in the "Affected" Public. *Poroi: An Interdisciplinary Journal of Rhetorical Analysis and Invention.* 2(1): 125–142.
Condit, Celeste Michelle. 1985. The Functions of Epideictic: The Boston Massacre Orations as Exemplar. *Communication Quarterly* 50(4): 284–299.
Crable, Richard E., and Steven L. Vibbert. 1983. Mobil's Epideictic Advocacy: "Observations" of Prometheus-Bound. *Communication Monographs* 50(4): 380–394.
Danisch, Robert. 2006. Power and the Celebration of the Self: Michel Foucault's Epideictic Rhetoric. *Southern Communication Journal* 71(3): 291–307.
Harding, Ford. 2006. *Creating Rainmakers: The Manager's Guide to Training Professionals to Attract New Clients.* Hoboken, NJ: Wiley.
Harpine, William D. 2004. "We Want Yer, McKinley": Epideictic Rhetoric in Songs from the 1896 Presidential Campaign. *Rhetoric Society Quarterly* 34(1): 73–88.
Hauser, Gerard. 1999. Aristotle on Epideictic: The Formation of Public Morality. *Rhetoric Society Quarterly* 29(1): 5–23.
Hayward, Mathew L. A., Violina Rindova, and Timothy G. Pollock. 2004. Believing One's Own Press: The Causes and Consequences of CEO Celebrity. *Strategic Management Journal* 25(7): 637–653.
Huang, Chye-Ching. 2012. *Recent Studies Find Raising Taxes on High-Income Households Would Not Harm the Economy: Policy Should be Included in Balanced Deficit Reduction Effort.* Washington, DC: Center on Budget and Policy Priorities.
Hungerford, Thomas L. 2011. An Analysis of the "Buffett Rule." *Congressional Research Service,* October 7.
Kirn, Walter. 2004. American Everyman: Warren Buffett's Billions—And the Oft Told Tale of How He Made Them—Have Become the Least Interesting Thing about Him: It's Buffett the Symbol that Matters Now. *The Atlantic Monthly,* November 1, 104–111.
Korczynski, Marek. 2005. The Point Of Selling: Capitalism, Consumption and Contradictions. *Organization* 12(1): 69–88.
Korczynski, Marek, and Ursula Ott. 2004. When Production and Consumption Meet: Cultural Contradictions and the Enchanting Myth of Customer Sovereignty. *Journal of Management Studies* 41(4): 575–599.
Lauer, Maceio Ilon. 2015. Epideictic Rhetoric. *Communication Research Trends* 34(2): 4–18.
Leslie, Larry Z. 2011. *Celebrity in the 21st Century: A Reference Book.* Santa Barbara, CA: ABC-CLIO, LLC.
Loomis, Carol J. 2013. *Tap Dancing to Work: Warren Buffett on Practically Everything, 1966–2013.* New York: Penguin.

Lowenstein, Roger. 1995. *Buffett: The Making of an American Capitalist.* New York: Broadway.
Matthews, Jeff. 2009. *Pilgrimage to Warren Buffett's Omaha: A Hedge Fund Manager's Dispatches from Inside the Berkshire Hathaway Annual Meeting.* New York: McGraw-Hill.
McArdle, Megan. 2009. What Would Warren Do? The Sage of Omaha Has Redefined the Idea of Value Investing. But Will Its Principles Survive His Inevitable Passing? *The Atlantic Monthly*, 304, September 1, 30–32.
McChesney, Robert W. 2001. Global Media, Neoliberalism, and Imperialism. *Monthly Review: An Independent Socialist Magazine*, 10, March 1, 1–19.
Miller, Carolyn R. 1993. The Polis as Rhetorical Community. *Rhetorica* 11(3): 211–240.
National Economic Council. 2012. The Buffet Rule: A Basic Principle of Tax Fairness. *The White House*.Accessed 14 November 2004. https://www.whitehouse.gov/sites/default/files/Buffett_Rule_Report_Final.pdf
Newman, Rick. 2008. The Paradoxes of Warren Buffett the Billionare. *U.S. News and World Report*, October 9, 27–28.
Oravec, Christine. 1976. Observation in Aristotle's Theory of Epideictic. *Philosophy and Rhetoric* 9(3): 162–174.
Perelman, Chaïm., and Lucie Olbrechts-Tyteca. 1969. *The New Rhetoric: A Treatise on Argumentation*, trans. J. W. Weaver. Notre Dame: University of Notre Dame Press.
Poulakos, Takis. 1987. Isocrates's Use of Narrative in the *Evagoras*: Epideictic Rhetoric and Moral Action. *Quarterly Journal of Speech* 73(3): 317–328.
Pratt, Jonathan. 2012. The Epideictic Agon and Aristotle's Elusive Third Genre. *The American Journal of Philology* 133(2): 177–208.
Rockwell, Donna, and David C. Giles. 2009. Being a Celebrity: A Phenomenology of Fame. *Journal of Phenomenological Psychology 40(2): 178–210.*
Rubin, Richard. 2012. Senate Blocks Buffett Rule 30% Tax Floor on Top Earners. *Bloomberg*,April17.Accessed14Oct2014.http://www.bloomberg.com/news/articles/2012-04-16/senate-blocks-buffett-rule-30-tax-floor-on-top-earners
Schroeder, Alice. 2009. *The Snowball: Warren Buffett and the Business of Life.* New York: Bantam.
Sheard, Cynthia Miecznikowski. 1996. The Public Value of Epideictic Rhetoric. *College English* 58(7): 765–794.
Singer, Ross. 2010. Neoliberal Style, the American Re-Generation, and Ecological Jeremiad in Thomas Friedman's "Code Green." *Environmental Communication* 4(2): 135–151.
Steele, Jay. 1999. *Warren Buffett: Master of the Market* New York: Avon Books.
Sullivan, Dale L. 1993a. A Closer Look at Education as Epideictic Rhetoric. *Rhetoric Society Quarterly* 23(3/4): 70–89.

———. 1993b. The Ethos of the Epideictic Encounter. *Philosophy and Rhetoric* 26(2):113–133.

———. 1994. Exclusionary Epideictic: NOVA's Narrative Excommunication of Fleischmann and Pons. *Science, Technology, and Human Values* 19(3): 283–306.

Vivian, Bradford J. 2006. Neoliberal Epideictic: Rhetorical Form and Commemorative Politics on September 11, 2002. *Quarterly Journal of Speech* 92(1): 1–26.

———. 2012. Up from Memory: Epideictic Forgetting in Booker T. Washington's Cotton States Exposition Address. *Philosophy and Rhetoric* 45(2): 189–212.

Rhetorical Agency in a Neoliberal Age: Foucault, Power, Agency, and Ethos

Robert Danisch

The Order of Things, Michel Foucault's historical account of the human sciences, ends with the provocative image of "man" being "erased, like a face drawn in sand at the edge of the sea" (1970, 387). Nine years later, Foucault began *Discipline and Punish*, his historical account of the modern penal systems, with the equally provocative image of the public torture and execution of Damiens. Taken together, these two images symbolically represent the ways in which human subjectivity has been transformed by social institutions and discursive regimes of rationality. For some, subjectivity is a given and natural attribute of human existence, but Foucault shows how such a basic feature of our conception of what it means to be human is a product of historical forces. The ending of *The Order of Things* hints at the possibility that some set of anonymous historical forces may wash away the modern sense of what it means to be human. The beginning of *Discipline and Punish* suggests that the transformation in our practices of punishment is also a transformation in the operations of power in our society more broadly. Foucault's concern with the human sciences, power relations, discourse, and the body (concerns that extended from his earliest work on madness to the final volumes of *The History of Sexuality*) seem especially prescient and troubling with the ongoing proliferation of

R. Danisch (✉)
Speech Communication, University of Waterloo, Waterloo, ON, Canada

© The Editor(s) (if applicable) and The Author(s) 2017
K. Hong Nguyen (ed.), *Rhetoric in Neoliberalism*,
DOI 10.1007/978-3-319-39850-1_4

neoliberal governmentality. In light of these two images, we may ask a straightforward, but complex, question: What kinds of agency or power do we have as citizens of a neoliberal state? Put in the terms of rhetorical theory, the cognate question is: What kinds of power or agency do we have in the creation of rhetoric, the use of language, and the ability to speak and express ourselves? What I take from these two images (and Foucault's work more generally) is that traditional answers to these questions that rely on a conception of subjectivity are insufficient to meet the demands of our present.

Rhetorical agency generally refers to the ability to speak or to express oneself. Most succinctly, it is the ability to create rhetoric. This means that rhetorical agency exists as a kind of empowerment—it relies on a conception of rhetoric as *dynamis*. Implied in the concept of rhetorical agency are a series of questions about the subject creating the rhetoric. Such questions touch on both a set of theoretical concerns regarding the status of subjectivity and practical concerns about the expression of subjectivity. This essay begins with a consideration of the classical Aristotelian concept of ethos as a mode of expressing and practicing rhetorical agency. For centuries, ethos has been continuously rethought in light of the vicissitudes of theories of subjectivity, but along the way it has remained essential to both the *dynamis* and *techne* of rhetoric. Ethos speaks directly to the potential of rhetorical discourse to produce social and political change. Foucault presents a unique and considerable challenge to both classical and modern conceptions of ethos, and helps explain how and why our neoliberal moment complicates ethos as a function of rhetorical agency. The main purpose of this essay is to consider the ways in which Foucault's work on power, discourse, and subjectivity helps us rethink how ethos works in sociopolitical affairs as an effective form of rhetorical agency. By showing how we are all subjects of regimes of discourse, Foucault's work points to the following difficult question: Do appeals to ethos, made possible by the discursive productivity of the neoliberal state, actually undermine or limit rhetorical agency? And by telling a fascinating combined history of the present and history of the subject, Foucault's work suggests that our notions of rhetorical agency are always already constituted by discourse. Given our historical moment and what we know about power, discourse and subjectivity, do our appeals to ethos express our agency and subjectivity or do they merely reproduce circulating discourses that serve only to render us all inhabitants of Bentham's panopticon? I hope to show that Foucault's insights can be combined with Aristotle's to help formulate a conception of relational power and relational agency that might ground an effective antidote to neoliberalism.

This essay is more committed to posing a set of questions than advancing a particular interpretation or argument about either Foucault or neoliberalism. Many within the rhetorical tradition have taken Foucault's work as an important resource in articulating a critical rhetoric and advancing or rethinking key features of rhetorical theory (McKerrow 1999, Vivian 2004). In an attempt to extend the work of other rhetorical theorists interested in Foucault, my purpose is to show how Foucault's conception of power and subjectivity combined with the conditions of neoliberalism pose significant challenges to basic considerations of rhetorical agency. In doing so, I hope to show how we might think about rhetorical power and rhetorical agency as commonplaces, or intellectual resources, for coping with the kinds of historical transformations that Foucault so eloquently described in his work. Foucault's challenge to our long-held beliefs about power and subjectivity need not result in a politics of resignation (as others have suggested). Instead, those challenges can sharpen and improve our ability to theorize and practice forms of rhetoric capable of generating political and social change. Comparing historical forces with waves from the sea crashing in on the sand is such a disturbing image because it renders change a matter of accident and not human intention. This essay goes in search of a way to take Foucault's insights into power, subjectivity, and discourse seriously while retaining the possibilities of rhetorical agency and rhetorical power to drive sociopolitical change. It ends by suggesting how we might reconceive such concerns as matters of relationality. Perhaps my entire understanding of what it means to be human and to use rhetoric will be washed away by a series of anonymous historical forces, but in the meantime I find the combination of Foucault and Aristotle a useful resource for articulating a conception of rhetorical agency and rhetorical power that could resist the proliferation of the neoliberal state by turning toward relationality and away from subjectivity.

Dynamis, Ethos, and Rhetorical Agency

Aristotle defines rhetoric as "the ability in each case to see the available means of persuasion" (*Rhetoric* 1355b). This translation renders the original Greek word *dynamis* as "ability." In some other translations, *dynamis* is understood as a faculty. Both translations miss an important feature of Aristotle's definition. Homer used *dynamis* to refer to bodily strength, power, or might. By extension, *dynamis* also referred to force, or more specifically to a kind of potentiality for force. Aristotle was most certainly aware of the ways in which Homer used *dynamis*, and so when he chose to define rhetoric as a *dynamis*, he knew it would have been interpreted as faculty or ability, on one hand, and force, power or strength, on the other. The meaning of *dynamis* is inextricably linked up with agency within the classical Greek world, either divine agency or human agency. It is an embodied concept, meant to highlight the different kinds of powerful capacities for doing that both humans and gods possessed. A better translation of Aristotle's definition of rhetoric might be: "The embodied power, ability, force, or capacity to see, in each case, the available means of persuasion." This would better highlight the ways in which rhetoric is a powerful capacity for doing located within the potentialities of human agents. Rhetoric is power in its nascent state, according to Aristotle. At the same time, rhetoric is also a *techne*, or a system of rules for the use of language. To learn these rules is to learn how best to practice rhetoric, or to direct human agency through discourse. We go in search of the rules governing the practice of rhetoric to better turn the potentialities of rhetorical power into actualities. To exercise rhetorical power (*dynamis*) demands that we know a body of rules and principles (*techne*) for the use of discourse and the practice of persuasion. If we simply take Aristotle's definition of rhetoric as a starting point, rhetorical agency is the power to actualize the principles and practices that constitute the *techne* of rhetoric in order to pursue the rhetor's desired end.

Aristotle admits that rhetoric is not easy to practice, and that exercising rhetorical power through rules or principles derived from experience is complicated by the presence of an audience: "But since rhetoric is concerned with making a judgment (people judge what is said in deliberation, and judicial proceedings are also a judgment), it is necessary not only to look to the argument that it be demonstrative and persuasive, but also to construct a view of himself as a certain kind of person and to prepare the judge" (1377b21–24). William Grimaldi interprets this commitment to audience by noting that Aristotle was quite aware that: "one is always speaking to a person who is a complexus of reason, feelings, emotions, and set attitudes" (1980, 9). It would, therefore, be wrong to pervert or manipulate the audience that is judging. A statement can only be persuasive, for Aristotle, "because there is somebody whom it persuades" (1365b25–28). *Dynamis*, or rhetorical power, is only realized through engagement with an audience. The audience decides the fate of discourse, and, therefore, has agency itself. Much of the *Rhetoric* is devoted to the action and agency of others as an audience in the formation of character and the rendering of judgments. This is why Aristotle claimed that ethos was the controlling mode of persuasion: "[There is persuasion] through character whenever the speech is spoken in such a way as to make the speaker worthy of credence; for we believe fair-minded people to a greater extent and more quickly on all subjects in general and completely so in cases where there is not exact knowledge but room for doubt. And this should result from the speech, not from previous opinion that the speaker is a certain kind of person; for it is not the case, as some of the technical writers propose in their treatment of the art, that fair-mindedness on the part of the speaker makes no contribution to persuasiveness; rather, character is almost, so to speak, the controlling factor in persuading" (1365a). Ethos is more than the intrinsic character of the speaker; it is the character of the speaker *made manifest by speech*. I highlight this characteristic of ethos because it will be essential to my argument about Foucault and neoliberal governmentality but also because it shows how ethos is constructed by the interaction between rhetor and audience. Rhetorical power, the *dynamis* of rhetoric, is made actual through speech predominantly by virtue of appeals to ethos that cause the audience to judge a piece of discourse favorably in the light of some trust in the rhetor that is constructed by that piece of discourse. The most fundamental aspects of the *techne* of rhetoric that one must master are the rules that allow one to manifest ethos through discourse. In other words, discursive appeals to ethos are the surest way, for Aristotle, to activate the *dynamis* of rhetoric. I don't mean to discount the use of logos and pathos in constructing discourse, and surely Aristotle suggested that a rhetor use those modes of proof as well. But one's discursive choices in using logos and pathos are also ways of manifesting one's ethos through speech (Garver 1995).

Both Aristotle and Isocrates agreed that personal character was often the strongest source of persuasion, but this was not just the aura of credibility or trust that accompanied a speaker. Ethos is a mode of proof, and, therefore, it is simply not enough to have a reputation as a likable person or a great communicator. These qualities must be manifested through discourse in order to tap into the potentiality of rhetoric. Character is not a constant, an entity that exists prior to rhetorical success. Instead, it is something performed and reformed through the rhetorical choices we make when we engage audiences. Specifically, Aristotle claims that audiences trust a speaker able to display *phronesis* (wisdom), *arête* (virtue), and *eunoia* (good will). (1378a). The rhetor's task is to display these three characteristics to the audience. When one considers how this might be accomplished, it begins to seem as if a rhetor must display a working knowledge or expertise regarding some subject matter, a cultural sense of the values of an audience, and the ability to identify with an audience. It is hard to imagine how rhetorical power might be used to drive radical (or revolutionary) sociopolitical change given such constraints. Instead, it seems more likely that a "good," and ultimately effective rhetor would simply understand the necessary moves of the reigning discursive mode of the audience and be able to work well within those constraints. In some sense, Kenneth Burke offers an updated take on this notion of ethos in *The Rhetoric of Motives*: "You persuade a man only insofar as you can talk his language by speech, gestures, tonality, order, image, attitude, idea, *identifying* your ways with his. Persuasion by flattery is but a special case of persuasion in general. But flattery can safely serve as our paradigm if we systematically widen its meaning, to see behind it the conditions of identification or consubstantiality in general" (1969, 55). Burke's theory of persuasion-as-identification sees the *dynamis* of rhetoric in the relationship between rhetor and audience, just as Aristotle saw it. The agency of the audience constrains and situates the agency of the rhetor, and discursive appeals to ethos must situate the rhetor within the audience's sense of wisdom, virtue, and good will in order for persuasion to take place.

A more careful reading of the modes of discursively producing ethos is beyond the scope of this essay. I want simply to point out that the *techne* of rhetoric includes rules for that kind of discursive production because, as Aristotle thought, that is one fundamental way to activate the *dynamis* of rhetoric. A classical reading of ethos and *dynamis* is unburdened by modern conceptions of subjectivity and freedom. No rhetor, from Aristotle's perspective, has the freedom and power to simply impose an arbitrary and idiosyncratic vision of the world on an unwitting audience. Rhetoric's power is relational; it does not belong to a subject but is activated in the relationship that a subject forms with an audience. Christopher Gill has shown that Classical Greek intellectuals simply did not have a modern conception of self-as-subject that we often have (and that Foucault so radically critiques). Modern ideas about the self, developed by and since Descartes, are "subject-centered," whereas Gill claims that Greek ideas were "objectivist" (1996, 4). A "subject-centered" concept of the self thinks of the "I" (the single reasoning, feeling subject) as the defining locus of selfhood, consciousness, and personality. What Gill calls the "objective-participant conception," by contrast, stresses shared, communal, nonprivate mental states as the defining characteristics of the self. If we think of the rhetor as in possession of an "objective-participant conception" of selfhood, then both the *dynamis* and *techne* of rhetoric are not properties of a subjective speaker but relational manifestations of interactions between speakers and audiences.

If we begin with Aristotle's definition of rhetoric, as I have done here, and we recognize that rhetoric is power in its nascent state, then much is at stake in the way we imagine how that nascent power is actualized. The *techne* of rhetoric was never, in its classical conception, a mode of self-expression—one's inner sense of self was never revealed or expressed through rhetorical action and audiences were never simply wooed, amazed, or moved by a powerful speaker-as-subject. Instead, the *techne* of rhetoric, especially as it relates to ethos, outlined a set of rules for meeting the constraints of the agency of the audience-as-judge in order to actualize the potential power of rhetoric in the communal, shared interactions of rhetor and audience. Rhetorical power did not operate from one single point or person; it existed as a potentiality in between, and within, a community of citizens. Rhetorical agency belonged to both the rhetor and the audience, constraining the freedom of both while being enacted and embodied through discursive choices. If we think about ethos with a modern notion of selfhood, then we limit our understanding of what rhetoric can be and how it might create sociopolitical change. As modern notions of selfhood and subjectivity have come under increasing attack, classical sources can be a useful reminder that we need not sacrifice commitments to deliberation or political rhetoric simply because we do not have a robust subject-centered form of agency on which to rely. We simply need a more nuanced understanding of power and subjectivity in order to use Aristotle's insights about rhetoric in our own circumstances. Michel Foucault offers just such a nuanced understanding of power and subjectivity.

Foucault on Power and Subjectivity

Power, in *Discipline and Punish* and Foucault's later works, tends to occupy an anonymous place—it is, in a sense, everywhere and nowhere at the same time, without location, identity, or boundaries. Accordingly, power has no direction, no point of departure, and no definitive end. Instead, power is a kind of force that ensnares us all. Foucault even complicates and challenges questions of power and agency in several stylistic/rhetorical ways by using reflexive verbs, infinitives, and the impersonal and anonymous "one"; by writing about strategies and tactics without indicating whose strategies or tactics they are; and by telling us that certain historical realities "can be viewed as" having a certain significance, with the question of historical actors absent (Baldwin 1989). One way to make sense of this conception of power is to consider Foucault's relationship to Nietzsche (see Thiele 1990). *Discipline and Punish* employs the method of genealogy, and this coincides with Foucault's turn to a Nietzschean conception of power. Foucault's work in the 1960s is mostly negative in character —he himself suggests this in a 1977 interview with Lucette Finas (1980, 183–184). Power in *History of Madness* "excludes," "represses," "censors," "abstracts," "masks," and "conceals." But in the 1970s, Foucault contends that power is not exclusively negative; it is actually a positive phenomenon: "We must cease once and for all to describe the effects of power in negative terms . . . In fact power produces; it produces reality; it produces domains of objects and rituals of truth. The individual and the knowledge that may be gained of him belong to this production" (1977, 194). *Discipline and Punish* eloquently attests to this new attitude toward power—the central argument of the work is that the social role of the prison is to create delinquency not just to repress it. By producing a threat to social stability, the prison provides a justification for the formation of the apparatus of discipline and control that permeates present society.

Foucault also develops this argument in *Discipline and Punish* by subjecting the notion of visibility to inspection. The visibility of power, in the form of Bentham's "panoptic" prison, is challenged. The "major effect" of the panopticon was "to induce in the inmate a state of conscious and permanent visibility that assures the automatic functioning of power." The aim was "to arrange things" so that "surveillance is permanent in its effects, even if it is discontinuous in its action; that the perfection of power should tend to render its actual exercise unnecessary; that this architectural apparatus should be a machine for creating and sustaining a power relation independent of the person who exercises it; in brief, that the inmate should be caught in a power situation of which they are themselves bearers" (1977, 201). This argument is not confined to the prison. It is his contention that *all* of us are trapped within disciplinary systems—systems of micro-power. These systems exist throughout society and control our behavior unbeknownst to us, and they have formed an essential characteristic of the neoliberal state. A regime of observation, surveillance, and inspection (less obvious than Bentham's Panopticon) controls the functioning of these systems of micro-power. The operation and function of discipline within modern society presupposes "a mechanism that coerces by means of observation" (1977, 170). This disciplinary power "is exercised through its invisibility"; yet it "imposes on those whom it subjects a principle of compulsory visibility," and so controls, limits, or destroys individual agency (1977, 187). Accordingly, a major concern of *Discipline and Punish* is the active play of forces in the present and their genealogy, and it is this presentism that becomes clear alongside Foucault's full articulation of power's productivity.

In a very practical sense, one can effectively resist repressive powers in the deliberative realm—at least that is the place in which resistance to power is, and has generally been located. But if we take Foucault's work on power seriously, resistance and agency based on public sphere deliberation is limited. First, issues of identification on which this kind of resistance or agency relies run counter to the way power operates. We miss the focus of Foucault's insight if we try to identify some person, policy, or law as that which possesses power. As Foucault so clearly points out in *Discipline and Punish*, power has no agent through whom it operates, but rather we are all already *in* power. By trying to identify some person, policy, or law as that which possesses power, all of power's other operations are missed; in fact, it is these operations of power (the ones that cannot be seen so easily) that seem to be the most efficient and effective according to Foucault. Second, by making public arguments, we are caught within the "trap of a grammar" that compels us to make true assertions. Such public arguments must contain truth claims in order to be effective. Foucault rejects such true assertions in favor of "true" assertions, which in his style can only be made in an ironic fashion (as his reliance on a type of positivism in his work demonstrates). Making ironically "true" claims in a public forum would undermine the validity of the arguments made in such a way that the goal of rational decision-making would be very difficult to attain. Third, the seriousness and earnestness of argument taking place in the public sphere would be a manifestation of the type of agency Foucault wants to avoid. Public argument makes it obvious who has power and who does not, which allows power to operate more efficiently by leading us to a false sense of identification. Moreover, earnest argument would seem to preclude an ironic, playful style of discourse—the type that Foucault employs.

Foucault is actively trying to rethink both power and resistance by examining how we are all subjects of discourse. This requires him to show that the modern notion of subjectivity and selfhood is an invention of historical forces and that "subjects" do not possess and exercise power as autonomous agents. If we focus too squarely on the agency of individual subjects, then we miss the ways in which we are all ensnared within discursive regimes. If we return to Aristotle's use of *dynamis* and *techne*, we can see Foucault's analysis of power in a new light. For Foucault and for Aristotle, power is relational, not a possession of a particular subject, and it is made actual by discourse practices. One major difference is that Foucault is able to brilliantly track the practices of social institutions, while Aristotle attends only to the individual rhetor and the discourse practices at his disposal. But in both cases, agency is constrained by the presence of a judge—Aristotle calls that judge the audience while Foucault sees social institutions as judges. Interestingly, Aristotle turns to the rhetor as a kind of public figure, openly engaged in an ethical life by virtue of a series of interactions with audiences. Foucault turns, instead, back to the private individual instead of the public rhetor. This is a difference that I will try to address in the third section of this essay. For now, however, Foucault cannot turn to rhetorical agency in the same way that Aristotle or other classical rhetoricians may have because he sees that form of agency as already determined by the social institutions and systems of micro-power that govern our lives. From Foucault's perspective, we might say that ethos, as a discourse practice, is nothing more than the knowledge of what constitutes a legitimate subject position within a system of discourse. To make appeals to ethos would be to practice a way of being within a system of micro-power. This is the productivity of these systems of power—they teach us all how to occupy subject positions and proliferate discourse conventions, which further ensnares us in those systems. The kind of public, political rhetor championed by Aristotle and other classical rhetoricians cannot avoid such a predicament, and thus is not an option for Foucault.

In the final two volumes of *A History of Sexuality*, Foucault turns to the question of the self in antiquity and the relation between the self and aesthetics: "The elaboration of one's own life as a personal work of art, even if it obeyed certain collective canons, was at the center, it seems to me, of moral experience, of the will to morality in Antiquity" (1985, 49). He extends this concern with an aesthetics of existence in "Friendship as a Way of Life," "The Social Triumph of the Sexual Will," and "Sex, Power, and the Politics of Identity." In each of these essays, the focus is on gay rights in some way. Of course, any discussion of gay rights tends to point one to deliberative rhetoric, the practice of which can lead to securing such things as "rights," alongside a modern conception of selfhood with a subject that possess such things as rights. However, Foucault is uncomfortable with that kind of analysis. He is more interested in envisioning different possibilities for altering the very way that gay people live their lives. When discussing possibilities for gay culture, Foucault has in mind a "culture that invents ways of relating, types of existence, types of values, types of exchanges between individuals which are really new and are neither the same as, nor superimposed on, existing cultural forms" (1997, 160). In other words, new power relations can and should be produced by a gay culture. This analysis need not be limited to gay culture—it extends and applies to everyone. The central concern here is with the aesthetic creation of new possibilities for everyday lived experience. The method by which one can realize such new possibilities is by first refusing the accepted categories of existence (mostly heterosexual categories) and then producing and displaying new categories. The production and display of new ways of living would be more than just resistance. In the sequence from refusal to production to display, one moves from a method or mode of living that simply resists to one that makes and lives within new power relations. Aesthetic self-creation is not equivalent to resistance for Foucault, nor is it a question of simply expressing oneself. Instead, it is a process of understanding the structures and values that order individuals about, refusing those structures and values, and using them to produce and display new ways of living.

Foucault's historical analyses in *The Use of Pleasure* and *The Care of the Self* run parallel to his arguments about gay culture. *The Use of Pleasure* begins with the claim that the object of these new volumes of *The History of Sexuality* is to learn "to what extent the effort to think one's own history can free thought from what it silently thinks, and so enable it to think differently" (1985, 9). Again, the presentist concern is obvious, but now the emphasis is no longer on power relations or structures of repression. The emphasis is now on "what might be called 'arts of existence.'" Foucault explains: "what I mean by that phrase are those intentional and voluntary actions by which men not only set themselves rules of conduct, but also seek to transform themselves, to change themselves in their singular being, and to make their life into an *oeuvre* that carries certain aesthetic values and meets certain stylistic criteria" (1985, 10–11). This is not to say that techniques of the self do not involve power relations at all: "To form oneself as a virtuous and moderate subject in the use he makes of pleasures, the individual has to construct a relationship with the self that is of the 'domination-submission,' 'command-obedience,' 'master-docility' type" (1985, 70).

The relation one has with oneself is perhaps the most "local" power relation possible, but this power relation does not turn into a form of resistance. Instead, a person can become an ethical subject without relying on structures of domination that provide or impose a system of ethics. Speaking about pleasure in antiquity, Foucault explains: "Ethical conduct in matters of pleasure was contingent on a battle for power," but it is a power that one has over oneself (1985, 66). Moderation, then, was "an art, a practice of pleasures that was capable of self-limitation through the 'use' of those pleasures that were based on need" (1985, 57).

The Care of the Self moves down a similar path. Here Foucault claims that it is a "matter of forming and recognizing oneself as the subject of one's own actions, not through a system of signs denoting power over others, but through a relation that depends as little as possible on status and its external forms, for this relation is fulfilled in the sovereignty that one exercises over oneself" (1986, 85). One produces oneself, or produces relations with oneself, and then by displaying that very production forges new kinds of relations with others. Beginning with refusal (or moderation) in *The Use of Pleasure*, Foucault moves from the self's need to resist pleasure to the process of self-production in *The Care of the Self*. Resistance and production are clearly connected for the individual, just as they were clearly connected in Foucault's work on structures and discourses. The panopticon is such a devastating metaphor because any form of resistance is futile when power is everywhere at once—resistance can never turn into the production of new power relations on this level because one can never precisely identify all of power's polymorphous operations within a given structure. The relationship between the self and a social structure within which a self is located does not hold the potential for producing new kinds of power relations. That is why Foucault turns to the relations one has with oneself as the remaining possibility for turning resistance into new kinds of power relations. But to get into relation with oneself, one needs to understand the content and quality of the structures that regulate the self.

It is at this point that Foucault's later work on governmentality is especially important. According to Foucault, "governmentality" is the approach to social regulation and control over populations that resulted from changes that gradually occurred between the fifteenth and the eighteenth centuries. Those changes were associated with the breakdown of the feudal system, demographic expansion, and the development of administrative states. By the eighteenth century, European governments began to think of their citizens in terms of populations in which groups of people were classified, managed, and controlled. The creation of statistics meant that populations could be broken into groups, about which we could produce knowledge. Through the creation and quantification of these populations, individuals learn how to act as subjects within groups. In other words, governmentality positions individuals within discourses that work to create self-regulating subjects (Miller 1993). Discourse functions to produce the parameters of what is sayable and knowable within our society. We become subjects of these discourses, and we learn a set of practices to perform the ways in which we are always already implicated within those discourses. As such, governmentality refers to "the tendency which over a long period of time and throughout the West, has steadily led towards the pre-eminence over all other forms (sovereignty, discipline, etc.) of this type of power which may be termed government, resulting on the one hand, in the formation of a whole series of specific governmental apparatuses and on the other hand in the development of a whole complex of *saviors*" (1991, 103–4). Toby Miller (1993) explains that "*savoir* describes the process through which the subject finds himself modified by what he knows, or rather by the labor performed in order to know." (xxii). In other words, it connotes the securing of governmental power, not through brute force but through a series of techniques for managing the population by having it manage itself. I take this to be a central feature of the neoliberal state.

Clearly Foucault's turn to the relation one has with oneself is a way of responding to and resisting this form of neoliberal governmentality. But what can we make of rhetorical agency or rhetorical power given Foucault's insights into power and subjectivity? If our conception of rhetorical agency and rhetorical power rests on a modern notion of subjectivity and selfhood, then any form of rhetorical agency or rhetorical power might seem like just another discourse practice that is always already constituted and constrained by the circulating discourse of the neoliberal state. But if we start with an Aristotlean conception of *dynamis* and *techne*, is it possible to think about politics and rhetorical agency in ways that could resist neoliberal governmentality? It is clear that Foucault thinks about historical change in terms of ruptures or breaks, and that those ruptures or breaks are not the direct result of human agency. The image of the man being erased like a face drawn in the sand at the edge of the sea is implicitly an argument about historical change. Some have interpreted this to mean that Foucault has little to offer us in terms of political theory or political practice. Perhaps that is because he cannot think about political rhetoric without a modern notion of subject and self. But agency is not simply reducible to subjectivity, as Aristotle and other classical rhetoricians surely knew. And Foucault was not the first person to think about power in relational terms (and not in terms of subjectivity). What Foucault does hint at when describing the relation that one has with oneself is the possibility and potential embodied in smaller, more local rhetorical practices. To think about political change in incremental, pragmatic terms may still be useful and desirable given the omnipresence and diffuseness of power within the neoliberal state.

Rhetorical Agency, Rhetorical Power, and Ethos in a Neoliberal State

Aristotle's notion of rhetoric as *techne* showed the power of discourse practices. Foucault's notion of governmentality and his analyses of modern social institutions also show the power of discourse practices. From the perspective of classical rhetorical theory, the agency and power of the rhetor are realized through those discourse practices. But from Foucault's perspective, our agency and subjectivity are lost within those discourse practices. We need not simply choose to believe one perspective or the other—the political empowerment of the classical rhetor and the modern subject of the governmental, neoliberal state are not opposites engaged in a contest to solicit our vote. They both teach us about relational power, its potential and the ways in which that potential is made real. They both also contain essential insights into political and social change. Foucault's challenge to rhetorical theory is to remind us that modern notions of subjectivity and selfhood are products of history and in danger of being erased. That reminder comes with a detailed analysis of the ways in which our modern institutions have produced extensive, elaborate, and omnipresent forms of discourse that govern our behavior, that allow us to know ourselves, and that condition our ways of being in the world. Therefore, the question in light of Foucault's work on power is as follows: Can we articulate and practice a form of rhetorical agency and rhetorical power without the modern conception of selfhood and subjectivity that Foucault claims is presently being erased, and that is, at the least, a central feature of the operations of power in our present? If we are not able to articulate and practice such forms of rhetorical agency and rhetorical power, then what becomes of our politics?

To answer the second question, one could read any part of the extensive scholarship on Foucault and governmentality. Miller's *The Well-Tempered Self* is admittedly my favorite example of such scholarship. The stark critique of citizens as consumers and cultural subjects gets much right about both Foucault and our political predicament. I have no doubt that the critiques of neoliberalism carried out in light of Foucault's work are important evaluations and warnings about the destruction wrought by modern social institutions. My interest, however, is not in extending these important forms of critique. My interest is in answering the first question, and I think that Foucault was equally as interested in this first question. Luckily, the classical origins of rhetoric are unburdened by notions of the modern subject or the modern self. I suggest some classical lines of thought that might aid a project that articulates rhetorical agency and rhetorical power in the presence of our massively productive social/political institutions of governance. In so doing, these suggestions may make our neoliberal predicament seem slightly less dire and impenetrable. Foucault was right to suggest that wherever we find power, we find resistance—the scale and scope of those forms of resistance may have been limited to individual projects of self-creation for Foucault but we may find, within the rhetorical tradition, examples and indications of how such projects may be made more public.

Let me first summarize the lessons we learn from Foucault: Social institutions (such as medicine, psychiatry, the human sciences, and penology) make the production of knowledge possible through discursive formations. These discursive formations authorize who may or may not speak, the style of communication or argument, and where/how speaking takes place. In such circumstances, power is everywhere and the conventions of social institutions discipline subjects because discourse speaks us. In light of these arguments, discursive appeals to ethos might always already be determined by the social institutions that produce discursive formations within which an appeal to ethos would be comprehensible. In other words, an appeal to ethos is just another way for discourse to speak us. Aristotle's insight that character was not the property of a person seems supported by Foucault's historical work. But for Aristotle, ethos is the most powerful source of persuasion, and thus holds potential for generating sociopolitical change. Additionally, Aristotle regards ethos as a matter of judgment. It is simply not enough to have a reputation as a likeable person—our character is an outcome of rhetorical success not a constant that exists prior to rhetorical practice. This implies that audience and rhetor engage urgent and unsettled matters together. Competence is a matter of recognizing and enacting the relational goods of civic friendship together with practical reason. In rhetoric, the character of both rhetor and audience can only be formed through reciprocal engagement. The power of rhetoric lies here. Rhetoric does not manifest some predetermined truth, but it does attempt something much more important. It puts us into relationship with others.

Discursive formations, of course, also put us into relationship with others, which is precisely what Foucault found so troubling about the social institutions that he studied. What Aristotle teaches us about power, however, is that the potentiality of *dynamis* is only made actual by the *techne* of rhetoric through discursive constructions of *phronesis*, *arête*, and *eunoia* that place us into a trusting relationship with others. Rhetorical power depends on *the quality of interactions among people made possible by symbols, discourses, and communication*. It does not depend on subjectivity or selfhood and it does not exist as a property of discourse itself. Ethos controls the process of persuasion because it goes furthest to determine the quality of the interaction between the audience and the rhetor. I believe that Foucault has deftly shown how the quality of our interactions with others has been diminished by modern forms of neoliberal governmentality. We may think that the state was a brutal force when we read the description of the torture of Damiens, but our modern state is far more cruel because of the ways in which it impacts our relations with ourselves and with others. We must take that critique seriously. But that outcome is a product of rhetorical practice and not a natural feature of any and all forms of social order. The concept of ethos puts the question of my relationship with others central in the process of persuasion. It, therefore, permits the possibility that those relationships can be rethought and remade. Nearly all great democratic reform movements, including those in Ancient Athens and the contemporary USA, relied on a rhetor's ability to leverage relational power through discursive practices. The modern neoliberal state attempts to do the same to its citizens. The first step in any political project, therefore, is the recognition that my character and my relationship to others is not predetermined but made in and through rhetoric.

If rhetorical power is relational power, then rhetorical agency is the ability to enact different kinds of relationships with others through discourse, speech, symbols, or communication. The great success of neoliberal governmentality is the proliferation of modes of discourse capable of regulating those relationships. Foucault's turn, toward the end of his career, to the relationships we have with ourselves was his initial attempt to think through a project capable of generating change through rhetorical agency. That same project can, and ought to be, directed toward the kinds of relationships we have with others—that is a form of politics as a way of life, championed by thinkers from Aristotle to John Dewey. Neoliberalism relies on a notion of agency in which I am an individual, subjective, economic, rational agent. The great success of the neoliberal state relies on my atomization and differentiation from others. The discourse forms of the social institutions that Foucault studied isolated us from one another and changed the shape of our relationships to ourselves and to others. All of this fundamentally undermines a rhetorical project based on *dynamis* and *techne*. This is what rhetoricians can learn from Foucault and from our neoliberal moment—if we think of agency as an autonomous property of a subject or self, then we have failed to realize the ways in which modern social institutions and forms of governmentality have brought us to see the world in such a way and, in so doing, emptied rhetoric of its dynamic power. The supposed economic, rational self-interest that is thought to be "natural" by many advocates of neoliberalism would have been unthinkable for an Athenian rhetorician and works precisely because it voids the relational characteristics of rhetorical agency and rhetorical power from our view.

Relationality and Occupy Wall Street

Ethos is a mode of proof for Aristotle, and, as such, it is an artistic project. It requires an awareness of the values and beliefs of the audience that sits in judgment of a rhetor's discourse, and the audience always constrains the possibilities of speech. But those constraints are also resources for artistic recreation. The *Care of the Self* and *The Uses of Pleasure* are, I think, Foucault's most provocative calls for an aesthetic/political project. Each investigated relational power at the level of the individual. It seems clear that to push Foucault's project further would require a turn to ethos because that project would be a turn from a "care of the self" to a care of the audience. Ethos is the discursive manifestation of a care for the other; it is how the rhetorical tradition has long thought about the relationship between rhetor and audience and long thought about the dynamic power of the good will, good sense, and good intentions that rhetors display toward audiences. This seems directly in line with Foucault's concerns for the relationships we have with ourselves. It also seems like our best resource for leveraging the productivity of power by putting ourselves into different kinds of relationships with others and displaying those different kinds of relationships as a form of resisting the neoliberal state. A political project like Occupy Wall Street (OWS) is an example of how we might enact different kinds of relationships with others. OWS was perhaps more invested in developing and practicing an ethos, a politics as a way of life, than advancing or advocating for a particular agenda. This is a virtue in a neoliberal world that has succeeded by undermining the quality of our relationships with others. If we turn to ethos, rhetorical power, and rhetorical agency might we find additional ways of reimagining our relationships with others? The demise of the neoliberal state would seem to hinge on that outcome. Classical rhetoric might be more useful than any rhetoric based on modern subjectivity and selfhood. Regardless, that outcome will only be secured if we realize that power exists in between us and not in us, and that discourse practices, as a mediating force, determine the quality of that space in between. I believe that OWS is an initial example of this kind of commitment.

Members of OWS wrote a "Declaration of the Occupation of New York City" in 2011. That "Declaration" begins with the following phrase: "As we gather together in solidarity to express a feeling of mass injustice." This initial document emphasizes both solidarity and the act of assembly, two critical features of any attempt to leverage relational power. "Solidarity" signals the extent to which the occupiers were committed to the social dimension of politics (or the relationships between the members of the movement). The rest of the declaration is mostly devoted to an explanation of what the occupiers "feel" "mass injustice" means. This explanation ranges from an "illegal foreclosure process" to "colonialism," "torture," "outsourced labor," and the sale of "privacy as a commodity." In other words, the feeling of "mass injustice" is the grounds for the feeling of "solidarity" and makes possible a form of cooperation capable of uniting "as one people" a "formerly divided" group. Solidarity and cooperation, therefore, are driven by the felt presence of injustice and inequality, mostly caused by corruption at the hands of "economic power." In light of Foucault and Aristotle, a straightforward reading of such a document might suggest that the injustices of neoliberalism have made a commitment to relational solidarity possible and desirable.

The title of the "Declaration" clearly pays homage to the "Declaration of Independence," but a stark contrast between these two documents promotes different forms of political action. The "Declaration of Independence" also describes a list of grievances and the existence of injustice, and in response, it argues for the existence of "inalienable rights." The preamble to the "Declaration of Independence" promotes a general theory of government that is used as a justification for rebellion against the King. This general theory of government is different in kind than the one promoted by OWS because it understands the location and exercise of power and agency differently. The beginning of the "Declaration of Independence" does not announce the existence of a feeling, but rather the existence of a set of "self-evident" truths. A system of government founded on preserving the rights of its citizens becomes the basic mode of political life and underpins a modernist commitment to agency and subjectivity. "Inalienable rights" have a minor role in the "Declaration of the Occupation of New York City," and of all the rights mentioned, the right to assembly is clearly identified as the most important. Assembly is important because OWS refuses to see citizens as individual, autonomous subjects and accuses the neoliberal government and global corporations of injustice facilitated by a modern conception of subjectivity and agency that alienate us from one another. Thinking about agency and subjectivity in terms of political rights alone denies the possibility of solidarity and relational power and promotes corporate interests.

The "Declaration of the Occupation of Wall Street," therefore, does not assert or really use human rights as either a cause or motivating factor for the kinds of political action that issue from it. This is not a rights-based politics because it is not a politics based on the modern subject or a modern conception of agency. It is a politics with faith in assembly as an antidote to corruption and a key to equality because assembly makes relational power possible. This is why OWS has put so much effort into thinking about the structure and format of their general assembly meetings. These meetings are based on Athenian direct democracy and the Roman Republic. At the General Assembly, everyone is heard and equal opportunities for speech are made possible, but those moments for rhetorical action enact commitments to the kind of relational ethos that Aristotle articulated. The goal of the General Assembly is "modified consent," which simply means that "everyone is in agreement when we come to a decision… What we want, and what we're hoping to achieve, is an agreement by everyone. So that way no one is excluded and no one is stepped on." If that kind of consensus cannot be reached, "then we [the General Assembly] have to move to a nine-tenths vote. We don't want to have to do this. We're fighting against a system that oppresses people like voting. Voting means that some people are ignored, they're completely forgotten about. So that way the majority can enact something, so we want consensus. The reason it's nine-tenths is because that's almost impossible to get. That's an insurance policy to ensure something that conflicts with the group isn't being put through."

The commitment to, and faith in, assembly is one of the reasons that OWS was illegible or incoherent in the eyes of the mainstream press. Some argued that OWS was not a proper social movement or form of political dissent because it did not have a clear, definitive goal or policy solution that it sought. But OWS was intentionally violating discourse conventions around typical forms of political dissent because it sought to make claims about the very organization of political life around modern, neoliberal conceptions of subjectivity. What OWS calls "process" (the methods of meetings, facilitating discussions, and making decisions) reflects the movement's values and advances an argument about what democracy ought to look like. In other words, the processes employed to cultivate specific kinds of relationships of solidarity and sought to perform or enact democracy in a different manner from other more traditional modes of modern political action. Further, the meetings themselves (and any meeting that uses consensus) were long, often frustrating, and deeply ethical. The experiential side of the meetings held the potential for the personal transformation of the participants and could not be captured in more basic forms of political analyses. These meetings attempted to produce solidarity, which would ultimately facilitate the productive capacity of what I've been calling relational power.

Although OWS employed many different kinds of meetings, the working group meetings and the general assembly meetings stand out as the two most important. The General Assembly meetings were typically larger and more formal, while the working group meetings were smaller and more informal. But both typically included facilitators, a note taker, the use of hand gestures, a speaking stack, and the need for consensus. These functional characteristics of the meetings have probably become the central identifying feature of OWS, more than any particular policy goal or political proposition. While the political agenda of OWS may have been illegible to the mainstream press, the hand gestures, as the most visible form of the process employed at the meetings, were perhaps the clearest representative feature of the kind of politics preferred by the occupiers. There were seven specific hand gestures used during the meetings. First, holding one's hand up, with palm open, and fanning one's fingers back and forth signaled that the person agreed with the proposal or like what she heard. Second, holding one's hand down and fanning one's fingers back and forth signaled disagreement with a proposal or dislike of what was being said. Third, holding one's hand flat while fanning one's fingers up and down signaled a neutral stance on a proposal. Fourth, curling one's hand and fingers into a letter "C" shape signaled either the need for clarification or that the person making the gesture had clarifying information. Fifth, raising one's index finger up signaled that the person had information pertinent to the discussion. Sixth, making a triangular shape with one's hand by joining one's index fingers and thumbs signaled that the process governing group discussion was not being followed properly. Seventh, crossing one's arms in front of one's chest to form an "X" signaled strong moral or ethical reservations about the proposal being considered. Collectively, these gestures insured that everyone at the meeting was physically incorporated into the communicative practices of the group and into the decision-making process. These gestures ritualized participation and concretized the language from the declaration that insisted on the importance of the "horizontal" dimension of politics. As a set of communicative practices, these hand gestures helped to distribute the process of reaching consensus equally among all the participants in the meetings. Further, these hand gestures prevented the possibility of any vertical or hierarchical organization from emerging. In other words, privileging the communicative practices that belonged to everyone at the meetings maintained and reproduced the feeling of solidarity while at the same time barring any potential fractures between those who might attempt to assume more power or control to direct meetings. This is relational power at work.

The other practices in place at the meetings worked toward the same ends. The "stack taker's" job was to organize a list of people who wanted to speak. The "stack taker" was required to make a "progressive stack," which meant that people in minority groups were moved up to the top of the list to make sure that everyone had an opportunity to speak and to make certain that old and enduring forms of creating hierarchical divisions between people were not reproduced at the meetings. Members of the meetings were also encouraged to practice "step up, step back" which meant that those members of the group who had traditional advantages would step back to allow others to be heard. This was a form of acknowledging that some people have been suppressed in their lifetimes and have not been given as many opportunities as others to speak and be heard. The meetings also typically used "temperature checkers" who would deliberately interrupt meetings to gauge how the group was feeling about a particular proposal or idea. These "temperature checkers" were another mechanism of insuring that the horizontal structure of the meetings remained and that the group was working toward consensus. All meetings were run by "co-facilitators" who implemented the rules for the meetings and kept the meetings to the established agenda. This was a "leadership role" but the facilitators were not "leaders." The facilitators were trained to introduce themselves into the group as authoritative figures with no real direct power. Each meeting strived to achieve more diversity of co-facilitators instead of less. The combination of these practices was necessary to achieve consensus, the goal of the meetings. These practices were necessary for eradicating the notion that particular "leaders" ran democracies and were important for turning all participants into leaders.

The combination of these practices gave OWS a texture and embodied the shift from vertical to horizontal democracy called for in the "Declaration of the Occupation of New York City." These practices, in other words, represented the most important political claim advanced by OWS—that the best way to redress inequality is through organizing our lives together in a more egalitarian manner whereby everyone participates in decision-making. The most fundamental entailment of both the meetings and the declaration was that democracy ought to be practiced differently if it is to produce something other than the massive inequality and injustice that plague present-day American society. The search for different practices was also a rejection of modernist conceptions of subjectivity and agency and a rhetorical commitment to relationality. From such a perspective, the means of democratic life ought to reflect the ends that democracy seeks to create. Therefore, the best available solution is to change the means of practicing democracy away from the conceptions of subjectivity and agency that prop up the neoliberal state. The process was slow, complicated, and frustrating, but it allowed everyone to be heard and that was, in itself, a kind of political transformation. I imagine any future shift of the kind that Foucault outlines in his work will entail the kinds of transformation for which OWS argued. I think we ought to remember what Aristotle taught us about ethos while being committed to rethinking rhetorical agency as relationality instead of subjectivity.

References

Aristotle. 1984. *The Rhetoric and Poetics of Aristotle*, trans. W. R. Roberts. New York: Modern Library.

Bladwin, David. 1989. *Paradoxes of Power*. New York: Basil Blackwell.

Burke, Kenneth.1969. *The Rhetoric of Motives*. Berkeley: University of California Press.

Foucault, Michel. 1970. *The Order of Things: An Archaeology of the Human Sciences*. New York: Random House.

———. 1977. *Discipline and Punish: The Birth of the Prison*, trans. A. Sheridan. New York: Random House.

———. 1978. *The History of Sexuality, Volume 1: An Introduction*, trans. R. Hurley. New York: Random House.

———. 1980. In *Power/Knowledge: Selected Interviews and Other Writings 1972–1977*, ed. C. Gordon. New York: Pantheon.

———. 1985. *The History of Sexuality Volume 2: The Use of Pleasure*, trans. R. Hurley. New York: Random House.

———. 1986. *The History of Sexuality Volume 3: The Care of the Self*, trans. R. Hurley. New York: Random House.

———. 1991. In *The Foucault Effect: Studies in Governmentality*, eds. G. Burchell, C. Gordon, and P. Miller. Chicago: University of Chicago Press.

———. 1997. *Michel Foucault: Ethics, Subjectivity, and Truth*, ed. P. Rabinow. New York: The New Press.

Garver, Eugene. 1995. *Aristotle's Rhetoric: An Art of Character*. Chicago: University of Chicago Press.

Gill, Christopher. 1996. *Personality in Greek Epic, Tragedy, and Philosophy: The Self in Dialogue*. New York: Oxford University Press.

Grimaldi, William. 1980. *Aristotle, Rhetoric I: A Commentary*. New York: Fordham University Press.

McKerrow, Raymie. 1999. Critical Rhetoric: Theory and Praxis. In *Contemporary Rhetorical Theory, A Reader*, eds. John Louis Lucaites, Celeste Michelle Condit, and Sally Caudill, 441–463. New York: The Guilford Press.

Miller, Toby. 1993. *The Well-Tempered Self: Citizenship, Culture, and the Postmodern Subject*. Baltimore: Johns Hopkins University Press.

Thiele, Leslie Paul. 1990. The Agony of Politics: The Nietzschean Roots of Foucault's Thought. *American Political Science Review* 884(3): 907–925.

Vivian, Brad. 2004. *Being Made Strange: Rhetoric Beyond Representation*. Albany: SUNY Press.

The Capable American: Ethos, Pathos, and the Governance of Education

Samuel M. Jay

On July 24, 2009, the Obama Administration officially launched the Race to the Top program, an initiative aimed at "providing a high-quality education to every young American" and a response to the Great Recession that recognized the student as "vital to the health of our nation's democracy and the strength of our nation's economy" (The Office of the Press Secretary 2009, para. 2). By improving K-12 education in the USA, students would be better prepared to achieve success in college and in their careers; the cumulative effect would be a USA that was more competitive in the world marketplace ("Race to the Top Executive Summary" 2009, 2).

According to President Obama and Secretary of Education Arne Duncan's blueprint, Race to the Top was to function as a "competitive grant program designed to encourage and reward" for those states that effectively governed education and emphasized five areas of reform: designing and putting into place "rigorous standards and high-quality assessments," hiring and retaining "great teachers and leaders in America's classrooms," using state-of-the-art data systems to inform better decisions in regard to teaching and to improve instruction, "using innovation and effective approaches to turn around struggling schools," and "demonstrating and

---

S.M. Jay (✉)
Department of Communication Arts and Sciences, Metropolitan State University of Denver, Denver, CO, USA

sustaining education reform" (The Office of the Press Secretary 2009, para. 6). States had the option to implement previously established reform rubrics (e.g. Common Core State Standards Initiative) or create their own. Those states that "demonstrated success in raising student achievement" and developed the "best plans to accelerate their reforms in the future" could enter into the Race to the Top contest ("Race to the Top Program Executive Summary" 2009, 2).

States were then evaluated according to criteria that incentivized various achievements, including creation and implementation of statewide educational standards and reform; closure of knowledge gaps; development and application of "common, high-quality assessments"; creation of data systems to inform, improve, and support the decisions made by instructors; recruitment, evaluation, and retainment of effective teachers; improvement of the lowest-achieving schools; and whether or not states spent more of their own money on funding education ("Race to the Top Program Executive Summary" 2009, 8). Those states and their respective school districts that best met the criteria were then awarded up to $700 million in grant money depending upon performance and the number of K-12 students going to school ("Nine States and the District of Columbia Win Second Round Race to the Top Grants" 2010, para. 16).

Since the summer of 2009, President Obama and Secretary Duncan have continually advertised the benefits of Race to the Top and have developed more educational programs under the banner of the original initiative, including Race to the Top Assessment, Race to the Top-Early Learning Challenge, and Race to the Top-District ("Setting the Pace: Expanding Opportunity for America's Students Under Race to the Top" 2014). As recently as March 2014, the Administration has asked for an additional $300 million in discretionary spending to be used toward Race to the Top and its ancillary programs ("Setting the Pace: Expanding Opportunity for America's Students Under Race to the Top" 2014). Still, evaluation of the initiative has been mixed with judgments about whether or not it has been successful often depending upon political ideologies. For example, assessments of the Race to the Top program by conservative think tanks such as the American Enterprise Institute and the Economic Policy Institute have been negative while evaluations by progressive policy research groups such as the Center for American Progressive have shed more positive light on the program (Bowen 2010; Weiss 2013; Miller and Hanna 2014).

These conflicting evaluations of Race to the Top as a partisan educational policy are typical of deliberation in the modern political ecosystem and its established approaches to argumentation. As G. Thomas Goodnight (1989), an argumentation and rhetoric scholar, claimed over two decades ago, if "public deliberation is a way to share in the construction of the future," then the technical sphere of argumentation that is modern politics—conservative/Republican and liberal/Democrat in this situation—inevitably "create[s] social knowledge in order to uncover, assess, and resolve shared problems," but in doing so impacts a public understanding that is in accordance to respective political logics (198). In the case at hand, Republicans viewed Race to the Top as the federal government's attack of free choice because their discourse always already evaluated the policy actions of a Democratic president as negative due to the ideologies disdain for state intervention. Democrats evaluated government intervention within education positively because their sphere was favorable toward actions of government involvement. Simply put, these deliberators argued from standpoints tethered more to the good of a political philosophy (either conservative or liberal) than to the progress of the American public.

Changes to processes of reasoning and deliberation can be further recognized in Michel Foucault's work on modern governance, specifically in the era of neoliberalism. Although Foucault (2008) does not use the language of argumentation or rhetorical theory in his work on neoliberalism, he does theorize that the validity and correctness of the ideological argument need not matter. Instead, what matters is that practices of reasoning, arguing, and persuasively communicating function as autonomous actions by politically engaged and capable individuals that further legitimate neoliberal governance through the creation and circulation of emotional energy and credibility. In a rhetorical sense, we might say that these components of *pathos* and *ethos* work alongside the logical components to habituate neoliberal processes of decision-making by individuals who feel and think themselves capable of being the rational, liberal citizens needed to harness their economic potential.

It is the celebration of self-governance and content that works in favor of subtraction of the state from market activity and the predominance of an economic logic used to evaluate all decisions according to success within a competitive marketplace that seem to really stick as a result of these ongoing practices (Foucault 2008). Thus, the technical arguments made on both sides of the aisle matter in the sense that they create value for the logic of neoliberal governance. It is the process of making one's argument, not the argument itself that comes to matter as both further entrench goods such as self-governance and minimal intervention by central government within the sphere of democratic, public deliberation.

As a result, those who claimed Race to the Top was an interventionist policy did so through a neoliberal evaluative lens and concluded the following: Race to the Top limited the ability for states, school districts, and students to govern themselves because it implemented blanket reform and evaluation; it did not subtract the federal government out of the state, local, and personal spheres, but injected more federal oversight into all; and it hindered unfettered competition and subsequent evaluation because the state was in many ways rigging the system, forcing state and district education agencies to increase the possibilities for the "*risks* constituencies" to succeed (Goodnight 1989, 60).

When reading Foucault's work in combination with Goodnight's perspective, it appears that the logic of neoliberalism further structures political deliberation as a technical knowledge, with its own "characteristic modes of argumentation [...] constitutive of difference[,] human activities" which "make possible different sorts of human choices" and "communicative reasoning" (61). However, as Goodnight then predicted, this technical knowledge becomes the logical structure of the larger, non-technical sphere of deliberation as well (61). The way sense is made in the technical sphere offers up credibility and emotional weight, subsequently taking over the sense-making structure in the public sphere as well. As this occurs, every action, decision, or choice made by the liberal subject is a value-creating one, that is, all further entrench and legitimate specific ways of understanding the world. Race to the Top and the deliberation it incited comes to function as a technology of governance that actually reaffirmed and added value to the neoliberal governing rationality no matter what side of the debate one was on. Race to the Top was *not* a program that somehow threatened neoliberalism, but rather functioned as a practice through which neoliberalism was further legitimated and its logic further affirmed.

With an awareness that neoliberalism now functions not just as an economic and technical discourse, but rather as the social argument and the shared logic informing all decisions made in the contemporary moment, this chapter seeks to problematize the Obama Administration's Race to the Top education reform program as a technology of self-governance made up of practices and discourses that when employed gave additional rhetorical value to neoliberalism as a social truth and further habituated already established ways of being (Foucault 1988).

In order to highlight how this new arena of argumentation impacts and is impacted by modern discourse, this chapter will begin by problematizing the Race to the Top program and through analysis of speeches and interviews given by President Obama and Secretary Duncan, show how Race to the Top worked as value-creating, neoliberal discourse and knowledge that generated competitive value for the USA through governance of K-12 education. Such a process will involve examination of the ways in which the Obama Administration challenged state leaders, administrators, teachers, and parents to implement reform, adding rhetorical value and effectiveness to the learning environment within which K-12 students were made capable of becoming the responsible decision-makers needed to help regain America's competitive advantage. Delving further into the working of this process, I will examine the *ethos* and *pathos* inherent in the rhetoric of Obama and Duncan, which influenced community members to see the credibility of Race to the Top while simultaneously taking advantage of the emotional environment in which these community members resided. The chapter concludes by discussing the "rhetoric of capacity," which I argue is the defining discursive characteristic of modern, neoliberal governance.

Before moving on, it is worth noting that the decision to look beyond the *logos* of Obama and Duncan's rhetoric, which no doubt matters for the validity of what they attempted to do with the Race to the Top program. However, in this situation, it seems that the reasoning and justification for their education reform is sufficiently housed in the shared belief that access to a good education is something all Americans should have. In other words, for their *logos*, Obama and Duncan rely on the enthymematic components of this shared belief then turn to *ethos* and *pathos* as a means of giving Americans the capacity to make this belief possible.

Make America Competitive (Again), One Student at a Time

The critical method of problematization is a product of scholarly work informed by Foucault's (2008) concept of "governmentality" developed during his lectures at the Collège de France in the late 1970s. In terms of its value as a method of critical analysis, governmentality gained significant steam in the early 1990s when Foucault's writings and lectures were translated into English and taken up in the work of social scientists such as Nikolas Rose and Mitchell Dean who used Foucault's work to structure their reading of how modern societies are governed.

It is in this uptake of Foucault that the clearest characteristics of governmentality were developed, characteristics that focused on problematization or questioning items such as "how we think about governing others and ourselves in a wide variety of contexts," "the way different ways of governing is thought about in the contemporary world," "the trajectory by which government through processes comes to be displaced by a government of governmental mechanisms themselves," and "the long-term trajectory by which the exercise of sovereignty comes to be articulated through the regulation of populations and individuals and the psychological, biological, sociological and economic processes that constitute them" (Dean 2010, 267).

In its most simplistic terms, governmentality might be known as the "conduct of conduct" or how populations are led, directed, and guided, and the power relations and assumed knowledge in place and reaffirmed through such conduct (Dean 2010, 17). It includes a plethora of different practices, institutions, discourses, and technologies that impact how we see, what we see, how we think, how we question, how we act, and how we become governable subjects. In terms of rhetoric, it includes patterns of argumentation and sense-making functions that must be problematized or called into question via a thorough unpacking and critique of their development across contexts. In terms of the Race to the Top program, it helps unpack the complex systems through which students are led toward becoming capable democratic citizens.

A rationality of governance will adhere to its own truth or grid of intelligibility that will guide and simultaneously be reaffirmed by the conduct that is governed and the discourse through which that governance is made possible (Foucault 2008). To study governmentality then is to problematize an apparatus or technology of governance, tracking its evolution through disparate eras of governing rationalities and the truths they circulate. For example, one might question how the argument in favor of financial education worked to minimize financial risk-taking during American "New Deal" liberalism in the 1940s and 1950s, but was then utilized to make financial actors more confident and willing to embrace risk during the neoliberalism of the 1990s and 2000s. The technology remained (financial education), but its sense-making function—and the emotional disposition engendered—was dependent upon the rationality in place at the time (social liberalism vs. neoliberalism) (Jay 2014).

Governmentality is a move away from ideological criticism and is concerned not with tracing power to a starting point, but rather recognizes that "any origin is the effect of a present; history is already multiple and diffuse and it is the task of the [researcher] to play up, rather than tame, this multiplicity" (Colebrook 1998, 42). It is not a linear backtracking to a beginning point, but rather a mapping of disparate elements and relations—including discourses and knowledge—that come together to make a truth possible. Rhetorical scholars have produced a significant amount of scholarship problematizing the role of communication as a technology at work within this network. For example, in my own rhetorical criticism I have attempted to outline how financial education might be an institution, but also works together with communicative practices and discursive knowledge within that institution to give staying power to a particular governing rationality (Jay 2014). Thus, teaching the value of risk-taking is valuable, but so is the act of taking risks and talking about the value gained by taking said risks.

For Ronald Walter Greene (2004), complex process is an example of communicative labor and of a new rhetorical agency as each communicative act gives further value to the habitual acts that define neoliberalism. Greene sees communicators within neoliberalism as agents in the sense that their acts of communication produce value for the dominant governing logic even when they seem to work against the status quo. Some of the most obvious of acts that Greene has problematized include items such as deliberation on campaign finance reform and making political donations.

Jodi Dean (2005) has come to a similar, although more pessimistic conclusion about the role of communication in neoliberalism. In particular, in her work, everything can be traced back to an ideological structure that protects and promotes the values of neoliberalism. Therefore, all acts of communication work to benefit a mainstream ideology. Greene and other rhetorical scholars share similarities with Dean, but are not as quick to discount the self-promoting and positive value of such acts, instead recognizing communicators as responsible for the further entrenchment of neoliberalism as they circulate such discourse.

Such rhetoric scholarship includes the work of Greene and Darrin Hicks (2005) who have talked about switch-sided debate as another communicative program through which liberal values are reaffirmed within a modern governing rationality. The act of debate is entered into voluntarily and with positive goals in mind. The end result may even be positive deliberation. However, for them, debate is but one discursive practice among many that give value to modern governance. Catherine Chaput (2010) has discussed the impact of modern communicative technologies on rhetorical value creation and argues that all communicators add rhetorical effectiveness and affective value to certain habits within neoliberalism and through communication, allow certain claims and arguments relevancy over others.

These rhetorical scholars offer is a way of showing how autonomous individuals exhibit power in their own right, but simultaneously how that power ultimately functions to reaffirm to validity and rhetorical effectiveness given to the contemporary governing rationality. They have performed the practice of problematization as they examined "specific situations in which the activity of governing comes to be called into question, the moments and the situations in which government becomes a problem" (Dean 2010, 38).

The ideal of never-ending critique of state action at the heart of neoliberalism was the driving force behind many of these moments, but there were times, such as the 2007–2008 financial crisis and the Great Recession, when problematization was more obviously called for as fissures in the fabric of governance become hard to ignore, that is, times when the seamless conduct of conduct was not working as seamlessly as it once had. This section focuses on the Obama Administration's response to the Great Recession and works to problematize these actions as evidence of "a particular context in which governing is called into question, in which actors and agents of all sorts must pose the question of how to govern" (Dean 2010, 38).

Three months prior to Obama's inauguration, then President George W. Bush and the US Congress enacted the Emergency Economic Stabilization Act of 2008, which authorized $700 billion in bailout money for distressed Wall Street banks. In February 2009, President Obama himself signed into law the American Recovery and Reinvestment Act (ARRA), a bailout package that included an additional $787 billion in stimulus money. These two acts, along with additional government interventions such as shifts in monetary policy and state-orchestrated bank mergers, months of economic recession, and the anxieties that accompanied all of these actions created a moment of problematization in which the Obama Administration had to recalculate the ways in which the American population was governed.

The Administration's overhaul of education involved refocusing the individual decision-maker as the motor behind the country's economic prowess. This had been part of the neoliberal truth standard throughout the 1980s, 1990s, and 2000s and exemplified in the passage of various bills that worked in favor of deregulation and the passing of economic responsibility to individual citizens. Such legislation included President Ronald Reagan's 1982 Garn–St. Germain Depository Institutions Act, which allowed banks to issue adjustable-rate mortgages and made consumers the party responsible for the new risks involved. With the economic downturn of 2007–2008, the state was motivated to act upon the economic sphere in order to salvage the American economy.

However, when considering the influence of the neoliberal discourse still revered at this time, it is evident that the Obama Administration's February 2009 ARRA bill was in fact an attempt to again subtract the state from the economic sphere and return the relationship between the government and the economy into one in which the state kept its economic intervention at a minimum while ramping up government of the social sphere through an economic perspective. The Race to the Top program is a valuable technique of governance to unpack and lay bare how this neoliberal form of government—specifically, the government of the social through an economic logic—worked rhetorically.

From the very beginning, justification for Race to the Top was to give American students the capability to become more competitive in the global marketplace, an application of an economic truth to the governance of the social sphere (in this case through education). In applying an economic logic to social relations, Race to the Top makes economic science—with its emphasis on items such as risk assessment and cost–benefit analysis—an influential factor in how humans evaluate decisions and make choices. A good example of scholarship that has unpacked such a phenomenon is Chaput and Joshua Hanan's (2015) work on the popularization of "freakonomics," which function as a "rhetorical dispotif," a discursive structure—colored by economics and its respective power relations—through which the social sphere is known (1).

Along these same lines, the economic perspective was also the guiding logic behind the Obama Administration's Race to the Top education reform. President Obama made this clear during an interview with *The Washington Post* on July 23, 2009, the day prior to the Administration's official announcement of the program. In the interview, Obama says:

We want to challenge all of the stakeholders—parents, teachers, unions, school administrators—to not only raise standards, but make the changes that are required to actually meet those standards, by having the best teachers and principals, by having the kind of data collection that tells us whether improvements are actually happening, and tying student achievements to assessments of teachers, by making sure that there's a focus on low-performing schools, by making sure that the standards that have been set are ones that mean a kid who graduates can complete at the international level (Shear and Anderson 1992, para. 2).

This quote demonstrates how the Obama Administration sought to make education something knowable through an economic logic, particularly through the principle of competition. As mentioned above, the goal of new reform was to remove the state from the economic sphere. Race to the Top did this, but in a typical, neoliberal way, turned the economic grid of intelligibility upon the social sphere and used economic science to structure education reform.

Modern governance is not simply about disciplining bodies to ensure they perform the correct duties and make the right choices, but rather securing the environment in which individuals make choices by managing the relations and connections between all things that exist within that environment (Foucault 2008). Moves such as "adopting standards and assessments," "building data systems," and "recruiting, developing, rewarding, and retaining effective teachers and principals" were all ways Race to the Top reform acted upon the learning environment to produce student-subjects that would, according to the 2009 "Race to the Top Program Executive Summary," "succeed in college and the workplace" and "compete in the global economy" (2). From a governmentality perspective then, Race to the Top functioned rhetorically as a program that reformed the learning environment in which students would be influenced and guided toward "achieving their fullest potential" that would, in the long run, benefit the US economy ("Setting the Pace" 2014, 5).

Secretary of Education Arne Duncan has provided several examples of how Race to the Top works to legitimate the neoliberal governance of education as well. For example, during a speech at the Fourth Annual Institute of Education Sciences Research Conference on June 8, 2009, Duncan told attendees "reforming public education is not just a moral obligation. It is absolutely an economic imperative. It is the foundation for a strong future and strong society" (6). Duncan would then reiterate this claim less than a month later when on July 2, he told those in attendance at one of the National Education Association's "Listening and Learning" meetings that viewing education reform in terms of its economic viability was the key to America's future:

> The president understands that the nation that out-teaches us today will out-compete us tomorrow. He understands that education is the foundation of our economic strategy and the only sure path to long-term economic strength. That's why he wants Americans to produce the highest percentage of college graduates by the end of the next decade. This is our moon shot. This is our call to action. It is an economic imperative and a moral imperative (6).

What Duncan and the Obama administration have exhibited in their comments and in the legislation they penned is that in no way have they attempted to dismantle the edicts of neoliberalism such as free choice, self-management, and the subtraction of the state from the economic sphere. Instead, what is clear is that Race to the Top is the governance of the social sphere, specifically education, through an economic logic, which *is* one of the defining characteristics of neoliberalism.

The lens through which these reformers viewed education in the USA and the lens through which they wished others to view the issue was an economic one. This was further affirmed in the Administration's desire to collect immense amounts of data about students and teachers in order to evaluate and take action, something Duncan mentioned several times during his 2009 campaign to garner support for Race to the Top ("Robust Data"). Collection and analysis of mountains of data is another common practice of neoliberalism as more data allow those governing to effectively rationalize the choices made (Foucault 2008). If the Administration chose to cut funding for education in some states, it would have the data necessary to legitimate the action. Examples such as these prove rich for problematization of Race to the Top reform and show that the intent was to order an environment in which students would be guided toward making the economically sound decisions needed to pull America out of the Great Recession.

The governance of the social in this situation is relatively concrete when looking at these quotes. President Obama and Secretary Duncan were clear in their desire to reform and manage education according to an economic truth, that is, according to the rationality of neoliberal governance.

Education then becomes a technology of governance for it was through education that students become governable subjects. However, the situation was a bit more complex. As much as Race to the Top was focused on reforming the learning environment, it would have to be through the self-governed actions of various stakeholders—parents, teachers, unions, administrators, and state officials—that this environment was rendered. It is through the self-guided actions of these individuals that Race to the Top changes were given the rhetorical value needed to take hold and to properly influence the educational environment the Obama Administration sought to reform. The next section will examine how ethical and emotional appeals (*ethos* and *pathos*) were employed to persuade stakeholders into taking the actions necessary for Race to the Top to gain its rhetorical effectiveness.

Governing the Stakeholders

Much of Foucault's later work focused on the complexities and interconnectedness of power, especially within various discursive spheres. As a result, he was more interested in how power circulated and how mechanisms of power functioned differently in different historical epochs than he was with uncovering the origins of power and subordination. And for Foucault, especially in his understanding of liberalism, the individual who is free to make his/her own choices was as implicated in the reaffirmation and circulation of power as the institutions of power that ideological criticism has examined.

Several social scientists have taken up this perspective to examine the role that individuals play in their own governance, especially in modern liberal societies. For example, Nikolas Rose (1999) has unpacked how one's ties to his/her community, especially their ethical and moral obligations, gave effectiveness and affirmed power within British liberal governance. Toby Miller (1993) took a similar approach to unpacking the ways in which acts of cultural criticism affirmed notions of governance through ethical incompleteness. And Richard Grusin (2010) looked at how Internet users gave value to apparatuses of security and modern governance, particularly in the years since the September 11, 2001 attacks.

However, while all of these studies have taken up Foucault to show the role of the liberal citizen in his/her own subjectification, it has been rhetorical scholars who have truly shown an understanding of the effectiveness that individuals add to neoliberalism not only as an economic truth but also as a social sphere of influence. A few of these scholars have been mentioned above, including Greene (2004) who critiqued the role of modern day communicators as laborers who add value to the tropes of neoliberalism, but for the purpose of examining the Race to the Top program, it is Chaput's (2010) theory of "rhetorical circulation" that seems the most fitting for analysis. This is due to the fact that Chaput is interested in the ways communicative acts function to create rhetorical value in modern liberalism, particularly when the circulation of information is made easier with changes to communication technologies.

For Chaput, the habituated practices of neoliberalism are better understood when thinking not of the situatedness of rhetoric but rather of its "transsituational and transhistorical connectivity" (20). Rather than seeing rhetoric as the response to or creation of a problem or dilemma in any given moment, in neoliberalism, rhetoric and persuasion must be understood as a product that comes from processes of communication connected across contexts. Affective energy is key to this connectivity as it provides the extra-discursive glue that holds understandings together across different communicative moments. This is the energy that creates the "pathways that invite human connectivity and constitute knowledge as an ongoing, creative pursuit" (22). When individuals communicate, past, present, and future processes of communication have always already inundated the act with rhetorical energy and influenced it. This influence then guides what is thought, felt, and said, and when these responses occur, affective and rhetorical energy is recirculated into the energy stream, finding its way into and out of habituated experiences. In sum, what Chaput offers to the conversation on the rhetoric of governance is an awareness of the role communicators have in their own subjectification for he/she reaffirm power while simultaneously circulate it with each communicative act.

The Obama Administration targeted stakeholders such as parents, teachers, school administrators, and state officials as the parties responsible for Race to the Top education reforms because it is through their actions that the new learning environment—one laden with neoliberal principles—is circulated and habituated. True to the logic of modern governance, it would be through the guided actions of these individuals that a more competitive education system was made possible. However, in order to compel these stakeholders to play this role, the Administration employed the Aristotelian appeals of *ethos* and *pathos*. In other words, to persuade teachers, parents, and others to play the role of rhetors, President Obama and Secretary Duncan first had to make themselves credible and then take advantage of the emotional atmosphere in which these stakeholders resided.

The first way in which Obama and Duncan established credibility was through their treatment of the Bush Administration's No Child Left Behind educational program. Rather than an outright attack on the previous policy, there was a clear desire to erase its weaknesses. For example, during his address at the Fourth Annual Institute of Education Sciences Research Conference, Duncan (2009b) said:

> There's a lot I don't like about No Child Left Behind, but I will always give credit for exposing our nation's dreadful achievement gaps. It changed American education forever and forced us to take responsibility for every single child, regardless of race, background, or ability ("Robust Data", 1).

During the summer of 2009, Duncan would continue to make comments about the need to "fix" and "change" No Child Left Behind, but not to dismantle it (4). President Obama himself commented on the value of No Child Left Behind as an idea, but through Race to the Top wanted to make the application of such reform more practical (Shear and Anderson 2009, para. 2).

What these examples showed was the Obama Administration carefully treating the previous policy as something in need of reform, but not something to attack. This was an ethical appeal in the Aristotelian sense as it conveyed the tone of change, but not blame. It also specifically reaffirmed Duncan's expertise in education reform. During several speeches, he brought up No Child Left Behind in order to explain what needed to be overhauled. By showing knowledge of the previous policy, both Obama and Duncan have told those who would be implementing reform—teachers, governors, and others—that they knew the problems and would be working to eliminate them.

The second way Obama and Duncan established credibility was by highlighting their experience with and/or commitment to education reform. In his July 24, 2009 remarks on the launch of Race to the Top, the president made it clear that he had been a proponent of reform "from the moment I entered office" (para. 3). He continued by saying:

> In recent months, I've spoken about the different parts of this strategy. I've spoken about what we're doing to prepare community college students to find a job when they graduate; to make college and advanced training more affordable; and to raise the bar in early learning programs. Today, I

want to talk about what we can do to raise the quality of education from kindergarten through senior year. Because improving education is central to rebuilding our economy, we set aside over $4 billion in the Recovery Act to promote improvements in schools. This is one of the largest investments in education reform in American history. And rather than divvying it up and handing it out, we are letting states and school districts compete for it. That's how we can incentivize excellence and spur reform and launch a race to the top in America's public schools. That race starts today (para. 9–11).

In these comments, the President reaffirmed his commitment to education as a producer of economic growth and accentuated the fact that this was something he and his Administration had been a part of for a long time. Such a move connects Obama to his claim for reform and establishes his credibility in relation to the topic.

Secretary Duncan made a similar appeal during his speech at the National Alliance for Public Schools Conference on June 22, 2009. Throughout the speech, Duncan referenced his experience as head of the Chicago Public School system and discussed the tough decisions he was forced to make. He talks about his choice to close some schools due to low performance and the personal connections he formed with teachers, administrators, and parents who trusted him to do the "right thing" even if that meant moving kids to another school or firing school officials (2). Duncan mentions his experience again during later speeches, including one at the Governors Education Symposium, in which he mentioned his relation to education reform by saying, "I am very sensitive to the issue. As I said before, I was a local educator before I came to Washington" ("States Will Lead the Way Towards Reform" 2009c, 4).

What the Obama Administration did through the rhetoric of President Obama and Secretary Duncan leading up to and during the implementation of Race to the Top was affirm their knowledge of the education, their commitment to it, and their authority to do what needed to be done to make the learning environment better. And while this improvement was evaluated through a neoliberal and economic logic, there was still a clear desire to show stakeholders that they knew what they were doing in hopes of getting them on board with the changes to be made.

Obama and Duncan's appeals to audience emotion were also used to make this happen and to guide stakeholders toward actions that would make a new competitive educational environment possible. The best way to summarize this appeal would be to say that in the wake of the

Great Recession and the fear, doubt, and anxiety it produced, the Obama Administration made stakeholders responsible, but hopeful engines of reform. When Duncan was talking to members of the National Education Association, he spoke of reform as a "call to action," the "fight for social justice," and "the civil rights issue of our generation" ("Partners in Reform" 2009a, 6). Duncan ended his speech with these comments as a way of engendering hope and energy in his audience of education administrators and finished by saying "Now we—all of us together—must act on [the understanding that education is the most important work in our society] and move forward" ("Partners in Reform" 2009a, 6). Duncan played upon his audience's emotions throughout the speech and gave them the call to action needed for change. There was hope and promise in his words and in lieu of the Great Recession these words were the pathetic appeal that would make change possible.

President Obama used emotional appeals during his initial remarks on Race to the Top as well. During his announcement of the program, the president told his audience:

> I'm issuing a challenge to our nation's governors, to school boards and principals and teachers, to businesses and non-for-profits, to parents and students: if you set and enforce rigorous and challenging standards and assessments; if you put outstanding teachers at the front of the classroom; if you turn around failing schools—your state can win a Race to the Top grant that will not only help students outcompete workers around the world, but let them fulfill their God-given potential ("Remarks" 2009, para. 11).

Through emotion, he is attempting to motivate his audience and make them the harbingers of reform. The Administration could enact Race to the Top legislation, but the success of reform would depend upon the actions of stakeholders.

In *The Well-Tempered Self*, Miller (1993) discusses the role of cultural critique as a practice of ethical self-governance. Through reading and analyzing culture, citizens find themselves in need of ethical reform and come to "embrace one's ethical incompleteness" (231). If citizens view themselves as ethically incomplete, they will continue to govern themselves in hopes of making themselves ethically whole. For Miller, this incomplete citizen is the desired product. The argument the Obama Administration made to stakeholders in education reform—teachers, parents, administrators, and state officials—functioned in a similar way. Using *ethos* and *pathos*, President Obama and Secretary Duncan attempted to persuade these individuals to work toward ethical completeness for the betterment of America's educational system.

However, ethical stakeholders were but a means to an end for Race to the Top, a fact that separates the program from Miller's conclusions about cultural critique. Parents, teachers, and others who saw serving K-12 students as their ethical duty was itself a technology of governance through which a new learning environment could be created. Like cultural critique, their actions would become the ways through which student subjects would provide the competitive energy needed to pull the USA from its economic woes.

Ideally, once persuaded to act, the stakeholders would be the targets of reform and implement changes to the learning environment in which students would become governable, competitive in the global marketplace, and valuable. The stakeholders, through communicative action—school reforms, teaching, administrative actions, and so on—would provide the value needed to structure the new social sphere of education in which all decisions made by students would add further value to the neoliberal governing rationality. Each action within this sphere would produce and circulate the value necessary to habituate actions—actions that were inherently beneficial for stakeholders and students—and further the legitimacy of the deliberative and communicative ecosystem of modern liberal governance.

Concluding with Capacity

This chapter attempted to challenge the argument that the Obama Administration's Race to the Top program worked against modern liberal governance. As mentioned, many believed federal regulation of education would hinder competition and hurt notions of market-based relations and individual success. By problematizing Race to the Top, its discourse, and the discourse that surrounded it as a networked technology of governance, it becomes clear that the Administration was not hindering neoliberalism, but was in fact working in favor of the rationality as it governed the social sphere according to an economic logic for the benefit of the US economy and not to its detriment.

Race to the Top functioned as an ideal example of how neoliberal governance works rhetorically. The state subtracted itself from the economic sphere and instead turns its attention to the social. It is then through the social that economic viability was made possible. Also, in true neoliberal fashion, Race to the Top attempted to persuade stakeholders to be the creators and circulators of rhetorical value and effectiveness as these were the components needed to order and legitimate the learning environment, its relations, and its processes, all of which worked together to influence actions of students that would ultimately make America more competitive.

I would like to conclude this chapter by making the claim that Race to the Top functioned as one particular form of governance *within* neoliberalism. This new program works in favor of capacity and thus, I would like to claim the discourse it involves functions as a "rhetoric of capacity." The *New Oxford American Dictionary* defines capacity as "the maximum amount that something can contain," "the amount that something can produce," and "the ability or power to do, experience, or understand something."

Part of the success owed to neoliberal economics' emergence in the 1960s and 1970s was its belief in the rational individual, that is, someone who would make the best decision according to his/her situation (Foucault 2008). This was the justification needed to legislate the state out of the economic sphere because if all economic actors were rational, there was no need for intervention. Through the rational analysis of risk, all free individuals would make the right choice for themselves. Neoliberal governance has attempted to influence and structure those choices since the logic became the truth of all social relations.

What is key to this construction of education as a social sphere is that the process of education continues to function according to the neoliberal logic of market competition. If all act, think, and feel within the same sphere, all are guided toward achieving the same level of capacity. However, by nature, not all will achieve and be made capable. When this is the case, the governing rationality is reaffirmed because if one does not succeed, especially when all are given the same knowledge, the same chance, and the same support, it becomes the failing individual's burden to bear.

As Thomas Lemke (2001) makes clear in his reading of Foucault's work on modern liberal governance, "Neoliberal policy [...] focuses not on the players, but on the rules of the game, not on the (inner) subjugation of individuals, but on defining and controlling their (outer) environments" (200). If one cannot succeed and profit in the game everyone has been prompted into playing, that is his/her problem and no one else's.

Bibliography

Bowen, Daniel H. 2010. Politics and the Scoring of the Race to the Top Applications. American Enterprise Institute. http://www.aei.org/publication/politics-and-the-scoring-of-race-to-the-top-applications. Last modified 10 Sept 2010.

Chaput, Catherine. 2010. Rhetorical Circulation in Late Capitalism: Neoliberalism and the Overdetermination of Affective Energy. *Philosophy and Rhetoric* 43(1): 1–25.

Chaput, Catherine, and Joshua S. Hanan. 2015. Economic Rhetoric as *Taxis*. *Journal of Cultural Economy* 8(1): 42–61. doi:10.1080/17530350.2014.942 349 .Accessed 10 Aug 2015

Colebrook, Claire. 1998. Ethics, Positivity, and Gender: Foucault, Aristotle, and the Care of the Self. *Philosophy Today* 42(1): 40–52.

Dean, Jodi. 2005. Communicative Capitalism: Circulation and the Foreclosure of Politics. *Cultural Politics* 1(1): 51–74.

Dean, Mitchell. 2010. *Governmentality: Power and Rule in Modern Society*. Thousand Oaks, CA: Sage Publications.

Duncan, Arne. 2009a. Partners in Reform: Address to the National Education Association. Department of Education. http://www2.ed.gov/news/speeches/2009/07/07022009.pdf. Last modified 2 Jul 2009.

———. 2009b. Robust Data Gives Us the Roadmap to Reforms: Address at the Fourth Annual Institute of Education Sciences Research Conference. Department of Education. http://www.ed.gov/news/speeches/robust-data-gives-us-roadmap-reform. Last modified 8 June 2009.

———. 2009c. States Will Lead the Way to Reform: Address at the 2009 Governors Education Symposium. Department of Education. http://www2.ed.gov/news/speeches/2009/06/06142009.pdf. Last modified 14 June 2009.

———. 2009d. Turning Around the Bottom 5 Percent: Address at the National Alliance for Public Charter Schools Conference. Department of Education. http://www2.ed.gov/news/speeches/2009/06/06222009.pdf. Last modified 22 June 2009.

Foucault, Michel. 1988. Technologies of the Self. In *Technologies of the Self: A Seminar with Michel Foucault*, eds. Luther H. Martin, Huck Gutman, and Patrick H. Hutton, 16–49. Amherst, MA: University of Massachusetts Press.

———. 2008. *The Birth of Biopolitics*. New York: Picador.

Goodnight, G. Thomas.1989. Toward a Social Theory of Argumentation. *Argumentation and Advocacy* 26: 60–70.

———. 2012. The Personal, Technical, and Public Spheres of Argument: A Speculative Inquiry into the Art of Public Deliberation. *Argumentation and Advocacy* 48: 198–210.

Greene, Ronald Walter. 2004. Rhetoric and Capitalism: Rhetorical Agency as Communicative Labor. *Philosophy and Rhetoric* 37(4): 188–206.
———. 2007. Rhetorical Capital: Communicative Labor, Money/Speech, and Neo-Liberal Governance. *Communication and Critical/Cultural Studies* 4(3): 327–331.
Greene, Ronald Walter, and Darrin Hicks. 2005. Lost Convictions: Debating Both Sides and the Ethical Self-Fashioning of Liberal Citizens. *Cultural Studies* 19(1): 100–126.
Grusin, Richard. 2010. *Premediation: Affect and Mediality After 9/11.* New York, NY: Palgrave MacMillan.
Jay, Samuel M. 2014. Governing Confidence: Rhetoric, Affect, and Post-Crisis Financial Education. PhD dissertation. University of Denver. ProQuest (3641996).
Lemke, Thomas. 2001. 'The Birth of Bio-Politics'—Michel Foucault's Lecture at the Collège de France on Neo-Liberal Governmentality. *Economy and Society* 30(2): 190–207.
Miller, Tiffany D. and Robert Hanna. 2014. Four Years Later, Are Race to Top States on Track? *Center for American Progress.* https://www.americanprogress.org/issues/education/report/2014/03/24/86197/four-years-later-are-race-to-the-top-states-on-track Last modified 24 Mar 2014. Note to Paginators and QC: we are raised the query to CE for new reference afer reply from CE need to annotate the reference.
Miller, Toby. 1993. *The Well-Tempered Self.* Baltimore, MA: The Johns Hopkins University Press.
New Oxford American Dictionary. s.v. "capacity."
Nine States and the District of Columbia Win Second Round Race to the Top Grants. 2010. Department of Education. http://www.ed.gov/news/press-releases/nine-states-and-district-columbia-win-second-round-race-top-grants. Last modified 24 Aug 2010.
Obama, President Barack. 2009. Remarks by the President on Education. Office of the Press Secretary. http://www.whitehouse.gov/the_press_office/Remarks-by-the-President-at-the-Department-of-Education. Last modified 24 Jul 2009.
Race to the Top Program Executive Summary. 2009. Department of Education. http://www2.ed.gov/programs/racetothetop/executive-summary.pdf. Last modified 4 Nov 2009.
Rose, Nikolas. 1999. Inventiveness in Politics. *Economy and Society* 28(3): 467–493.
Setting the Pace: Expanding Opportunity for America's Students Under Race to the Top. 2014. Department of Education. http://www.whitehouse.gov/

sites/default/files/docs/settingthepacerttreport_3-2414_b.pdf. Last modified 24 Mar 2014.

Shear, Michael D, and Nick Anderson. 2009. President Obama Discusses New 'Race to the Top' Program. *The Washington Post.* http://www.washingtonpost.com/wp-dyn/content/article/2009/07/23/AR2009072302938.html. Last modified 23 Jul 2009.

The Office of the Press Secretary. 2009. Fact Sheet: The Race to the Top. *WhiteHouse.gov.* http://www.whitehouse.gov/the-press-office/fact-sheet-race-top. Last modified 4 Nov 2009.

Weiss, Elaine. 2013. Mismatches in Race to the Top Limit Educational Improvemen. Economic Policy Institute. http://www.epi.org/publication/race-to-the-top-goals. Last modified 12 Sept 2013.

Constitutive Rhetoric in the Age of Neoliberalism

David W. Seitz and Amanda Berardi Tennant

Constitutive rhetoric is a theory of speech regarding the ability of language and symbols to create a collective identity for an audience. Traced back to the Greek Sophists, who appreciated the contingent nature of knowledge and the constitutive power of language (the capacity of speech to call reality into being), and developed by ancient thinkers and modern scholars alike, constitutive rhetoric is commonly understood as a genre of public discourse in which a speaker establishes and provides an addressed audience with a common identity that theretofore had not been named or realized. Constructed upon an allegedly shared value system, this newly formed identity can subsequently foster conditions for persuasion, collectivism, political action, or the defense or challenge of some authority (Charland 2001, 616–19).

Focusing on constitutive rhetoric's potentially radical, emancipatory power and relevance to democratic public life, this essay seeks to understand how constitutive rhetoric functions in a world presently dominated

---

D.W. Seitz (✉)
Department of Communication Arts and Sciences,
Pennsylvania State University, Mont Alto, PA, USA

A.B. Tennant
Department of English, Carnegie Mellon University, Pittsburgh, PA, USA

by neoliberal ideology. Broadly understood as economic philosophy that advocates globalization, deregulation, privatization, Social Darwinism, and the commodification of nearly every aspect of life, neoliberalism deprives citizens of their power and instead benefits the interests of a small dominant class. Advancing the power and wealth of the few at the cost of the agency and wellbeing of the many, neoliberalism is fundamentally antithetical to the ideals of democratic politics (Harvey 2007; Steger and Roy 2010).

Against this grim social backdrop, how might constitutive rhetoric successfully generate identification around democratic principles of equality and freedom, and advocate the extension of citizenship and rights to previously forgotten, excluded, or oppressed peoples? The answer, we believe, may be found in French philosopher Jacques Rancière's counterhegemonic, anti-neoliberal political theory of "the part of no part." Rancière (1999, 2010, 27–44) suggests that contemporary democratic political action (seen, e.g., at various moments throughout the recent Arab Spring) becomes possible when people who evade the code governing the system (the invisible or marginalized "uncounted") emerge and transform from unintelligible "noise" to a powerful "voice"; as a new, yet identifiable, political form, this "voice" enables a collective, societal reexamination of who "counts" and, ideally, a redistribution of equality.

In this chapter, we argue that Rancière offers rhetoricians an alternative perspective and vocabulary for understanding how identities emerge rhetorically to foster equality within "the new way of the world" (Dardot and Laval 2009) and the obstacles these new identities must overcome in the neoliberal age. The remaining pages are divided into four sections. The first section traces the history of thought on constitutive rhetoric. The second section explains the fundamental challenge that neoliberalism poses to democratic constitutive rhetorical action. The third section presents Rancière's political theory as an innovative conceptual framework for understanding the nature, limits, and rich potential of constitutive rhetoric as it often occurs today. Finally, the fourth section offers a brief case study of the 2010 Levi Strauss "We Are All Workers" multimedia ad campaign. Here, we show how the clothing company effectively appropriated the aesthetics and identity of the people of Braddock, Pennsylvania—a poor, "forgotten" community devastated by neoliberal economics that nonetheless, through a radical, collective effort, had recently come to "voice"—in its attempt to "rust wash" its brand (a rhetorical strategy that other corporations regularly used during the so-called Great Recession). This case, we believe, is a representative example of the promise, tensions, complexities, and fragility of (what we term) 'Rancièrian constitutive rhetoric.'

Constitutive Rhetoric Through the Ages

Straddling the traditional fault line between rhetoric and philosophy for 2500 years, constitutive rhetoric encapsulates the fundamental question with which some of the greatest minds have grappled: What is rhetoric's nature? Is it "an art without substance, a *techne* [...] divorced from any outcome other than the instrumental relationship between intent and effect"—in other words, speech that alone creates (or constitutes) truth and reality for a given audience? Or is it, as Aristotle posited, the necessary "handmaiden" to philosophy—the uniquely human practice that enables speakers to give effectiveness to verified truths (Condit and Lucaites 1993, x)? Falling in the first camp were the Sophists, who believed that rhetoric was capable of, and typically responsible for, producing "the very categories by which the world, and indeed the self, are understood" (Charland 2001, 616). Plato, the great champion of philosophy and "Big-T Truth," concurred with the sophistic view of rhetoric as an empty if highly potent *techne*. But whereas the Sophists accepted and valorized rhetoric's constitutive powers and central place in a democratic society, Plato abhorred rhetoric's alleged corruptive effects on public morality and state affairs. If the judgment, beliefs, and behaviors of the *demos* are so easily influenced by the dubious logic, flowery language, and constitutive powers of rhetoric, Plato claimed that ideally all political power should reside in a small class of qualified rulers ostensibly capable of basing their decisions on knowledge, reason, and ethics alone (Condit and Lucaites 1993, x–xi).

Situating himself somewhere between the Sophists and Plato, Isocrates sought to "recombine rhetoric and philosophy as the basis for a culturally specific, public discourse that exploited the radical potential of Athenian democracy both to critique itself and adapt to social and political exigencies in an orderly and liberating manner." Isocrates' project rested on two assumptions: (1) that nothing good in human affairs comes about without the help of speech (therefore rhetoric is inherently ethical) and (2) that instances of rhetoric should be judged not on their artistic or persuasive merits, but rather on "the value of the political world they create." Isocrates envisioned an ideal Athenian state in which leaders issued public statements that drew upon reason and "commonly used allusions, aphorisms, characterizations, ideographs, images, metaphors, myths, narratives, and *topoi*" to constitute a collective identity between potentially diverse and competing individuals and groups of the *demos*.

By reminding the rulers and the ruled alike of a shared identity based on Athenian ideals and virtues through speech, leaders would foster conditions for consensus—represented by the assent of the public—as to the "best course of action" within any given moment of political or social exigency (Condit and Lucaites 1993, x–xiii). Rhetoric's value, Isocrates posited, was located in a particular feature: rhetoric's ability to constitute collective identity around piety to "a natural (or supernatural) order that provides the pre-existing conditions of one's existence and identity" (Chase 2009, 3, 239–62).

These ancient thoughts on constitutive rhetoric have informed modern conceptions of the term. Most notably, Kenneth Burke's theory of "identification" very much aligns with the sophistic view of rhetoric's constitutive powers. Words, Burke (1966) argues, often serve as "terministic screens" that filter what people see, how people act—seemingly even the contours of their reality itself (44–62). Likewise, through language an orator can "rearrange the meaning of terms, so that one thing becomes more or less like another, or members of an audience are brought to share a common identity with each other or the speaker" (Charland 2001, 617). Such identification between speaker and audience—the verbal constitution of an "us" (and, necessarily, an implicit or explicit "them")—is crucial to Burke's view of rhetoric, for as he famously proclaimed: "You persuade a man only insofar as you can talk his language by speech, gesture, tonality, order, image, attitude, idea, *identifying* your ways with his" (Burke 1969, 55). Rhetorically produced, rather than a prior given, identity is, in Burke's estimation, a fundamental prerequisite for persuasion.[1]

Perhaps effective speech "both depends upon and validates" an "always already" shared identity, worldview, or *ēthos* (as thinkers like Maurice Charland and Michael McGee contend). Perhaps it simply relies on articulating (or constituting) a collective identity that serves as "a place from which the audience is called upon to judge and act," regardless of that identity's prior existence or nonexistence. Whatever the case, today constitutive rhetoric is commonly understood as a discursive process "that arises [...] usually in the face of a threat that is itself presented as alien or other," in which "audiences are called upon to materialize through their actions an identity ascribed to them" (Charland 2001, 616). Notable instances of this process include:

- Solon's rhetorical transfiguration of the Athenian underclass from "slaves" to "the people" and "citizens," a speech act that helped set the table for Athenian democracy;
- The frequent appearance of "free man" in the Magna Carta, a term that implied the extension of unprecedented rights, not just to aristocrats, but to a broader swath of less "noble" Englishmen and women as well;
- The Preamble of the US Constitution, which named and unified the populations of 13 disparate colonies with the seemingly simple phrase, "We the People of the United States";
- Martin Luther King, Jr., casting Americans of every pigmentation as "all of God's children" in his monumental *I Have a Dream* speech.

Whether general ("worker," "mother," "citizen," "feminist") or specific (abolitionist, Chicano, Suffragette, Black Panther, Guerrilla Girl, Black Lives Matter), collective identity generated through the constitutive rhetoric has always been a central component of emancipatory democratic politics.

Neoliberalism's Challenge

Citizenry group identity formation, the lifeblood of democratic politics, is increasingly hard (seemingly even impossible) to achieve in our current epoch: the age of neoliberalism. Rising to prominence in the 1980s, neoliberalism is an ideology that "promotes a consumerist, free-market world" in which "the production and exchange of material goods [is] at the heart of the human experience" (Steger and Roy 2010, 11–15). In their examination of "the new way of the world," Pierre Dardot and Christian Laval argue that neoliberalism is, above all else, a "rationality"—an "existential norm" that "tends to structure and organize not only the action of rulers, but also the conduct of the ruled." In their view, "this norm enjoins everyone to live in a world of generalized competition; it promotes the justification of ever greater inequalities; it even transforms the individual, now called on to conceive and conduct him- or herself as an enterprise. In other words, it reduces human beings to "neoliberal subjects" (Dardot and Laval 2009, 3–4). Self-disciplined in thought and behavior, the neo-liberal subject is one who: must constantly compete to maximize advantage and survive; assumes all responsibility for her own lot in life; and works for her employer as if she were working for herself. As neoliberal modes of governance continue to dismantle social services and protections, transfer public wealth to private coffers, and equate freedom with the right to buy, the unfortunate and downtrodden of the world, "often already marginalized because of their race and class, are viewed as redundant or a burden on the economy and labeled 'disposable'" (Giroux 2012, 62–63). In a world where citizens are compelled to pursue self-preservation and united only by a common state of detachment, employing constitutive rhetoric to generate identification around democratic principles of equality, freedom, justice, and civil rights—principles that, on a day-to-day level, have been all but abandoned—is an increasingly futile proposition.[2]

Hope, however small, may reside in the political theory of French philosopher Jacques Rancière. Developed over the past 30 years and recently introduced to English speakers in *Dis-agreement: Politics and Philosophy* (1999) and *Dissensus: On Politics and Aesthetics* (2010), Rancière's theory of "the part of no part" offers an alternative way of thinking about 'constitutive rhetoric' (a term that Rancière never explicitly evokes, per say). According to Rancière, democratic political action emerges from a particular process of identity formation. "Against Habermas," Steven Corcoran writes in the introduction to *Dissensus*,

> Rancière emphasizes the fact that genuine political speech above all entails a dispute over the very quality of those who speak […] Political struggle proper is therefore not a matter of rational debate between multiple interests; it is above all, a struggle to have one's voice heard and oneself recognized as a legitimate partner in debate (Rancière 2010, 8–9).

Rancière's (1999) concern, then, is not with the now-commonsensical positivist relationship between speech and political identity and action, but rather with the more fundamental question of who is able to speak (i.e., take part in politics) in the first place. Who has an equal place at the table in Habermas's coffee house, and who does not (23)?

For Rancière (1999, 59), true democratic moments and change result not from rational argumentation or dramatic proclamations,[3] but instead when those without voice display their previously unrecognized capacity for *logos*—when "the part of no part" emerge as a comprehensible (though not necessarily named or branded) political identity whose *mere existence and undeniable ability to speak* call into question the social order's seemingly natural yet always arbitrary logic that determines who can take part in politics and who cannot (Rancière 2010, 8–9). Irreducible to mere protest and affixed to no particular setting,[4] this radical process of constituting identity, termed "dissensus,"[5] is often fleeting[6] and/or effectively suppressed by the all-encompassing social order or (in Rancièrian terms) "police."[7] As distant and recent historical events reveal, prominent acts of "dissensus" can draw stiff resistance from the "police" order. This resistance tends to manifest in one of two ways. The first is state-sponsored violence—a prevalent, intimidating, and highly conspicuous response that can clear particular spaces of bodies yet simultaneously draw greater attention to both "the part of no part's" plight and the inherent injustice and inequality of the status quo. The second and far more productive response is "consensus"—the insidious rhetorical deflection, deflation, or appropriation of "the part of no part's" voice, image, argument, and momentum that stabilizes or reaffirms the standing social order. The following section unpacks these ideas in greater detail.

Rancièrian Constitutive Rhetoric

Rancière's political critique is based on the friction between two opposing entities: "police" and "politics." "Police" refers to something much greater and more abstract than commonplace law enforcement or military personnel. In Rancièrian terms, "police" refers to the "symbolic constitution of the social," the social order that determines who can speak, who is visible, what can be said, seen, and done, and where (Rancière 1999, 22–23). Ubiquitous (and something akin to neoliberalism itself), police is the seemingly natural yet manufactured "configuration of the political community"—the arrangement of society and power that bestows equality (the ability to take part in political discourse and action) to some, determines who counts, and separates "those who are born for politics from those who are born for the 'bare' life of economic and social necessity" (Rancière 2011, 3). Police is the code of governance that categorizes and divides groups "by differences in birth, and by the different functions, places and interests that make up the social body to the exclusion of every supplement" (Rancière 2010, 36). The whole of the "social body" is always less than the total sum of the populous, as those deemed fit for "bare" life (the poor, the unemployed, the disenfranchised, manual laborers, minorities, immigrants—in other words, the "disposable") are excluded from the count (Rancière 1999, 14). These are the invisible masses, "the part of no part," the uncounted "supplemental" who are denied the capacity to speak, whose voices are reduced to silence or, at best, unintelligible, animal-like noise.[8]

The police order's geometrical and asymmetrical (as opposed to arithmetical and equitable) allocation of rights and recognition disproportionally serves the interests of a small elite class (i.e., the rich), yet survives on the basis of perpetuating "consensus," the "general agreement that the partition of the sensible and its distribution of roles is a reasonable one, and that there is no reasonable alternative to it" (May 2010). Certainly, those afforded some measure of equality—those allegedly in possession of *logos*, those whom the governing code claims to recognize (the "middle class," etc.)—are *not* encouraged to pursue emancipatory democratic political action of any kind. On the contrary, the "counted" are conditioned to become inured to, and accept as inevitable, "consensus" politics, which reduces: equality to "commercial equality"[9]; people down to demographics; government to an affair of the officials and experts; politics to the struggle for and maintaining of power; and civic participation to essentially inconsequential undertakings (e.g., casting votes once a year, speaking at town hall meetings, writing letters to representatives, and so on) (Rancière 1999, 101–102). Rancière (1999, 16–17) claims that the police order depends upon the deference and conformity of those considered "born for politics"—deference and conformity made possible by a "primary contradiction":

> There is order in society because some people command and others obey, but in order to obey an order at least two things are required: you must understand the order and you must understand that you must obey it. And to do that, you must already be the equal of the person who is ordering you […]. In the final analysis, inequality is only possible through equality.

In Rancière's view, the peculiar sense of equality that this seemingly inescapable paradox affords to those deemed part of the "whole" makes *real* politics—political action that might challenge the basis of a ruler's authority, the inequitable "partition of the sensible," or the exclusion of "those having no part"—highly unlikely, undesirable, and even unimaginable.

The police order depends upon the configuration, depoliticization, and management of both public and private spaces. Rancière claims the police "consists, before all else, in recalling the obviousness of what there is, or rather of what there is not, and its slogan is: 'Move along! There's nothing to see here'" (Rancière 2010, 37–40). Public areas are cast as spaces for circulation and commerce, not congregation and political discourse. In those rare moments of mass demonstration, the police order contains and defuses the politicization of public space by enforcing protest permits, designating "free speech zones," or clearing the area with military force. Meanwhile, spaces like the workplace and factory floor are legally and culturally distanced from public life. Today, the average worker (blue collared or white) is no longer a political subject capable of speaking in solidarity with others for more rights, better pay, or equality, and must engage those (upper management) who have neither the inclination nor ability to comprehend workers' arguments *as* arguments (Rancière 2010, 5).

In Rancière's schema, "politics," or "dissensus" (as against "police" and "consensus"), is the idiosyncratic process by which "the part of those who have no part"—"the supplementary subjects that are a surplus in relation to any (ac)count of the parts of society"—disrupt the logic of the police order in a struggle to be heard. Politics occurs when, either out of necessity or chance, "surplus" actors manifest themselves as intelligible political beings in spaces that were once demarcated as apolitical, and bring to light the typically unacknowledged void between the "whole" of society and those left uncounted. An "intervention upon the visible and the sayable," politics renders apparent "the presence of two worlds in one" by refiguring the moving-along space of the police "into a space for the appearance of a subject: i.e., the people, the workers, the citizens" (Rancière 2010, 37–40). As evidenced, for example, by the 2011 Egyptian protest at Tahrir Square, when hundreds of thousands of ordinary citizens gathered and asserted their humanity to an oppressive regime and (via Twitter and YouTube) the world at large, Rancièrian politics entails the "uncounted" asserting "a most peculiar platform of argument"—behaving "*as though* such a stage [from which to speak] existed, as though there were a common world of argument" (Rancière 1999, 52–53). This activity—this demonstration or reenactment of equality[10]—illuminates, if only for a brief moment, visions of a social order in which no one is left out and everybody counts.[11]

According to Rancière (1999), equality is not an effect of dissensus, but rather the presupposition upon which acts of dissensus are based.[12] Dissensus is not the act of arguing for equality, rights, and greater representation within the status quo.[13] Instead, dissensus entails demonstrating one's equality as *logos*-possessing human beings in such a way as to call the police order's distribution of the sensible (and thus the police order itself) into question. Therefore, dissensus, or Rancièrian politics, should not be identified with a Habermasian model of rational argumentation, since this model presupposes the partners in communicative exchange to be pre-constituted, and that the discursive forms of exchange imply a speech community whose constraint is always explicable [...] Political argument is at one and the same time the demonstration of a possible world where the argument could count as argument, addressed by a subject qualified to argue, upon an identified object, to an addressee who is required to see the object and to hear the argument that he or she 'normally' has no reason to either see or hear. It is the construction of a paradoxical world that relates two separate worlds (Rancière 2010, 38–39).

In simpler terms, the Habermasian model of communication presumes a mutually recognized equality between speakers that, in the real world, is rare and, for "the part of no part," systemically and effectively voided through law, force, economics, and customs. Drawing attention to this crucial blind spot within traditional conceptions of politics and rational argumentation, Rancière conceives dissensus not as what is said around the proverbial café table, but as the radical act of conjuring up a chair that had not existed; of emerging as a comprehensible yet unprecedented political form that inherently stands as an argument for the arithmetic, uniformed redistribution of equality to all.

A twist on the traditional conception of constitutive rhetoric, "Rancièrian constitutive rhetoric" is not a matter of identification, division, or consensus building, though it may entail these phenomena to varying degrees (Rancière 1999, 19). Instead, politics is a matter of disidentification, a process in which "the part of no part" shirk their delegated role as the silent, invisible, and surplus "uncounted," and emerge as an unprecedented, theretofore unnamed, yet viable political form that the status quo can neither accommodate as is nor simply ignore.[14] Dissensus lays bare the illegitimacy of previously assigned classifications, the division of people into parts, the "partition of the sensible," and the seeming natural order of social relations between those who rule, those who are ruled, those who count, and those who do not. Demonstrating the humanity and social experience of the "uncounted,"[15] dissensus reveals the unspoken "miscount" and ruptures "the outrageous claim" that "there is no part of those who have no part" (Rancière 1999, 11, 14). In sum, dissensus attempts to bring *every person* into the fold by exhibiting the inherent equality of *all* people and the struggle and discursive abilities of the "uncounted" as universal.

Forever desiring the maintenance of or "return to the normal state of things—the non-existence of politics," the police order tends to respond to marked acts of dissensus in one of two ways (Rancière 2010, 43). The first, and most conspicuous, is the use of physical force. Countless historical instances attest to the police order's tendency to inflict violence upon even the most peaceful practitioners of dissensus.[16] By reacting to dissensus with extreme force, the police order may be able to clear bodies from public spaces, stifle political action, and intimidate those who might otherwise support "the part of no part" in their struggle to be heard. Such effects may be immediate and long lasting. Moreover, it is unlikely that those who pull the trigger or swing the truncheon will ever be held accountable for their deeds in a court of law (e.g., see *New York Court Dismisses Lawsuit* 2015). But heavy-handed repression of political actors can also backfire on the police order, particularly when mass-produced images of police brutality circulate and reach widespread audiences. In other words, documented violence can easily depict the police order as villainous, generate sympathy for the injured, and, in the eyes of the masses, justify acts of dissensus (Blair and Michel 2008, 139–155; Carlson 1983, 71; Ginsburg 2015, 8).

The police order's second option, of course, is "consensus." Subtle yet highly effective, consensus primarily entails disqualifying "the political quality of the speech of those who demonstrate their equality" (Rancière 2010, 9). Instead of suppressing "the part of no part" with brute force or draconian laws, the police order may find symbolic means of rejecting or falsely recognizing a given, dissensus-generated (and, typically, theretofore *unnamed*) political identity so as to: (1) redefine it; (2) appropriate its voice and visibility; (3) neutralize its meaning, message, and radical potential; (4) fold it back into the logic of social order/neoliberal hierarchy of disposability; and (5) preserve the status quo. Less turbulent—less likely to generate wider sympathy for, interest in, or understanding of, a particular act of dissensus—consensus can deflate a Rancièrian political moment, discourage "the part of no part," and reinscribe the "symbolic constitution of the social" (Rancière 2010, 36). Rancière cites the suppression of Scythian slave revolt (per Herodotus's telling) as an archetypical, if dramatic, example of consensus in action. After reaching "the conclusion that there was no particular reason why they should be slaves, being born the same way their distant masters were and with the same attributes," a younger generation of conquered Median slaves took up arms to prove themselves equal to their Scythian masters. When an assault on the rebellious slaves failed, a quick-thinking Scythian warrior told his comrades:

Take my advice—lay spear and bow aside, and let each man fetch his horsewhip, and go boldly up to them. So long as they see us with arms in our hands, they imagine themselves our equals in birth and bravery; but let them behold us with no other weapon but the whip, and they will feel that they are our slaves, and flee before us.

"And so it was done," Rancière writes, "with great success: struck by the spectacle, the slaves took to their heels without a fight." In refusing to meet the slaves as equals and employing the aesthetic violence of the master's whip, the Scythians devastated the slaves' psyche and effectively demonstrated the apparent intransience of the existing social order (Rancière 1999, 12).

Given the predominantly visual world in which we now live, consensus may involve hijacking, manipulating, and subsequently redeploying the image of "the part of no part" in a fashion that is favorable to the neoliberal/police order. If dissensus is the process of making visible "that which has no place to be seen" (Rancière 2010, 39), consensus may be the process of visually reframing "that which has no place to be seen" in a way that is conducive to the maintenance of the normal state of affairs. Somewhat similar to "cool hunting," the corporate appropriation and commodification of African-American culture (Klein 1999, 73–76), this form of consensus can be identified in:

- Apple's reductive "Think Different" ad campaigns, which have employed images of practitioners of dissensus—for example, Martin Luther King, Jr., Mahatma Ghandi, Rosa Parks, Cesar Chavez, Nelson Mandela—to identify the massive multinational corporation with the "The crazy ones [...] rebels [...] troublemakers [and] ones who see things differently" (Siltanen 2011);
- The Washington Redskins' "Original Americans Foundation," a charitable organization that claims "to address the challenges in the daily lives of Native Americans," but in reality is merely a carefully constructed website that exploits the stories and images of struggling "Tribal communities" in the service of justifying the NFL team's racist name and logo (Newell 2014);
- Corporate media news coverage of the 2015 Baltimore riots in which young Black protesters were cast as "thugs" and "criminals" (Rothkopf 2015).
- The mainstream media and political establishment's marginalization and vilification of the Black Lives Matter movement, as well as the

attending rise of the "Blue Lives Matter," "White Lives Matter," and "All Lives Matter" 'counter-movements' (Blue Lives Matter; Cherry 2015; Craven 2016; Victor 2016; "White Lives Matter").

Visually reframing the meaning, voice, and image of "the part of no part" into Gramscian "common sense" notions and legabilities (Gramsci 2012, 419), this type of consensus tempers, rejects, and/or negates acts of dissensus through symbolic action, rather than overt and potentially disadvantageous physical force, to demonstrate effectively that there has not been a miscount of any kind—that the system has accounted for all.

In order to bring the ideas above into starker relief, we would like to conclude this essay with a brief case study that exemplifies both the potential of Rancière's political theory and the ease with which the neoliberal/police order can appropriate the aesthetics of newly formed, emancipatory democratic identities. In 2010, the international clothing company Levi Strauss sent a film crew to Braddock, Pennsylvania (a largely abandoned former steel town near Pittsburgh) to shoot a multimedia marketing campaign for its trademark denim jeans attire. At that time (the high point of the Great Recession), the people of Braddock had become nationally visible for a marked act of dissensus. In the few remaining pages, we hope to explain how Levi's (a powerful representative of the neoliberal/police order) appropriated Braddock's image (and thus the town's voice and message) for its own corporate purposes, and thereby defused the radical potential of the Braddock project. This case is instructive for understanding the challenge of practicing "Rancièrian constitutive rhetoric" in the current neoliberal age.

Braddock/Levi's: A Case in Brief

In 2009, Levi's sought out Braddock, Pennsylvania as the backdrop for a multimedia ad campaign that might reconnect the Levi's brand to its blue collar roots. Long before, during the heights of the steel industry, Braddock had once been "a flourishing city of 20,000 residents" (*What is Braddock* 2014). In 1875, Andrew Carnegie had chosen Braddock as the location for his first steel mill, a decision that placed Braddock at the center of the US steel industry. Furnishing thousands of jobs for local residents for 100 years, the steel industry had boosted Braddock's economy and supported the town's many shopping districts, churches, schools, furniture stores, restaurants, and breweries. However, beginning in the 1970s, as US steel production was outsourced to Japan and Germany,

Braddock's economic stability proceeded to deteriorate (*List of Act 47 Distress Determinations* 2014); rapidly, the community experienced "a complete and utter implosion of everything that comprised its socioeconomic fabric over the years" (Fetterman 2012). With few job prospects and rising crime rates, the majority of residents left for good and most shops closed their doors. In 1988, the borough was officially designated a "financially distressed municipality" (*List of Act 47 Distress Determinations* 2014). By 2000, Braddock's population had decreased to less than 3000 residents, all of whom struggled to survive in this hollowed out, shell of a town (Kline and Brill 2014). As the spirit of Braddock decayed, so did its physical landscape and infrastructure; by the 2000s, "ninety percent" of the borough had come to resemble "a landfill" (Fetterman 2012).

When Levi's arrived a decade later, Braddock was under the leadership of a new mayor who envisioned an alternative future for the community. Elected in 2005, John Fetterman had set a radical initiative (dubbed "Braddock Redux") in motion that sought to transform this neglected "moving along space" (to use Rancièrean parlance) from a post-industrial wasteland into a progressive, self-sufficient, racially diverse community of workers of all ages. Imagining "groups of people with wide varieties of skills, knowledge, resources, drive, and abilities sharing ideas and developing collaborative efforts," Fetterman actively courted artists, anarchists, skilled laborers, and micro-green tech companies to the town (*Braddock Redux* 2015). Working in collaboration with longtime residents and recent transplants, Fetterman oversaw the erection of a new community center, the establishment of an organic urban farm (a source of affordable produce for Braddock citizens), the restoration of dilapidated buildings and the Braddock Carnegie Library, and the provision of affordable housing to local poor. Though progress was slow and violent crime rates remained high (Streitfeld 2009), Braddock's revitalization project began gaining attention from local, then national, press. As the head of the movement, Braddock's young, gruff-looking, tattoo-covered mayor became its de facto spokesperson. Following a series of profiles in the *Pittsburgh Post-Gazette*, Fetterman and "Braddock Redux" were featured in the *New York Times*, Comedy Central's *The Colbert Report*, and many other mainstreams, mass media outlets (*A Once Booming Steel Town Looks to Future* 2009; Streitfeld 2009; *The Colbert Report* 2009).

Thus, at the very peak of the "Great Recession," Fetterman publicly and cogently articulated and championed Braddock's rebellious approach to community revitalization. In turn, the "new Braddock worker" started to emerge as a counter-voice to the neoliberal forces that had negatively shaped Braddock (not to mention the nation and the world) for decades.

In an interview with Public Broadcasting Service (PBS), Fetterman flatly stated, "We need to reinvent the overall operating paradigm in these communities" (*A Town Revitalized* 2010). Fetterman's call for reinvention extended to other struggling post-industrial communities (particularly American "rust belt" cities), thereby exemplifying the power of constitutive rhetoric to establish new, collective identities and inspire action. The radical potential of Braddock's emerging voice existed in the longtime residents' and new workers' willingness to invest in the neighborhood with no guarantee of personal financial gain, their acts of collective responsibility to Braddock thereby challenging neoliberal ideals of individualism and assumptions of what it means to be a "productive" worker. The fact that Braddock's new identity was both difficult to comprehend and impossible to ignore (as evidenced by the numerous national media sources that featured Braddock's story) helps us to understand this unprecedented voice as a moment of Rancièrian dissensus (Pilkington 2009; Jacobs 2010; Stroud 2006; *Brave Thinkers* 2009). When speaking with PBS, Fetterman was not shy with his critique of the unjust conditions that led to Braddock's demise. He stated:

> Braddock is emblematic of what happens when there is no intervention, there is no bailout. And if you contrast the energy that was spent and the resources that were used to bailout the financial service sector last year in 2008 versus this complete laissez-faire approach to industry and steel and what have you, and that's the logical conclusion [...] You can't put a sparkly gauze over it. It is a community that has endured a great deal of suffering at the hands of forces that were well beyond the control of any residents (*A Town Revitalized* 2010).

Fetterman's outspokenness revealed the nature of Rancièrian dissensus, which "consists in the often short-lived moment when those who are excluded from the political order or included in it in a subordinate way, stand up and speak for themselves" (Rancière 2010, 6). For a relatively brief moment (2007–2009), the previously unrecognized, unheard, and "uncounted" community of Braddock emerged as a new, democratic, and radical yet viable political identity with which the police order might have to contend. The power of the 'Braddock identity' was not located in Fetterman's diacritical, personal voice and image, but rather in the undeniable, radical potential of the democratic, collaborative, long-term action that his voice and image represented.

When Levi's approached Fetterman in 2009, the company was in the process of closing its last US factories (the type of outsourcing that, ironically and grotesquely, mirrored what the US steel industry had done decades before), a move that distanced the brand from its once well-known "all-American values" (Greenwood 2014). By partnering with Braddock, Levi's aimed to identify their brand with the voice of the "new Braddock worker," and to effectively reconnect the company to its working-class roots. In exchange for their participation in the campaign, Levi's paid Braddock Redux approximately 1.5 million dollars to assist in renovating their community center and developing their urban farm—a sum that Fetterman apparently found too hard to resist (Greenwood 2014). The company then filmed the work being done on these projects during a two-year period and used portions of the recordings for the advertisements.

The collaboration resulted in a collection of print and television advertisements featuring Braddock residents wearing faded denim clothing in urban gardens, construction sites, and various abandoned landscapes (Elliott 2010). Though local, these individuals appear for the most part indistinguishable from the models featured in other Levi's campaigns. Attractive, svelt, and mostly white, the "Braddock workers" on display hardly represent the realities of the borough's residents who struggled (and continue to struggle) daily to secure safety, employment, and healthcare for themselves and their families. As Tony Buba, a filmmaker and resident of Braddock, remarked: "I never knew there were so many thin people in Braddock until I watched these spots—or that many people with six-pack abs. You don't see anybody 300 pounds and wearing a pair of Levi's jeans walking across the screen" (Newman 2010). Partially due to Levi's strategic selection of Braddock models, the images strikingly depict working-class life in a ruggedly attractive style that Jesse Pearson compares to "Depression-era photographer Walker Evans" (Pearson 2011). However, in the majority of the advertisements, the actual work being done in Braddock is left unclear—a man warms his hands over a fire as a train passes to his front, a child hangs playfully from the flexed bicep of a man, and so on (Hillcoat 2010; McDaniel 2010). Throughout the campaign, Braddock's true political identity is unrecognizable; the community's powerful message essentially left unheard.

Rather than amplifying the radical political identity that Fetterman had so effectively promoted up to that point, the advertisements merely (what we term) rust washed[17] the Levi's brand. In appropriating and repackaging the image of Braddock, Levi's was able to identify its designer denim wear (clothing that few in Braddock could ever afford themselves) with the ethos of the working-class—an ethos that was once an integral aspect of Levi's image and thus easily marketable to potential consumers in a time of economic downturn. For example, one of the print advertisements features a black and white image of a man in a denim shirt and vest holding a shovel over his shoulders. The following words appear above his right arm: "Everybody's Work is Equally Important, Levi's, Go Forth." In this and other Levi's/Braddock media products, the voice of the "new Braddock worker"—with its resistance to the status quo and eagerness for reinvention—was effectively reconfigured into a hollow, commercial Trojan Horse of sorts for the brand's more general and mythic (yet by any measurement *dubious*) working-class identity.

As the people of Braddock were rendered flesh-and-blood mannequins for hip attire, their history, plight, and act of Rancièrean dissensus were effectively cast to the margins. As Sarah Banet-Weiser (2012) explains in her analysis of the campaign, these pioneers fit comfortably into Levi's "capital friendly narrative" which "[authorizes] the American working class to deal with the crisis [of Braddock's downfall] individually, rather than [calls] a flawed capitalist structure into question" (107–131:108). This narrative depicts Braddock as a land of unforeseen opportunity where individuals can pick themselves up by their bootstraps and save themselves (i.e., conduct themselves as neoliberal subjects). Standing hand-in-hand with Levi's—a clear representative of the very social order responsible for Braddock's real-world plight—the community was effectively folded back into the police logic.

Displayed in billboards, television commercials, YouTube clips, and print ads, the "Braddock worker" was seen by hundreds of thousands of people across the country and the world in a manner that was conducive to the status quo. By virtue of the Levi's campaign, the people of Braddock were "accounted for"—superficially restored to a "part of the part," per say. Cast not as the epicenter of a radical movement or the long-lost heart of US steel, Braddock was, if only for the timebeing, the center of a working class-ethos-based ad campaign. Instead of creating possibilities of identification with Braddock's plight within the Great Recession and larger neoliberal age, Levi's urged consumers to find common ground with Braddock on the plane of denim wear. In our view, Levi's fictionalized version of Braddock made the community's actual material and political realities negligible. How bad could things there be, after all, if Braddock residents were apparently on an upward trajectory and, moreover, earning money as clothing models?

Critically minded observers and those familiar with Braddock's past and current state were not so easily duped, however. Many criticized the Levi's campaign for its willingness to conveniently gloss over Braddock's history, its current economic struggles, and its powerful political message. In the local press, on social media boards, and elsewhere, commenters criticized the advertisements for depicting Braddock as a land of opportunity and future prosperity at a time when jobs and resources were quickly disappearing from the borough.[18] For example, Kathy M. Newman, Carnegie Mellon University Professor of Literary and Cultural Studies, publicly argued that despite the campaign's claim that "everybody's work is equally important," Levi's had done little to increase employment opportunities in Braddock; that Levi's contradicted its emphasis that all workers matter equally by mistreating workers in their overseas factories; and, that the Levi's/Braddock catchphrase "We Are All Workers" could be interpreted as a slogan for Marxist class theory—a radical message that would be better applied to a "progressive political party" than a multinational clothing corporation (Newman 2010). In a 2010 blog post, Pittsburgh's Justseeds Artist Cooperative described the Levi's campaign as "a genius melding of amnesiac musings, blue collar fetishism, and astoundingly brazen brand-name posturing." The post continued:

> A town built and destroyed by a goliath industry which decimated American cities by outsourcing labor overseas (Carnegie Steel) being touted as a "frontier" by another massive company which has, itself, outsourced a majority of its labor overseas (Levi's)? If we were thirsty for a primer on how slick corporate campaigns can rewrite history and ignore contemporary fact, we sure got a compelling one (*Go Forth [and Step In It]* 2010).

Sticking to his unconventional methods, Mayor Fetterman responded directly to such claims by emphasizing Levi's role in funding the community's youth center and expanding the urban farm. Describing the church-turned-youth center, Fetterman stated, "In seven years, NO ONE, NO ONE cared enough to help or gave any money to fix this church up. The whole thing was ready to come down, and it was Levi's that helped" (*Go Forth [and Step In It]* 2010). Despite its community impact, Levi's contribution to Braddock did not indicate a long-term investment in the borough. In May of 2013, the company announced its commitment to give $220.3 million over a period of 20 years to fund Levi's Stadium, home of the San Francisco 49ers, thereby investing nearly 150 times the amount of money in the stadium that the company contributed to the Braddock community (Rosenberg 2013). Still, Fetterman's eagerness to stand behind the Levi's partnership despite these obvious discrepancies reveals the trade-offs of Rancièrean dissensus in the neoliberal age. Whereas the campaign diffused the power of Braddock's political voice, the Levi's partnership did, in all fairness, enable Fetterman to meet some of the most immediate needs of the community he served and make Braddock more of a household name. And despite the criticism provoked by his partnership with Levi's, Fetterman and Braddock have continued to take slow yet measurable steps forward. In the years since the campaign's release, the borough has opened a free clothing store (*Free Store 15104* 2012) and a brewery (*The Brew Gentleman Beer Company* 2015), and announced plans for a new urgent care facility (Krauss 2014). Still, while the borough's progress continues to receive local media attention,[19] Braddock's powerful political message has lost momentum[20]; a message initially difficult to comprehend was easily overshadowed by hauntingly beautiful images too difficult to ignore.

The Levi's/Braddock case serves as a prime example of the promise and fragility of "Rancièrian constitutive rhetoric." As the "Braddock Redux" project has shown, acts of dissensus can make previously silenced voices heard, constitute political identities around which pro-democracy forces can rally, and promote alternative visions of an ideal social order in which every person counts and every human life matters. Sadly, however, Rancièrian moments almost always seem to fail or lose steam in the face of brute police force or, as evidenced by the Braddock example, subtler acts of consensus. Our hope is that this essay has made Rancière's political theory and his challenge to traditional conceptions of constitutive rhetoric apparent to the reader. Looking ahead, we encourage rhetorical scholars to consider both as the vital search for counter-neoliberal rhetorical strategies continues.

Notes

1. Like any influential theory, Burkean identification is not without its detractors. For instance, Arabella Lyon offers a compelling critique of Burkean identification's apparent inability to account for lingering, crucial differences—"gender, culture, and all manner of contingencies"—inherent to any collective, as well as its preoccupation with present-moment speech acts that tend "away from understanding coalition and solidarity as achieved through action over time." Such salient appraisals notwithstanding, Burkean identification maintains its place among foundational and accepted rhetorical concepts (Lyon 2013, 62–65).

2. As multiple examples show, today, emancipatory, democratic, antineoliberal attempts at identification and constitutive rhetoric are routinely co-opted, demonized through ad hominem attacks, silenced, or legally suppressed (*#IAmGeorgeZimmerman* 2015; O'Reilly 2014; Kirkpatrick 2015, A1; Herszenhorn 2012).
3. Of course, true democratic moments and change may entail instances of rational argumentation or dramatic proclamations (self-naming).
4. "The names of the actors, sets, and props might change," Rancière writes, "but the rule remains the same. It consists of creating a stage around any specific conflict on which the equality or inequality as speaking beings of the partners in the conflict can be played out" (Rancière 1999, 51).
5. For Rancière, "dissensus" is interchangeable with "politics" (Rancière 2010).
6. Dissensus is "an activity that is always of the moment and provisional" (Rancière 2010, 43).
7. Rancière states that "politics doesn't always happen—it actually happens very little or rarely." This is due primarily to the fact that politics "runs up against the police everywhere." Still it is in the rare moments when the incompatible "police logic and egalitarian logic" conspicuously collide that emancipatory politics and the repartition of equality become possible (Rancière 1999, 17, 32).
8. Rancière compares the police to an "animal tamer" who knows "what vocal effects make the great animal growl and those that make it nice and gentle." In this scenario, "the part of no part" is cast as a "phonic animal," a being that can comprehend the speech of the police, but whose own speech "is merely perceived as noise signaling pleasure or pain, consent or revolt"
(Rancière 2011, 22–23).
9. By "commercial equality," Rancière means the freedom to experience "the effects of the simple law of *owing* and *having*," the law that makes "wealth [...] immediately identical with domination" and, needless to say, inherently benefits the few over the many (Rancière 1999, 8–9).
10. Dissensus (i.e., politics, democracy, the 'Rancièrian moment' per say) is not simply reducible to moments of public protest (political demonstrations and the like), for dissensus "has no 'proper' place," "specific locale," or form. Simply put, dissensus is any activity that effectively demonstrates the inherent equality of "those of no part" and the arbitrary nature of the status quo, no matter where, when, or how long the activity occurs (Rancière 2010, 37–40).
11. Dissensus can be identified, for example, in the anti-police violence/racism, public protests that have swept across the USA in recent years. Whereas mass unrest over police violence has been normalized for some

time in European nations where police shootings are practically unheard of (e.g., France and England), the notion that Americans not only should but *can* take to the streets to argue for the humanity, dignity, and rights of all citizens is a relatively new and, from a Rancièrian perspective, welcome phenomenon that has brought the issue of police violence to the fore of national consciousness (Rancière 2010).

12. Per Rancière: politics "is that activity which turns on equality as its principle" (Rancière 2010, ix).
13. "Equality," Rancière argues, "turns into the opposite the moment it aspires to a place in the social or state organization" (Rancière 2010, 34).
14. The Lesbian and Gay Community Services Center in New York's formation of ACT UP, the AIDS Coalition to Unleash Power, in 1987 stands as an exemplar of such Rancièrian "politics" (Christiansen and Hanson 1996, 2, 157–170).
15. Rancière writes: "'Workers' or 'women' are identities that apparently hold no mystery. Anyone can tell *who* is meant. But political subjectification forces them out of such obviousness by questioning the relationship between a *who* and a *what* in the apparent redundancy of the positing of an existence." In other words, politics is that which makes the experience of "the part of no part" apparent in order to reveal the gap between identities/names *(who)* and the reality *(what)* that is so often obfuscated. Here, too, we see how Rancière's theory challenges traditional assumptions regarding the efficacy of constitutive rhetoric (that is, the power of calling groups into being through language) (Rancière 1999, 35–36).
16. Consider the armed suppressions of the Homestead Strike in Pittsburgh (1892), the Bonus Army March in Washington (1921), anti-Soviet student protests in Hungary (1956), demonstrators in Sharpeville, South Africa (1960), countless African-American marchers activists during the Civil Rights Movement, the Tahrir Square protests in Cairo (2011), and the civil unrest in Ferguson, Missouri (2014).
17. By rust washing, we refer to a set of marketing strategies a company uses to associate itself with the working class. This concept is similar to greenwashing, which "is what happens when a hopeful public eager to behave responsibly about the environment is presented with 'evidence' that makes an industry or a politician seem friendly to the environment when, in fact, the industry or the politician is not as wholly amicable as it or he might be" (Hoffman 2009).
18. During the same year that the "Ready to Work" campaign was released, the University of Pittsburgh Medical Center (UPMC) closed the Braddock Hospital, cutting off residents from a primary source of healthcare and one of the last major providers of local employment opportunities (Glassman 2010).

19. In large part, echoes of Braddock's revitalization effort still reverberate due to Fetterman's recent US Senate campaign (Simon 2015).
20. In 2016, Braddock once again appeared in *The New York Times* in Teju Cole's article on LaToya Ruby Frazier, Braddock native and acclaimed photographer. Cole depicts Braddock as a quickly deteriorating and crime-ridden post-industrial town and tells of Frazier's efforts to "[trace] out a web of related concerns" for the people who live there in her recent photography project. Unlike earlier *New York Times* articles that focus on Braddock as a place of hope and possibility, Cole makes no mention of Fetterman or the revitalization efforts that once earned him national attention (Cole 2016).

Bibliography

#IAm George Zimmerman. 2015. *Twitter*. https://twitter.com/hashtag/IAmGeorgeZimmer-man. Accessed 2 Feb 2015.

A Once Booming Steel Town Looks to Future. 2009. *National Public Radio*, March 15. http://www.npr.org/templates/story/story.php?storyId=101926763. Accessed 30 Apr 2015.

A Town Revitalized?. 2010. *PBS*, April 9. http://www.pbs.org/now/shows/615/. Accessed 30 Apr 2015.

Benet-Weiser, Sarah. 2012. Branding the Crisis. In *Aftermath: The Cultures of Economic Crisis*, eds. Manuel Castells, João Caraça, and Gustavo Cardos, 107–131. Oxford: Oxford University Press.

Blair, Carole, and Neil Michel. 2008. Reproducing Civil Rights Tactics: The Rhetorical Performances of the Civil Rights Memorial. In *Visual Rhetoric: A Reader in Communication and American Culture*, eds. Lester C. Olson, Cara A. Finnegan, and Diane S. Hope, 139–155. Thousand Oaks, CA: Sage.

Braddock Redux: Working Toward a Better, More Sustainable Braddock. 2015. Braddock Redux. http://braddockredux.org. Accessed 30 Apr 2015.

Blue Lives Matter. http://bluelivesmatter.blue/.Accessed 16 Sep 2016.

Brave Thinkers. 2009. *The Atlantic*. Last modified 1 Nov 2009. http://www.theatlantic.com/magazine/archive/2009/11/brave-thinkers/307692/?single_page=true. Accessed 10 Dec 2014.

Burke, Kenneth. 1966. *Language as Symbolic Action: Essays on Life, Literature, and Method*. Berkeley: University of California Press.

———. 1969. *A Rhetoric of Motives*. Berkeley: University of California Press.

Carlson, Peter. 1983. *Roughneck: The Life and Times of Big Bill Haywood*. New York: W.W. Norton & Company.

Charland, Maurice. 2001. Constitutive Rhetoric. In *Encyclopedia of Rhetoric*, ed. Thomas O. Sloane, 616–619. New York: Oxford University Press.

Chase, Kenneth R. 2009. Constructing Ethics through Rhetoric: Isocrates and Piety. *Quarterly Journal of Speech* 95(3): 239–262.

Cherry, Tyler. 2015. How Fox News' Primetime Lineup Demonized Black Lives Matter In 2015. *Media Matters*, December 29. http://mediamatters.org/blog/2015/12/29/how-fox-news-primetime-lineup-demonized-black-l/207637.Accessed 12 Sep 2016.

Christiansen, Adrienne E., and Jeremy J. Hanson. 1996. Comedy as Cure for Tragedy: ACT UP and the Rhetoric of AIDS. *Quarterly Journal of Speech* 82(2): 157–170.

Cole, Teju. 2016. The Living Artist. *New York Times*, February 10. http://www.nytimes.com/2016/02/14/magazine/the-living-artist.html?smid=nytcore-iphone-share&smprod=nytcore-iphone&_r=0. Accessed 18 Feb 2016.

Condit, Celeste Michelle, and John Louis Lucaites. 1993. *Crafting Equality: America's Anglo-African Word*. Chicago: University of Chicago Press.

Craven, Julia. 2016. Leaked 2015 Memo Told Dems: 'Don't Offer Support' For Black Lives Matter Policy Positions. Huffington Post, August 31.http://www.huffingtonpost.com/entry/dnc-black-lives-matter-memo_us_57c6f80de4b07 8581f1072ca. Accessed 12 Sep 2016.

Dardot, Pierre, and Christian Laval. 2009. *The New Way of the World: On Neoliberal Society*. London: Verso.

Elliott, Stuart. 2010. Levi's Features a Town Trying to Recover. *New York Times*, June 23. http://www.nytimes.com/2010/06/24/business/media/24adco.html?_r=0. Accessed 11 Dec 2014.

Fetterman, John. 2012. Rebuilding Braddock. Lecture at Juniata College, Will Judy Lecture Series, Huntingdon, PA, September 25. http://services.juniata.edu/jcpress/voices/pdf/2013/jv_2013_17-22.pdf. Accessed 30 Apr 2015.

Free Store 15104. 2012. *Braddock Redux*. http://www.freestore15104.org/. Accessed 1 Jul 2015.

Glassman, Sharon. 2010. What is Work? Small Town Hospital Closing Opens Health-Care Debate. *Huffington Post*, March 18. http://www.huffingtonpost.com/sharon-glassman/what-is-work-small-town-h_b_332256.html. Accessed 10 Dec 2014.

Ginsburg, Benjamin. Spring 2015. Is There Value in Violence? *Johns Hopkins University Arts & Sciences* 12 (2): 8.

Giroux, Henry A. 2012. *Twilight of the Social: Resurgent Publics in the Age of Disposability*. Boulder: Paradigm.

Go Forth (and Step In It): Levi's and All Those Frontiers the Rest of Us Can't See. 2010. *Justseeds' Artists' Cooperative*, July 16. http://www.justseeds.org/blog/2010/07/go_forth_and_step_in_it_levis_1.html. Accessed 11 Dec 2014.

Gramsci, Antonio. 2012. *Selections From the Prison Notebooks*. New York: International Publishers.

Greenwood, Jess. 2014. Case Study/Levi's/Get to Work/. *Contagious Magazine* 24. http://www.slideshare.net/KristinBannister/leviscasestudy-53987421. Accessed 11 Dec 2014.

Harvey, David. 2007. *A Brief History of Neoliberalism*. New York: Oxford University Press.
Herszenhorn, David M. 2012. Anti-Putin Stunt Earns Punk Band Two Years in Jail. *New York Times*, August 17. http://www.nytimes.com/2012/08/18/world/europe/suspense-ahead-of-verdict-for-jailed-russian-punk-band.html?_r=1. Accessed 3 Feb 2015.
Hillcoat, John. 2010. To Work. *YouTube.com*, Levi Strauss, June 30. https://www.youtube.com/watch?v=635XItRDU7g&list=PLE0EDF6DA393A206D. Accessed 11 Dec 2014.
Hoffman, Jane. 2009. What is Greenwashing? *Scientific American*, April 1. http://scientificamerican.com/article/greenwashing-green-energy-hoffman/. Accessed 11 Dec 2014.
Jacobs, Samuel P. 2010. Mayor of Inspiration. *The Daily Beast*, October 10. http://www.thedailybeast.com/articles/2010/10/10/mayor-of-inspiration.html. Accessed 10 Dec 2014.
Kline, Jonathan, and Christine Brill. 2014. Layers of Braddock's History. http://15104.cc/history/. Accessed 10 Dec 2014.
Kirkpatrick, David D. 2015. Coming to Mourn Tahrir Square's Dead, and Joining Them Instead. *New York Times*, February 3. A1.
Klein, Naomi. 1999. *No Logo*. New York: Picador.
Krauss, Margaret J. 2014. Apartment Hunting? Check out Braddock's Creative Studios. *Next Pittsburgh*, September 14. http://www.nextpittsburgh.com/city-design/apartment-hunting-check-braddocks-creative-studios/. Accessed 10 Dec 2014.
List of Act 47 Distress Determinations. 2014. Pennsylvania Department of Community and Economic Development. http://www.newpa.com/local-government/services-we-provide-local-governments/request-assistance/list-act-47-distress-determinations. Accessed 10 Dec 2014.
Lyon, Arabella. 2013. *Deliberative Acts: Democracy, Rhetoric, and Rights*. University Park: Pennsylvania State University Press.
May, Todd. 2010. Dissensus: On Politics and Aesthetics. *Notre Dame Philosophical Reviews*, July 1. https://ndpr.nd.edu/news/24403-dissensus-on-politics-and-aesthetics/. Accessed 23 Dec 2014.
McDaniel, Melodie. 2010. We Are All Workers. *YouTube.com*, Levi Strauss, September 27. https://www.youtube.com/watch?v=V2tBDhowRr8&list=PLE0EDF6DA393A206D&index=1. Accessed 11 Dec 2014.
New York Court Dismisses Lawsuit Over Occupy Wall Street Arrests. 2015. *Reuters*, February 24. http://www.reuters.com/article/2015/02/24/us-usa-occupywallstreet-idUSKBN0LS2CU20150224. Accessed 22 May 2015.
Newell, Jim. 2014. Redskins Propaganda Takes Vile Turn: How Team Seeks to Buy Off Opposition. *Salon*, August 13. http://www.salon.com/2014/08/13/redskins_propaganda_takes_vile_turn_how_team_seeks_to_buy_off_opposition/. Accessed 29 May 29 2015.

Newman, Kathy M. 2010. Levi's & Braddock: Exploitation or Invisibility? October 17. https://workingclassstudies.wordpress.com/2010/10/17.levis-braddock-exploitation-or-visibility/. Accessed 28 June 2015.

O'Reilly, Bill. 2014. ObamaCare and Socialism. *Fox News*. July 23. http://www.foxnews.com/transcript/2014/07/24/bill-oreilly-obamacare-and-socialism/. Accessed 2 Feb 2015.

Pearson, Jesse. 2011. No Jobs Here. *Playboy Magazine*, July. http://jesse-pearson.com/writing/no-jobs-here/. Accessed 11 Dec 2014.

Pilkington, Ed. 2009. Coolest Mayor in America? Why John Fetterman Has His Postcode Tattooed on His Arm. *The Guardian*, July 14. http://www.theguardian.com/world/2009/jul/15/us-mayor-postcode-tattoo. Accessed 10 Dec 2014.

Rancière, Jacques. 1999. *Disagreement: Politics and Philosophy*, trans. Julie Rose. Minneapolis: University of Minnesota Press.

———. 2010. *Dissensus: On Politics and Aesthetics*, ed. and trans. Steven Corcoran. London: Bloomsbury.

———. 2011. The Thinking of Dissensus: Politics and Aesthetics. In *Reading Rancière*, eds. Paul Bowman, and Richard Stamp, 1–17. London: Continuum.

Rosenberg, Mike. 2013. Levi's Stadium: 49ers' New Santa Clara Home in $220 Million Deal. *San Jose Mercury News*, May 8. http://www.mercurynews.com/ci_23198944/levis-stadium-49ers-new-santa-clara-home-gets. Accessed 10 Dec 2014.

Rothkopf, Joanna. 2015. CNN Guest Slams Media for Saying Protesters Are 'Thugs': 'Just Call Them N***ers. *Salon*, April 29. http://www.salon.com/2015/04/29/baltimore_councilman_slams_media_use_of_thugs_for_protesters_just_call_them_nggers/. Accessed 29 May 2015.

Siltanen, Rob. 2011. The Real Story Behind Apple's 'Think Different' Campaign. *Forbes*, December 14. http://www.forbes.com/sites/onmarketing/2011/12/14/the-real-story-behind-apples-think-different-campaign/. Accessed 29 May 2015.

Simon, Jeff. 2015. The Tattoos Are Not the Most Interesting Thing about This Mayor. *CNN*, November 23. http://www.cnn.com/2015/11/23/politics/senate-candidate-john-fetterman-braddock/. Accessed 30 Nov 2015

Steger, Manfred B., and Ravi K. Roy. 2010. *Neoliberalism: A Very Short Introduction*. New York: Oxford University Press.

Streitfeld, David. 2009. Rock Bottom for Decades, but Showing Signs of Life. *New York Times*, January 31. http://www.nytimes.com/2009/02/01/us/01braddock.html?pagewanted=all&_r=1&. Accessed 30 Apr 2015.

Stroud, Matt. 2006. A Call to Arms: Braddock Mayor John Fetterman Wears His Allegiances on His Sleeve. *Pittsburgh City Paper*, August 31. http://www.pghcitypaper.com/pittsburgh/a-call-to-arms/Content?oid=1337397. Accessed 10 Dec 2014.

The Brew Gentleman Beer Company. 2015. http://www.brewgentlemen.com/#home. Accessed 1 Jul 2015.
The Colbert Report. 2009. *The Colbert Report video* 5: 37. February 25. http://www.nytimes.com/2016/07/16/us/all-livesmatter-black-lives-matter.html . Accessed 10 Dec 2014.
Victor, Daniel. 2016. Why 'All Lives Matter' Is Such a Perilous Phrase. *New York Times*. July 15. http://thecolbertreport.cc.com/videos/jyyb0h/john-fetterman. Accessed 12 Sep 2016.
What is Braddock? 2014. http://15104.cc/braddock/. Accessed 10 Dec 2014.
White Lives Matter. 2016. *Southern Poverty Law Center*. https://www.splcenter.org/fighting-hate/extremist-files/group/white-lives-matter. Accessed 12 Sep 2016.

Branding Citizens: The Logic(s) of a Few Bad Apples

Jennifer Wingard

The 2003 documentary *The Corporation* contains a compelling segment wherein directors Mark Achbar and Jennifer Abbot assemble news media clips blaming corporate financial and ethical misconduct on the behavior of "a few bad apples" instead of systemic problems of corporate oversight. Achbar and Abbot's pacing of the segment draws attention to the branding work of "bad apples," and by the end of the segment, they have created a rhythmic montage of major news outlets uttering "bad apples" and "a few bad apples" repeatedly. Their focus on the language of "a few bad apples" argues that the media is complicit in protecting corporate interests by disarticulating wrongdoing from the greater corporate logics, which govern our world. Instead, "a few bad apples" take the blame for the wrongdoing that is enabled by the legal and economic systems that allow corporations to behave "like psychopaths with no regard for others and no remorse for their harmful behavior" (Akbar et al. 2003).

The Corporation argues for an understanding of and resistance to the overbearing and non-humanist control corporations have over governments and private citizens' daily lives. It exposes the intricate neoliberal logics that undergird corporate behavior as well as the governmentality that enables the wholesale adoption of those logics. The work of Achbar

---

J. Wingard (✉)
Department of English, University of Houston, Houston, TX, USA

and Abbot demonstrates how neoliberal nation-states organize the daily lives of citizens in the name of economic gain for a small group of individuals. In other words, much like corporations whose only requirement is to make profits for their shareholders, the nation-state that adheres to neoliberal governmentality works solely to create surplus value without much regard for the collective lives of its citizens.

As *The Corporation* demonstrates, the branding of "bad apples" allows corporations to continue to commit both economic and human rights violations by placing the blame on individual corporate entities, thus never having to examine the laws or procedures that enable these behaviors. To forward the work of the state as "fair and balanced," branding "bad apples" becomes a critical means by which to assign blame, create threats, and define boundaries of who can and cannot be protected by the state. Even the "bad apple" corporations are not completely excised from corporate culture. Instead they are seen as instances of individual behavior gone awry, thus needing to be either reeducated or made of example of, but never expelled.

I begin discussing "bad apples" because it is a brand that is both seemingly innocuous and ubiquitous. The invocation of the "bad apple" works to mystify the structural dimension to any social problem or event. In the case of the "bad apple," it is not merely about excising others from our midst. It is about placing blame on individuals so that the offending system can remain intact. In the case of *The Corporation,* the "bad apple(s)" allowed for corporate misconduct to continue while certain corporations faced fines and public scrutiny. But the legality or ethics of corporate behavior, or profit motive itself, were never called into question. The "bad apple" served to assign blame to a particular individual in order to save the system. The brand of the "bad apple," then, could be seen as a red herring or the *pharmakon*—the limb you excise to save the body (Plato 1952). The "bad apple," then, is a brand applied to certain citizens in times of state or economic crisis.

Branding, as a form of neoliberal rhetorical practice, cultivates an ethos that allows the US public to identify and make choices within a given set of circumstances. These choices seem to be dictated by rational responses to those circumstances, but are mostly influenced by *affect*. Therefore, when the media reports on a violent confrontation, for example, and contends that each man acted out of hyper-vigilance, racism, and/or mental illness and uses the brand of "the bad apple," it occludes the logics of US exceptionalism and protectionism that enable state violence inside and outside the US. Branding creates affective, emotional responses, not analytical ones.

Violent events may seem the perfect sites for discussions about policy and/or law, but instead, through the media's use of the "bad apple," these potentially substantive discussions are silenced by the spectacle of individual motive. Tragedies such as the Sandy Hook school shooting or the Aurora, Colorado, movie theater attack, become sites where public debate on gun control or the ideology of hyper-masculinity are eschewed because the shooters are seen as "bad apples" or anomalies. Therefore, the purpose of this analysis of branding is not to explicitly argue about the criminal status of individuals at the center of violent incidents, but rather to show how an ethos that isolates them as exceptions, "bad apples," is exemplary of current neoliberal technologies and logics.

To demonstrate these processes, I draw on the rhetorical assemblage[1] to examine how particular citizens are branded "bad apples" to protect institutional and economic practices that enable violence. The "bad apple" is defined as deficient or deviant in their individual choices, but not a product of the larger economic, historical, or political systems they inhabit. Branding in this instance works much the same as *affective identification(s)* that are not always created through logical recognition. Instead these "brands" are often affective responses based on affinities that are created through intangible or unintelligible contexts such as memory, emotion, and preference (Hesford 2005). And because of these schemata of organization, neoliberal subjects come to know the world through their identification (or non-identification) with those specific categories. Branding works, then, almost synecdochally as a means to represent and circulate these identities. This is because these histories and identities are ingrained into our memories and understandings of our current cultural moment.

In this essay, I will discuss two cases that forward the "bad apple" brand as a means to occlude the neoliberal social and economic logics that enable the violence in both scenarios. The first case I will discuss is the shooting of Trayvon Martin in Florida, and the second, the shootings of 16 Afghan civilians[2] by US Army Staff Sergeant (SSG) Robert Bales. Both of these cases demonstrate extreme violence against unarmed victims at the hands of armed gunmen. In the case of Trayvon Martin, George Zimmerman was a self-designated neighborhood watch volunteer who had been "working with the Sanford, Florida, police to protect The Retreat at Twin Lakes from theft of and threats to private property—missing bikes, grills and a few times [...] strangers [...] casing [...] town houses" (Robles 2012). In the case of the Afghan civilians, SSG Robert Bales was a US soldier who was there to protect the Afghan people from Taliban insurgents. He had served four tours in Iraq, and was now in Afghanistan to presumably bring freedom to the Afghan people.

In the media discussions of the actions of Zimmerman and Bales, they are both characterized as "unstable." Bales faced economic hardship at home, and it is speculated that he was facing psychological damage from his multiple tours of duty. Zimmerman is portrayed as a gun-loving, paranoid protectionist whose desire to police his suburb went far beyond his neighborhood watch authority. Both of these characterizations, regardless of whether or not they are realistic, place the blame for the shootings on "bad apples." Thus, the events are isolated and non-representative of any logics of racism, US exceptionalism, or state violence which might enable these actions. In other words, by branding Bales and Zimmerman as "bad apples," there need not be a discussion of racism in Florida or US exceptionalism in Afghanistan. Instead, each instance is the work of an "unstable" individual who cannot become representative of any larger social or political issues or elements.

I argue, however, that by placing these stories together, and viewing them as an assemblage[3], we can begin to see how branding not only defines the state, but also serves to protect the interest of the nation-state by sacrificing even those who are seen to be "part of the whole" of the nation. And it is through the practice of rhetorical assemblage, which allows these news stories to be placed together contiguously rather than analogously or causally, scholars can begin to "code and decode" the meaning of the "bad apple" and begin to read a counter-narrative to US state and public discourse (DeLanda 2006). Within these counter-narratives, the systems and laws which support the actions of the "bad apples"—corporate personhood, "Stand Your Ground" laws, military actions—become visible. Instead of seeing each accused citizen as a separate case, the assemblage allows for a larger context, one in which policy and law are consistent even if the crimes and details are not. In other words, Zimmerman and Bales become "bad apples" to provide US citizens a place to which to forward anger and remorse about state violence without questioning the logics of the state. Instead, the violence is connected to the individuals who commit the acts, but the state policies that enable those acts are never questioned.

The rest of this chapter will first define the brand of the "bad apple" and discuss its *affective value* as an acutely neoliberal rhetorical strategy. Then it will focus on the media coverage of Trayvon Martin and the 16 Afghan civilians who were killed. Through the assemblage of these stories, I will show that neoliberal governmentality enables the actions of both George Zimmerman and Robert Bales. And by defining Zimmerman and Bales as "bad apples," the media and the state not only occlude their implication in the shootings, but they also sacrifice US citizens in order to maintain the neoliberal logics of the government. However, as I will discuss in the conclusion, Zimmerman and Bales are not the citizens who are exiled. Instead, they are the citizens who are used to mystify the violence of the state, all the while maintaining their status as citizens. Therefore, the "bad apple" is not in exile, but rather an exception that creates an ethos that allows citizens to maintain their faith in the status quo of the state, even when the violence of the state continues.

OTHERING THROUGH BRANDING "BAD APPLES": A NEOLIBERAL MEME BEGINS

The brand of the "bad apple" can be applied to any member of any group—majority, minority, insider, or outsider. It is not a brand that distinguishes an inside or outside, but instead it serves as a protective measure to insure the continuation and propagation of the system itself. And it is my contention that the brand of the bad apple is borne of neoliberal governmentality. The bad apple can now be forwarded fairly efficiently because of the erosion of liberal governmentality, which has allowed for a lapse in the maintenance of the public good by both governmental and social institutions.

However, as I discussed in my book *Branded Bodies, Rhetoric, and the Neoliberal Nation-State* branding does more than simply construct false identities for various groups of people (Wingard 2013). Those identities resonate not because they create logical connections, but instead, they create *affective* understandings of current contexts and happenings. According to Wendy Hesford, *affective identification* is created in the cultural context from which the rhetor is speaking or writing. Hesford argues that instead of looking at identification as a means to find similar traits and identities, we must attend to the embedded and seemingly commonplace "cues" that help us to navigate and communicate in a particular context (Hesford 2005). These "cues" are not always created through logical recognition, but instead are often affective responses based in *affinities*, created through intangible or unintelligible contexts such as memory, emotion, and preference.

Affective identification uses language and images to create responses that are often extra-linguistic—in most cases, visceral or somatic. Affective identification works as a backdrop of feeling that resonates with histories, rhetorics, and images that are not evoked directly, but that circulate to connect our memories and bodies. Though not explicit, these circulate through the brand, much as "[n]eoliberalism organizes material and political life *in terms of* race, gender, and sexuality as well as economic class and nationality, or ethnicity and religion" (Duggan 2004, 3). Because of these schemata of organization, neoliberal subjects come to know the world through their identification (or non-identification) with those specific categories, which are often destabilized by the very system they look to for stability.

The feelings of anxiety created through economic inequality (that is often supported by neoliberal inflected state policies) can shake an individual's sense of identity to the core.[4] And without strong governmental social services for support, citizens are left searching for a way to ground their identities—both individual and national. Jodi Dean, in her book *Democracy and Other Neoliberal Fantasies,* looks at the complexities of neoliberal capital in the context of identity formation. Building from Slavoj Žižek's theory of the decline of symbolic efficiency,[5] she argues that due to the erosion of the welfare state, state run disciplinary venues no longer hold the power over individuals that they once did. Instead, individuals now have a much more fluid sense of identity, which according to Dean, leads to great anxiety and fear among the general population. She writes: "The fluidity and adaptability of imaginary identities is accompanied by a certain fragility and insecurity. Imaginary identities are incapable of establishing a firm place to stand, a position from which one can make sense of one's world" (Dean 2009, 67). Although this may seem as if the lack of pre-determined or normative identities would provide a certain space for individual "play" (to use Derrida's term) with identity, Dean demonstrates that without a clear means of identification, most neoliberal subjects are left searching for stable ways with which to define themselves.

Branding offers just this kind of succor in a time of subjective anxiety. Adam Arvidsson states: "Like commercial brands, the political brand is an answer to the homelessness of post-modern subjects. [...]. This identification is generally framed, not in terms of rational interest, but in terms of emotional experiences" (Arvidsson 2006, 92–3). Part of what we see with branding and the formation of identity under neoliberalism, in terms of their connection to varied sources and the responses they draw to a multiplicity of attractors, is that both are necessarily fragmentary and conjunctural. Although at any given moment, branding seems to present a seamless and non-complicated image of a whole, it really can be a shifting representation of an item or body evacuated of its material value.

Branding, then, works as a means to circulate these identities relying on the fact their histories and identities are ingrained into our memories and understandings of our current cultural moment. Therefore, it is not about explicitly arguing the legal status and/or morality of the "bad apple," but rather it is about creating an image wherein the accused becomes sympathetic or revolting. Much like the corporate bad apples with which I began, Zimmerman and Bales are brands that allow the media, citizens, and the state itself to maintain the status quo of how language defines identities, all the while giving voice to the tragedies of Trayvon Martin and "the sixteen nameless civilians in Afghanistan" who lost their lives. Therefore, the state can be caring and attentive to the violence that befell its victims, while never taking any responsibility. And thus the neoliberal logic of the criminal justice system creates the popular belief that if violence was committed by individual actors, it is because of the individual's own personal beliefs, investments, and mental state(s).

The call to the individual is key to the rhetoric of neoliberalism and is echoed in the cultivation of the "bad apple" brand. The rhetoric of personal responsibility is cited as central to the shift from Keynesian to neoliberal economics. Scholars such as Lisa Duggan (2004) and Rebecca Dingo have both made clear how the rhetoric of personal responsibility and the pursuit of economic self-interest demonstrate the clear logic of neoliberalism (Dingo 2012, 15). The rhetoric of the "bad apple" follows this logic, but it also provides the state with material gain. Once isolated through claims of mental or economic instability, those who are deemed "bad apples" are both personally responsible for their actions, thus alleviating the state and society from becoming implicated in their crimes, and legally absolved from taking responsibility because those individuals were "scared" or "not in their right mind." Therefore, the brand of the "bad apple," like in the George Zimmerman case, can work as a get-out-of-jail-free card for the individual in question, while still reinforcing the systems which supported and or helped to create these "bad apples."

Branding creates both economic and identificatory value. As a practice, it developed as a corporate marketing strategy designed to connect consumers with products not by extolling the uses or qualities of that product, but instead by selling what that product can *mean* to a consumer's life. Again, Arvidsson states: "The purpose of brand management is to guide the investments of affect on the part of consumers (or other subjects). [...] It is a matter of creating an affective intensity, an experience of unity between the brand and the subject" (2006, 93). It is not how the brand is defined, but it is the interaction between the brand and the subject that creates value in the process of branding. In other words, Nike and its representational "swoosh" is not a successful brand because of the swoosh logo. Instead, it is successful because of how that swoosh translates into an emotional identification for consumers. Consumers do not purchase Nike because of the swoosh. Rather they recognize the swoosh to represent all the meanings and investments they hope to gain from interaction with the products that possess the swoosh—athleticism, endurance, and strength. As a marketing strategy, then, branding focuses on affective value. It is about connecting the symbols attached to products to consumers in an emotional way. In its purest form, branding can be seen as a semiotic endeavor wherein the sign of the product is given meaning through the affective exchange with the consumer (Lury 2004).

Branding, as a facet of advertising, is not about product placement or the product at all. Instead it is about developing an identity or "lifestyle" into which groups of products then fit. And in this sense, it can be understood how easily it could be shifted to realms outside of what can be seen as purely economic exchange. Branding developed over the course of the twentieth century, and as global corporate power continues to be the reigning political and economic logic of our time, branding will continue to grow until people's lives will be so completely dictated by this consumerist model that they can "move right into their lifestyle choice" and watch their consumption habits become their reality (Klein 2000). Much like Trayvon Martin or the "sixteen nameless Afghan victims," the products are *almost* insignificant in this exchange, or the products are secondary to their affective identification. It is the product's representational (or surplus) value that becomes meaningful. And if the value of the product is not considered in the brand-driven transaction, the labor of the product is completely invisible.

Branding, then, is the ultimate technology[6] of a hyper-capitalist society defined by extreme economic inequality. As Dean states: "[Neoliberalism] makes a few winners—top 1 percent—and a lot of losers. [N]eoliberal competition is select (partial), brutal, and for the benefit of the top one percent." (emphasis in original, Dean 2011). By exploiting the anxieties of those who are not in the top one-percent, the media and government use branding to make the other 99 percent of Americans "feel better" and like a part of the very system that insures a select few remain rich. In order to quell those anxieties, branding offers a vision of America wherein the 99 percent are still valued members of society—a citizenry with meaningful histories and values to which they can attach.

The branding of "bad apples"—as others who no longer fit easily within the values of this anxious citizenry—is at the heart of neoliberal governmentality today, in order to mask the blatant state-reified economic inequalities at work. Branding draws on identification, intensity, and affect to move US citizens and give them objects with which to identify or dis/identify when forming both individual and national identities. Furthermore, it enables the mystification of the state supported violence perpetrated by one branded body against another. In the instances of Zimmerman and Bales, this violence is occluded through branding leaving the bodies of the victims and perpetrators as objects of state discourse instead of active subjects of the state.

The Branding of George Zimmerman as "Bad Apple"

It is no disrespect to Trayvon Martin's memory to point out that our ability to make him into a slogan is based less on who he was as a person than on our desire to fit him into a mold that will allow others to see him as worthy and deserving of justice.—"Justice for Trayvon... but how?" (2012)

As the epigraph states, turning Martin into a slogan—or brand—in the Justice for Trayvon campaign was intended to allow him to represent the need for justice for all black bodies who have lost their lives to violent crime committed in the name of policing. Trying to separate Martin's image from the one created by Zimmerman was essential in attempting to recode and shift the ethos of the public. By trying to identify Martin as a scared, unarmed teen who was assaulted by a violent, paranoid vigilante, the media furthered the image of Zimmerman as the true threat on the streets of that Florida suburb that afternoon. Even though many media outlets reprinted Zimmerman's description of Martin as threatening, they did so alongside of descriptions of Zimmerman's violent history and his call to 911, wherein the police told him to "back off" and wait for help to arrive—a direction he did not follow.

One of the biggest issues surrounding the invocation of the "bad apple" involves the consequences it can bring for the victims of the crimes at hand. For example, George Zimmerman, the killer of Trayvon Martin, was acquitted for the shooting, not because he was a "bad apple" but rather because Florida has a "Stand Your Ground" law in place that protects those who shoot first when they feel threatened (leaving the questions to be asked later or not at all). Calling George Zimmerman a "bad apple," which was done to ameliorate the public outrage about Martin's death, was an attempt to prevent Zimmerman from being held up as an exemplar of the Stand Your Ground law, gun rights, or neighborhood watch. But this branding also involved an attempt to detach Martin from the notion that he was indeed a "good apple," an innocent unarmed kid. Instead, for many, including Zimmerman, Martin actually was representative of black, male youth across the country and the perceived threat they embody.[7]

Therefore, Zimmerman's description of Martin as one of "these assholes" only serves to reflect on Zimmerman in the presentations of the media. According to the 911 call log, the call began with Zimmerman following Martin and convinced he was up to no good:

> This guy looks like he's up to no good or he's on drugs or something," Zimmerman told the dispatcher. "It's raining, and he's just walking around looking about." The man tried to explain where he was. "Now he's coming towards me. He's got his hand in his waistband. And he's a black male... Something's wrong with him. Yup, he's coming to check me out. He's got something in his hands. I don't know what his deal is... These assholes, they always get away. (Weinstein 2012)

This reprinted call log served as a means to construct Zimmerman as unreasonable in many news stories and even racist in some.[8] His unwavering desire to police Martin, his assumption at first glance that he was "up to no good," combined with his lack of obedience to the dispatcher, were all used to present Zimmerman as "overzealous" or "hyper-vigilant" or in some articles "violent."[9] By discussing Zimmerman's emotional state and possibly even his motives through his own words, the media created an affective identification that draws upon the public's understanding of both the construction of black males as criminals, but also the construction of vigilantes as rogue, unsafe, and unstable.

The confrontation between Zimmerman and Martin, as unequal as it was, drew upon some seeming truths within the state of Florida and beyond. As stated on *Crunk Feminist Collective:*

It is not coincidental that Black men are routinely profiled for looking suspicious in nice neighborhoods "because they don't belong there." The battle over who belongs in neighborhoods—even though Trayvon's step-mother lived there!—is just a modern site for a long-standing warfare over white racial entitlement to control land and every thing that moves on that land. ("Re-nigging on the Promises" 2012)

As it happens, the Martin shooting drew upon embedded understandings not only of black males, but also stereotyping of Latino men being "hot headed" and "aggressive." In multiple articles in both local and national press, Zimmerman was constructed as "aggressive" with a "history of violence."

In fact, the longer the Zimmerman case was in the media, the more information about Zimmerman's neighborhood watch habits came to light. As Frances Robles, a reporter from the *Miami Herald*, reports: "'He would circle the block and circle it; it was weird,' said Teontae Amie, 17. 'If he had spotted me, he'd probably ask me if I lived here. He was known for being really strict.' Zimmerman called police 46 times since Jan. 1, 2011 to report disturbances, break-ins, windows left open and other incidents. Nine of those times, he saw someone or something suspicious" (Robles 2012). Even though Zimmerman focused on protecting his neighborhood, he was seen as "weird" in terms of how he would do it. His form of neighborhood watch did not actually "fit in" with the neighborhood he was so vigilantly protecting. And although multiple interviewees attempted to paint Zimmerman as a friend to black and Latino children in the neighborhood, those interviews fell flat in light of the mounting evidence of his violent temper. Once Zimmerman's own words began to circulate, coupled with his prior arrest record and actions within the neighborhood, he was seen as a hostile force who stalked Martin prior to shooting him.

Both Zimmerman and Martin were racially stereotyped and then branded in the media. It could be said that the racial stereotyping was done as a means of reporting what happened. However, the reprinting and circulating of the description of Martin as one of "those people" and the counter-media surge that worked to describe him as "not a thug" or "just a good boy in a hoodie," all served to construct an ethos, no matter how sympathetic it may be, steeped in assumptions about and images of black male youth. But instead of deconstructing these images or talking about them (much as the media did not deconstruct or talk about the use of violent associations in connection with the Latino Zimmerman), the medial allowed to circulate and constructed a narrative in which Trayvon was an "everyman" and Zimmerman was the "bad apple" who took his life.

Yet even the public's belief in these images did not change the verdict of the Zimmerman trial. He was still found not guilty due to Florida's Stand Your Ground law. And this is the ultimate damage done by the invocation of the "bad apple" in this case. It prevents a crime being tried on its own merits and prevents any interrogation of the culture of violence that Stand Your Ground Laws facilitate.[10] Because Zimmerman, as a resident of Florida, was protected by a law that states that anyone has a right to defend themselves against attack, he was not required to stand trial for killing an unarmed youth. Instead, he was acquitted for his crime, but tried in the media as a violent offender who got much less than he deserved. But because the focus was solely on Zimmerman and his actions throughout the entire case, no one seriously challenged the legitimacy of Stand Your Ground laws in Florida or anywhere else in the nation.

Stand Your Ground: Get Out of Jail Free and the Loss of Trayvon Martin

The Sunshine State was the first (there are now 33 states in total) to vote in a "Stand Your Ground" or "Shoot First" law. The law states:

> A person who is not engaged in an unlawful activity and who is attacked in any other place where he or she has a right to be has no duty to retreat and has the right to stand his or her ground and meet force with force, including deadly force if he or she reasonably believes it is necessary to do so to prevent death or great bodily harm to himself or herself or another or to prevent the commission of a forcible felony. (qtd in Weinstein 2012)

Unlike the 44 other states where the "Castle Doctrine" is in place—a law that makes it legal to shoot someone if they attack your home, no questions asked—Florida augmented those private property laws by removing the need to be at your own home or on your own land. To invoke the Stand Your Ground law, you must lawfully be in a place, but that place does not have to be lawfully yours. In addition, you must also prove that you are being threatened. If you meet both of those criteria, then the law states: you can shoot to kill if necessary. Since 2005, when Florida adopted the law, 32 other states have followed suit.

The repercussions of the law are vast. Not only have there been high profile cases, like the Martin case, wherein a civilian has killed an unarmed but seemingly threatening person and then been acquitted under the Stand Your Ground law. There are also issues with cases never being investigated or charged because of the difficulties of making a charge "stick." Many law enforcement officials complain that Stand Your Ground makes their jobs more difficult. In fact, "many Orlando-area cops reportedly have given up investigating 'self-defense' cases as a result, referring them to the overloaded state attorney's office for action. A 2010 study by the *Tampa Bay Times* found that 'justifiable homicides' had tripled in the state since the law went into effect" (Weinstein 2012).

However, none of these complaints have created adequate pressure to change the law. Neither did the actions of George Zimmerman. Although many were outraged by the not-guilty verdict, the Zimmerman ruling has not inspired mass protest or any substantial push to change the law. Instead there are protests reminding us that Martin's life matters, which of course it does. And that his death was senseless, which of course it was. But there has yet to be any sustained pressure on Florida to shift the legal burden from the victim to the perpetrator. As long as the Stand Your Ground law is in place, it really does not matter how the media constructs the victim or the perpetrator nor does it matter what ethos those constructions create. Instead, what matters is the occlusion of the true fight and seat of power in the discussion. Without a campaign to repeal or change the laws, these Martin and Zimmerman will serve as brands to obfuscate the real institutional racism and powerful assumptions at work in the state of Florida and beyond.

Instead, as cases arise, we will continue to focus on those cases as evidence of localized or individualized conditions. And that is where the "bad apple" is most effective. It allows for a disjoining of the cases of violence that happen in different spaces. These cases become specific to the people and locations involved. Instead of connecting larger patterns of rhetoric, power, and presentation, the media separates stories through specifics and particularities that foreclose the connections that should be made.

Therefore in this paper, I will now shift from the suburbs of Florida to the desert of Afghanistan, to demonstrate how the "bad apple" works to sustain the practices of the nation-state. Of course the practices within the state of Florida and a nation at war will by necessity be different. There are legal contingencies, as well as fundamental matters of scale. However, by placing these stories contiguously, I will show how both instances of violence are supported by state practice at home and abroad. Although SSG Robert Bales may not be the same variety of "bad apple" as Zimmerman, he is constructed as a "bad apple" to protect the work of the nation all the same.

Afghan Civilians: Collateral Damage of US Exceptional Protectionism

Why did they not stop the killings? These soldiers at the camp spy with expensive equipment on all that happens, from the ground and from the air. It's too difficult to believe that one of their colleagues could get away with this.—Haji Nuur Mohammed (qtd in Dam 2012)

As the epigraph shows, there have been many questions about the "official story" regarding the murder of 16 Afghan civilians by SSG Robert Bales. Afghan investigators, as well as eyewitnesses from several nearby villages, reported the presence of 16–20 armed and possibly inebriated soldiers in the villages of Balandi and Alkozai near Camp Belambai in Kandahar on the night of March 11, 2002. However, the US military and media refused to circulate any conflicting accounts. Instead, they uniformly circulated a narrative in which SSG Robert Bales, mere weeks from the end of his military service, entered two Afghan villages and killed 16 civilians (Dam 2012).

The difficulty with the US military and the media's story is that it does not align with the carnage of that night, nor with the known facts of operations that had been going on in Afghanistan during the time Bales supposedly went mad. As Nima Shirazi of *Salon.com* states: "According to a September 2011 study by the Open Society Foundation, 'An estimated 12 to 20 night raids now occur per night, resulting in thousands of detentions per year, many of whom are noncombatants.' These raids produce heavy civilian casualties and often target the wrong people" (Shirazi 2012). This study shows the strong possibility that the killing of civilians was the result of faulty intelligence or a military action gone wrong. However, the military and the news saw fit to maintain that it was an officer on his fourth tour who suffered a mental break. Again Shirazi states: "Based on the preliminary information we have this account is flatly wrong," the official said. "We believe one U.S. service member acted alone, not a group of U.S. soldiers" (Shirazi 2012).

Both the military and media's adherence to the story of a lone gunman is another instance of the invocation of the "bad apple." Bales is no longer seen as a soldier. In fact, in all of the articles about him, his mental health, possible PTSD, and anger issues come to the fore. Bales, then, has become another individual acting from a place of illness. He is a man who did not represent the ills of a mission gone wrong; instead, he represents a man who has cracked and could no longer handle the pressures of serving his country. As Owen Dorell and Jim Michaels state: "'He just snapped,' a high-ranking official told the *New York Times* on Thursday. 'When it all comes out, it will be a combination of stress, alcohol, and domestic issues'" (Dorell and Michaels 2012). Not only was Bales facing stress from being on his fifth tour; the military and media made it clear he also was experiencing financial and domestic troubles. No matter how much his friends and family disputed these claims, Bales' past history with anger helped solidify his image as a "bad apple." As Peter Beaumont of *The Guardian* writes: "[Bales] had been charged with assault in 2002 and asked to attend an anger management course, while in 2008 he is reported to have fled the scene of a car crash" (Beaumont 2012).

Some of the more sympathetic outlets attempted to explain Bales' behavior in connection to the high levels of PTSD in returning and redeployed soldiers. Again, Beaumont states: "Of particular concern is the increased risk of PTSD in soldiers who are deployed on multiple occasions. PTSD is known to be "dose dependent"—the risk of suffering from it increases after more exposure to its triggers" (Beaumont 2012). But much like the attempts to humanize Zimmerman, these sympathetic efforts just did not work. The media and the military were too set on seeing him as a "bad apple" to remove any threat of repercussion against the practices of the US military in Afghanistan. It was very important to see this man as an anomaly.

Bales, much like Zimmerman, was used as a "bad apple" to maintain the status quo of military power abroad. It was not as if this crime was going unpunished. But any trial and/or inquiry into it was shouldered by Bales, not the US military as a whole. Therefore, the military maintained a presence in Afghanistan, and it did not have to change its policies due to a very public killing of the very civilians the US military had been sent to protect. Again, the "bad apple" brand serves to maintain the power and policies of the nation-state, all the while providing the citizenry of said state with the appropriate pathos—horror, sadness, repulsion—toward the act. Those feelings, however, are all focused on one soldier, SSG Robert

Bales, just as in Florida they were focused on George Zimmerman. This individual focus insures that broader considerations, such as whether the mission that sent Bales to Afghanistan in the first place was just or necessary, are averted.

Conclusion: "Bad Apple" and the Making of "Bare Life"

By assembling two cases which happened at the same time but in very different locations under very different circumstances, I demonstrate how the "bad apple" is not merely a solitary rhetorical device. Instead, it is used in many different scenarios when the state needs to maintain power, all the while admitting to the horrors of a crime. In both of these cases, the focus on hyper-vigilance, mental illness, and other individual particularities serves to both protect the state and those committing crimes recognized by the rule of law. In other words, a claim to being a "bad apple" does not create cause to eject or abandon a perpetrator from the state. Rather being a "bad apple" allows the accused to be seen as ill and/or in need of state support for their deviant behavior.

Therefore, the branding of a "bad apple" functions to not only mitigate the state's responsibility, but also protect the citizen from excessive violence that is reserved for those who need to be expelled from the state. Giorgio Agamben sees the expulsion of particular offenders as indicative of the move democratic states are making toward totalitarianism in order to maintain their national power in the face of global economic and migratory patterns. For Agamben, the most egregious misuse of power by the modern nation state is the development of "bare life" as a legitimizing force. According to Agamben, bare life is the ultimate exception [within a state's population], and it is deeply tied to life or the loss thereof (Agamben 1998). Citizens who are used as bare life are expelled from the state (often through death) in order to justify or maintain what Agamben calls "the rule of law," which is sovereign or state power. Therefore, in these instances, Trayvon Martin and the 16 nameless Afghan people are more than mere victims of "bad apples;" they are bare life who have died to maintain the rule of law. When SSG Bales and George Zimmerman kill innocent civilians, the deaths of those innocents become rationalized to maintain the rule of law of the state. In other words, these moments of violence, no matter how horrific, are rationalized to define the boundaries to those of us who seek protection and/or membership within the state.

The sacrifice of bare life is even further complicated in this mediated age because instead of making the state take responsibility for these sacrifices, the media develops a narrative of "bad apples" to shoulder the burden of the killings and reify the need for the state to protect and serve. And it is here that the "bad apple" performs its best work. The "bad apple" brand serves as a succor to the horror of bare life. It protects the state from seeming culpable in said violence, and instead creates a secondary sacrifice, one who remains part of the state, but who must be contained by it because these "bad apples" are no longer whole citizens. In other words, the "bad apple" not only supports bare life, it is *necessary* in creating the ethos that allows the rest of the citizenry of a state to live with institutionalized state violence every day.

Without the "bad apples," whether they be corporate or civil, citizens would have to acknowledge the legal systems in place, and our support of them, that allow for such unthinkable violence to continue. Therefore, the media must construct Zimmerman as "aggressive" and Bales as "insane." No matter the cause of those ailments, those men are branded as anomalies within the state—people who do not belong, but who must be taken care of. It is unfortunate, however that Trayvon Martin and 16 Afghan people had to be sacrificed, too.

Notes

1. Jasbir Puar defines the assemblage: "a series of dispersed but mutually implicated networks, drawn together by enunciation and dissolution, causality and effect" (Puar 2005, 127). Building from this definition, I argue that the assemblage can be a fruitful rhetorical analytic because it allows for the examination of the creation of affective value in our current neoliberal moment. Instead of having meaningful exchanges wherein references must be explained and connections coherently mapped through content, the assemblage allows for any referents to become meaningful just through the nature of their placement in a meme, news story, or piece of legislation.
2. I will refer to the Afghan people killed as "the 16 Afghan civilians" because that is how the US media has constructed them. Below is a list of the names of the Afghan people who died and were wounded in the massacre:

The dead: Mohamed Dawood *son of* Abdullah; Khudaydad *son of* Mohamed Juma; Nazar Mohamed; Payendo; Robeena; Shatarina *daughter of* Sultan Mohamed; Zahra *daughter of* Abdul Hamid; Nazia *daughter of* Dost Mohamed; Masooma *daughter of* Mohamed Wazir; Farida *daughter of* Mohamed Wazir; Palwasha *daughter of* Mohamed Wazir; Nabia *daughter of* Mohamed Wazir; Esmatullah *daughter of* Mohamed Wazir; Faizullah *son of* Mohamed Wazir; Essa Mohamed *son of* Mohamed Hussain; Akhtar Mohamed *son of* Murrad Ali

The wounded: Haji Mohamed Naim *son of* Haji Sakhawat; Mohamed Sediq *son of* Mohamed; Naim; Parween; Rafiullah; Zardana; Zulheja (Azimy 2012).

3. According to Manuel DeLanda (2006), we assemble meaning by placing words, phrases, and in the case of this study—brands—contiguously. They then become *territorialized* and *coded* or *decoded*, or as Rebecca Dingo would say *networked*, throughout their exchange. An assemblage is never complete, nor is it stable. It is always changing due to its context. Assembling brands, much like affect, only gain meaning and value through exchange. That exchange, however, is by no means performed in a vacuum. In fact, much of the value created in both consumer and political branding relies on historical narratives about identities and human characteristics in order for the brands to become affectively valuable.

4. Thomas Frank, in *What's the Matter with Kansas?* explores how economic insecurity and ideology function in political campaigns. When Frank inquired as to why the Kansans voted seemingly against their own "best interests," overwhelmingly, the voters did not cite economic platforms, but instead would cite candidates' position statements on "family values issues," such as abortion or gay marriage and "immigration" issues that were not even on the Kansas ballot. Frank's claim is that the results of the elections in Kansas reveal that American voters no longer want to engage with issues. Instead, voters are seduced by the ideology and branding that permeates politics today (Frank 2005). I, however, suggest that Frank's book reveals how branding in the political arena can serve to seemingly "simplify" and thus "soothe" the public during a time when politics and daily life are becoming both complex and destabilized. By focusing the discussion on brands, citizens do not have to understand the complexities of their job loss and political disenfranchisement.

5. So neoliberal ideology does not produce its subjects by interpolating them into symbolically anchored identities (structured according to conventions of gender, race, work, and national citizenship). Instead, it enjoins subjects to develop our creative potential and cultivate our individuality (Dean 66–7).

6. According to Aiwha Ong, a "technology" is the undergirding process(es) in which a logic becomes a logic. For her, a technology can be any practice which allows for the forwarding of a particular ideology. Ong implores us to look at neoliberalism not as an overarching ideology, but rather as a set of practices or technologies (e.g. privatization, rhetoric of personal responsibility) in order to understand how it can become a universalizing feature of a nation or transnational network. In other words, Ong calls for a more nuanced understanding of how neoliberal economics and the spread of regulatory power to individuals and corporations impact the claims and definitions that states can make on behalf of and about citizens.
7. Resistance to the death of Trayvon Martin was not the first time an African American teen's death was protested, but the image of Martin in a hoodie became representative of a growing concern about the construction of black male youth as violent, threatening, and unlawful. Since Martin's death there have been several organized attempts to draw attention to the disproportionate killing of black youth in confrontational situation: #blacklivesmatter and #icantbreathe are two of the most visible in response to the deaths of unarmed black males—Michael Brown in Ferguson, MO and Eric Garner in New York City by the police. These memes are attempts to fight against the "bad apple" and represent the systemic violence and pathological assumptions made against black men and youth.
8. See Blow, Charles M. "The Curious Case of Trayvon Martin." *The New York Times.* 16 March 2012. http://www.nytimes.com/2012/03/17/opinion/blow-the-curious-case-of-trayvon-martin.html?_r=0. Web.; Cadet, Danielle, "Trayvon Martin Case: George Zimmerman Made Racist Remarks at Work." *Huffington Post.* 18 May 2012. http://www.huffingtonpost.com/2012/05/18/trayvon-martin-george-zimmerman-evidence_n_1528268.html. Web.; "Racism and the Trayvon Martin Case." *The Washington Post.* 18 July 2013. https://www.washingtonpost.com/opinions/racism-and-the-trayvon-martin-case/2013/07/18/e380d58e-ee32-11e2-bb32-725c8351a69e_story.html Web.
9. See Capehart, Jonathan. "George Zimmerman's Relevant Past." *The Washington Post.* 28 May 2013. http://www.washingtonpost.com/blogs/post-partisan/wp/2013/05/28/george-zimmermans-relevant-past/. Web.; Lee, Trymaine. "George Zimmerman, Neighborhood Watch Captain who Shot Trayvon Martin, Charged with Violence Before." *The Huffington Post.* http://www.huffingtonpost.com/2012/03/09/george-zimmerman-trayvon-martin_n_1335984.html. Web.; "Zimmerman Accused of Domestic Violence, Fighting with a Police Officer." *NBC News.* 27 March2012. http://usnews.nbcnews.com/_news/2012/03/27/10894561-zimmerman-accused-of-domestic-violence-fighting-with-a-police-officer?lite. Web.

10. A 2012 Texas A&M Study by Mark Hoesktra and Cheng Cheng revealed that homicide rates were up at least 8% in all states wherein Stand Your Ground Laws are active. Furthermore, Joseph J. Vince, a task force member and former officer in the US Bureau of Alcohol, Tobacco, Firearms and Explosives states: "Instead of encouraging peaceful resolution through the rule of law, stand-your-ground laws encourage violent actions" (Prupis 2014).

References

Achbar, Mark, Jennifer Abbot, and Joel Bakan, directors. 2003. *The Corporation*. Vancouver, BC: Big Picture Productions.

Afghanistan shootings suspect set to face charges in US, says expert. 2012. *The Guardian*, March 18. http://www.theguardian.com/world/2012/mar/18/afghanistan-shootings-suspect-charges. 22 December 2014.

Agamben, Giorgio. 1998. *Homo Sacer: Sovereign Power and Bare Life*. Palo Alto, CA: Stanford University Press.

Arvidsson, Adam. 2006. *Brands: Meaning and Value in Media Culture*. New York: Routledge.

Azimy, Qais. 2012. No One Asked Their Names. *Al Jazeera*, March 19. http://blogs.aljazeera.com/blog/asia/no-one-asked-their-names. 22 December 2014.

Beaumont, Peter. 2012. 'He's a normal guy,' says neighbor of US Sniper Accused of Afghan Killings. *The Guardian*, March 19. http://m.guardian.co.uk/world/2012/mar/18/robert-bales-us-soldier-accused-of-afghan-massacre?cat=world&type=article. 19 March 2012.

Dam, Bette. 2012. Why did they not stop the killings? *Salon*, March 15. http://www.salon.com/2012/03/15/why_did_they_not_stop_the_killings/. 22 December 2014.

Dean, Jodi. 2009. *Democracy and Other Neoliberal Fantasies: Communicative Capitalism and Leftist Politics*. Durham, NC: Duke University Press.

———. 2011. Roundtable: Three Theses on Neoliberalism (or Contestants, but not Entrepreneurs). American Political Science Association. Septermber 2011.

DeLanda, Miguel. 2006. *A New Philosophy of Society: Assemblage Theory and Social Complexity*. London: Continuum.

Dingo, Rebecca. 2012. *Networking Arguments: Rhetoric, Transnational Feminism, and Public Policy*. Pittsburgh, PA: University of Pittsburgh.

Dorell, Owen, and Jim Michaels. 2012. Afghan massacre, mental health check could come first. *Veterans for Common Sense.com*, 19 March. http://veteransforcommonsense.org/2012/03/19/in-afghan-massacre-mental-health-check-could-come-first/. 22 December 2014.

Duggan, Lisa. 2004. *The Twilight of Equality? Neoliberalism, Cultural Politics, and the Attack on Democracy.* Boston, MA: Beacon Press.
Frank, Thomas. 2005. *What's the Matter with Kansas? How the Won the Heart of America.* New York: Holt.
Hesford, Wendy. 2005. Kairos and the Geopolitical Rhetorics of Global Sex Work and Video Advocacy. *Just Advocacy? Women's Human Rights, Transnational Feminisms, and the Politics of Representation,* eds. Wendy S. Hesford, and Wendy Kozol, 146–172. New Brunswick, NJ: Rutgers University Press.
Justice for Trayvon... but how?. 2012. *Words and Steel,* March 19. http://wordsandsteel.tumblr.com/post/19601359463/justice-for-trayvon-but-how. 22 December 2014.
Klein, Naomi. 2000. *No Logo.* New York: Picador.
Lury, Celia. 2004. *Brands: The Logos of the Global Economy.* New York: Routledge.
Ong, Aiwa. 2006. *Neoliberalism as Exception: Mutations in Citizenship and Sovereignty.* New York: Pearson.
Plato. 1952. *Gorgias.* New York: Pearson.
Prupis, Nadia. 2014. 'Stand Your Ground' Laws Linked to Rise in Homicides, Extreme Racial Bias: Study. August 14. Web. http://www.commondreams.org/news/2014/08/14/stand-your-ground-laws-linked-rise-homicides-extreme-racial-bias-study. 12 May 2015.
Puar, Jasbir K. 2005. Queer Times, Queer Assemblages. *Social Text* 84–85, 3–4 (November): 121–139.
Re-nigging on the Promises: #Justice4Trayvon. 2012. *The Crunk Feminist Collective,* March 16. http://crunkfeministcollective.wordpress.com/2012/03/16/3459/. 22 December 2014.
Robles, Frances. 2012. Shooter of Trayvon Martin a habitual caller to the cops. *The Miami Herald,* March 17. Web. http://www.miamiherald.com/2012/03/17/vfullstory/2700249/shooter-of-trayvon-martin-a-habitual.html#storylink=cpy%23storylink=cpy. 19 March 2012.
Shirazi, Nima. 2012. American Morlocks: Monsters of a murderous Afghan policy. *Salon.com,* March 14. http://www.salon.com/2012/03/14/american_morlocks_monsters_of_a_murderous_afghan_policy/. 22 December 2014.
Weinstein, Adam. 2012. The Trayvon Martin Killing, Explained. *Mother Jones,* March 18. http://www.motherjones.com/politics/2012/03/what-happened-trayvon-martin-explained. 22 December 2014.
Wingard, Jennifer. 2013. *Branded Bodies, Rhetoric, and the Neoliberal Nation-State.* Lantham, MD: Lexington Books.

The Psychotic Discourse of 9/11 Truth

Jodi Dean

In a 2004 poll conducted by Zogby international, 49.3 percent of New York City residents said that some US leaders "knew in advance that attacks were planned on or around September 11, 2001 and that they consciously failed to act" ("Americans Question Bush on 9/11 Intelligence" 2006). According to a *New York Times*–CBS News poll carried out in October 2006, only 16 percent of those surveyed thought the Bush administration was telling the truth about what it knew prior to September 11 about possible terrorist attacks on the USA ("Half of New Yorkers Believe" 2004). Fifty-three percent of respondents said that they thought the administration was hiding something. Twenty-eight percent thought the administration was mostly lying. A Scripps Survey Research Center-Ohio University poll carried out in July 2006 asked the more pointed question as to whether respondents thought 9/11 was an "inside job." Thirty-six percent of respondents found it very or somewhat likely that "federal officials either participated in the attacks on the World Trade Center and the Pentagon or took no action to stop them 'because they wanted the United States to go to war in the Middle East'" (Hargrove and Stemple 2006). The press release for the poll notes that

---

J. Dean (✉)
Department of Political Science, Hobart and William Smith Colleges, Geneva, NY, USA

this 36 percent is slightly less than the 40 percent convinced that a lone gunman was not responsible for the death of President John F. Kennedy and the 38 percent who believe the government is withholding proof of the existence of extraterrestrial life. It also reports that those suspecting 9/11 was an inside job are more likely to get their news from the internet than from mainstream media sources, which is hardly surprising given the hundreds of websites devoted to investigating the day's events, criticizing the official account, and finding patterns in facts scattered throughout and virtually ignored by the mainstream media.

What, if anything, might these numbers mean for progressive politics in the USA? Does the movement loosely organized around 9/11 truth involve dynamic political struggle? Is the movement an essential site of resistance against the Bush administration, its illegal wars, and its attempt to increase executive power and stifle civil liberties? Insofar as information at odds with the official story of 9/11 circulates primarily on the internet, do we find in the truth movement an example of the power of alternative and participatory media over the corporate-controlled mainstream media?

The conflict over 9/11 truth is a battle over facts, knowledge, who knew, who knows, and who has a right to know. Pervasive skepticism renders every fact, every claim, suspect. So does the push to uncover the truth of September 11 continue the democratic project of undermining the sovereign privilege of secrecy by making hidden knowledge public?

Most mainstream discussions of the 9/11 truth movement, as well as many who find the administration's account of the events of September 11 inadequate, dismiss truth activists as a lunatic fringe, as paranoid conspiracy theorists with a fragile hold on reality. This gap between the official and the alternative accounts raises the question of the possibility of facts credible both to those convinced by the official account and to those who reject it. Could any information exist that would disprove the suspicions of the MIHOP or made-it-happen-on-purpose segment of the 9/11 truth movement (the other segment is LIHOP, let it happen on purpose)? Conversely, could any facts be revealed that would firmly establish the Bush administration's complicity in the attacks on the World Trade Center (WTC) and the Pentagon? Differently put, is the matter simply one of revelation and disconcealment such that a smoking gun could emerge that all would agree is definitive proof of the truth of the event? Or is something else at stake, something that concerns the conditions of possibility for knowledge and credibility?

Confronting this dilemma is crucial for thinking through the role of media—old and new—as well as the setting of contemporary politics: if facts and information are introduced into a media environment wherein they are rejected or suspected in advance, that is to say, if facts are immediately presumed to be either lies in the service of ideology or the irrelevant factoids of the reality-based community, and if they circulate primarily as eyeball bait in communicative capitalism's endless circuits, then are they necessary for or relevant to Left political projects? What if the so-called facts circulate tribally, consolidating communities of the like-minded even as they fail to impress—or even register to—anyone else? Building movements, particularly of those alienated from the mainstream, is no trivial task; indeed, it's been a key tactic in culture war—as the success of the previously discredited school of neoliberal economics as well as of Christian fundamentalism indicates. Nonetheless, new media producers often proceed as if networked and participatory media—say, blogging, the introduction of videos onto the web, or even the independent journalism associated with indy-media—is necessarily progressive, as if radical and Left politics is somehow built into the technology. Moreover, some proceed as if their introduction of information into the media stream is a crucial element in progressive struggle or anti-capitalist resistance. Not only do they assume that the information or images they produce are visible and known, that it registers, but they presume as well that the information they provide is meaningful, credible, that standards for the assessment and evaluation of this information actually exist and that they are widely, rather than tribally, shared.

Most political discussion (as well as democratic theory) also takes for granted the existence of a consensus regarding the rules and conditions for establishing truth and falsity, not to mention a shared notion of reality. These presumptions are misplaced: our current political–medialogical condition is characterized by dissensus, incredulity, and competing conceptions of reality. Communicative capitalism thrives under these conditions—but can a progressive politics and a progressive media?

In *Publicity's Secret* (2002), I discuss the deep imbrications of conspiracy thinking and the hope for an American public, imbrications that demonstrate the ways democracy relies on publicity as a "system of distrust," to use the words of Jeremy Bentham (Dean 2002). Crucial to democracy's triumph over absolutism was the power of revelation, a power claimed for the people over and against the arcane mysteries of monarchy. As Carl Schmitt explained over 80 years ago, belief in openness as a value for its own sake is a product of this time, a product ill-suited to the practicalities of party politics under mass democracy where electoral victories and defeats depend on much more than a revelation here or there. I argue that belief in openness, publicity, and the power of revelation is not only ill-suited to a mass political age but also part of the ideological apparatus that furthers the expansion of networked information technologies to consolidate communicative capitalism. Materializing democratic aspirations and suspicions, the adoption, expansion, and intensification of communicative technologies is urged—on all sides, by left and right, privileged and disadvantaged—as vital to increasing democratic participation (as if a deficit in participation were the primary problem confronting democracy today). The ideal of publicity or openness functions ideologically, serving and protecting global capitalism's reliance on networked information technologies and consumers convinced that their every blog post, virtual march, or You Tube upload is a radical act rather than an entertaining diversion. Communicative capitalism mobilizes the faith in exposure animating democracy as the perfect lure: subjects feel themselves to be active even as their every activity reinforces the status quo; revelation can be celebrated, furthered, because it is ineffectual; its results are medialogical, just another contribution to the circulation of content with no impact on power or policy.

Is the 9/11 truth movement another instance of the convergence of conspiracy thinking and the internet, another manifestation of the desire to make the links, to enact the fantasy of publicity by revealing the secrets. No. Something different is going on. The movement associated with 9/11 truth manifests a shift in conspiracy thinking, a shift from questioning to certainty and from a logic of desire to a logic of drive. Moreover, this shift isn't confined to the conspiratorial fringes. On the contrary, it is symptomatic of a larger socio-cultural development that involves a new constellation of questioning, doubt, credibility, and certainty.

To make this argument, I draw from Jacques Lacan, Slavoj Zizek, and Eric Santner. I explain the shift as one from the discourse of the hysteric to a new form of psychotic discourse, a shift that replaces a logic or economy of desire with one of drive. For Lacan, the discourse of the hysteric is one of four kinds of social link. Its primary characteristic is questioning: the hysteric constantly asks the Master, "am I what you say am I? What are you saying and why are you saying that"? The discourse of the hysteric can thus be understood as providing the basic form of democratic discourse—which reminds us that these Lacanian terms are offered as analytical categories, not means of pathologization. Like the hysteric, democracy challenges claims coming from a Master. It is motivated by desire, a desire enabled by the very law that seems to block its fulfillment. By way of an example, we might note how various Democrats and journalists contested the Bush administration's classifying of previously public knowledge, its removal of all sorts of documents from the internet after 9/11. It's unlikely that these Democrats and journalists knew or even cared about this information while it was public. After it was secretized, however, then they desired it. Some conspiracy theorists echo democratic assumptions insofar as they don't provide theories but instead ask questions; they desire the truth; they want to know. They endeavor to reveal secrets and in so doing call into being a public that will get rid of the corrupt conspirators and restore legitimate government. In so doing, they situate themselves firmly in the democratic, anti-absolutist tradition (a tradition in which the American Declaration of Independence also belongs). Asking questions, making links, such conspiracy theorists try to persuade readers and hearers to think, to find out for themselves. Yet, this desire to reveal, under contemporary conditions of communicative capitalism, is a kind of trap: for all its aspirations to democracy it remains caught in a pseudo-activity that reduces politics to a single operation—revelation.

Appeals to "find out for yourself" appear in the videos, books, and websites of those involved in 9/11 truth. Frequently accompanying these claims appeals are claims to certainty. The mode of the injunction to "find out for oneself" thus changes: now it indicates less the openness of desire, a desire to know, than it does the closed circuit of drive: *the facts are already there; we can be certain of that; there's no need to accept anything on the basis of belief.* Commemorating the first anniversary of the group Scholars for 9/11 Truth, founder James Fetzer (2006b) writes:

> We have established beyond reasonable doubt that the Twin Towers were destroyed by a novel form of controlled demolition from the top down, that WTC-7 was brought down by a classic form of controlled demolition from the bottom up, and that, whatever may have hit the Pentagon, multiple lines of argument support the conclusion that it was not a Boeing 757.

Fetzer is certain. The Scholars for 9/11 truth know some things to be true. Persuasion retreats, replaced by confrontation with the actual facts.

Zizek explains that, unlike in desire, where the object emerges at the moment of its loss, in drive loss itself is an object (2006, 61). We can understand 9/11 as naming such a loss. The very term designates not just a day but a trauma. The term 9/11 has become a meme for loss, repeated endlessly in official accounts and reiterated in unofficial ones. In all these accounts, moreover, 9/11 marks loss resulting from excessive, impersonal, obscene power, power with little regard for life, power permeated with the *jouissance* of its conviction. Both the official and unofficial theories of the events of September 11 circle around this knot of obscenity and loss, albeit in different circuits. Zizek further links drive to constituent anxiety, to pure confrontation with the void (objet petit a) (2006, 61–62). Both the official and unofficial theories of the events of 9/11 rely on and reinforce this constituent anxiety as they confront the specific horror of the disintegration of the social link, the destruction of the symbolic pact promising security and holding society together.

In much of the production of the 9/11 truth movement, we find this confrontation with a hole in the symbolic order accompanied by *jouissance*—repetition, intensity, affect. The *jouissance* connecting each fact to another produces certainty as an effect. Indeed, *jouissance* arises through connectivity, through the specificity and systematicity of the facts circling the hole of loss. We see this in the excesses of connections: every specific fact—exact times and temperatures, flight schedules, and passenger manifests—is linked, everything is meaningful. Enjoyment is produced by the very drive to link, connect, document, by the intensity of detail and specificity. Because the most central component of the explanation remains unknown—who did it?—the evidence accumulates in extreme and specific detail, establishing connections without ever reaching its goal.

The 9/11 truth movement combines its intense certainty with an overwhelming skepticism. Explanations are doubted: why does the administration's story change over several years? Why are there differences in the official times of the planes crashing and the towers following? Why is a close associate of Condolezza Rice's, Philip Zelikow, appointed to head the commission investigating 9/11? A volatile mix of certainty and skepticism thus occupies the place of the lack of belief in the official story.

I read this combination in terms of what Lacan formalizes as the discourse of the university. In university discourse, the facts speak for themselves; experts claim objectivity even as they attempt to overlook the institutional power that supports their claims to expertise. We can understand scientific socialism, the press, and, economics all in terms of university discourse, for each the emphasis is on facts; facts are supposed to determine outcomes independent of power. Following Lacan, Zizek characterizes contemporary capitalism as well as the bureaucratic arrangements surrounding it in terms of the dominance of university discourse. With its emphasis on letting the facts speak for themselves, the 9/11 truth movement very much resembles university discourse. Yet, it lacks its authorizing support. Accordingly, I understand it as a clone of university discourse, a psychotic clone (Zizek 2006).

Why psychotic? Because of Lacanian psychoanalysis's account of psychosis in terms of a missing signifier, an absence and a foreclosure. Drawing from Lacan and Santner, I emphasize the loss of authority on September 11, the hole produced in the symbolic order. The Bush administration explains the events of September 11 as acts of terrorism. The psychotic response rejects this explanation and builds a discourse around the hole that is Left. In an effort to hold its speculations together, psychotic discourse models itself on other, more conventional discourses such as university discourse. Given the ubiquity of university discourse, it should come as no surprise that psychotic discourse might attempt to model itself, conform to precisely these terms and join it in letting the facts speak for themselves.

While I focus on the 9/11 truth movement as exemplary of the psychotic doubling or cloning of university discourse, I am more concerned with the likelihood of such discourses flourishing in the fragile discursive habitats of communicative capitalism. Characterized by the circuit of drive, by an intensity, certainty, and skepticism that circles around a fundamental loss, psychotic discourse perpetuates anxiety. It renders all that comes into contact with it suspect, uncertain, permeated with possible meaning.

The gap or blind spot emerging between the official story of 9/11 and the 9/11 truth movement, and reappearing within the movement suggests less an engaged political struggle than it does a political deadlock displacing action onto impossible subjects, futures, and terrains. I can put this as a question: what sort of politics is politics possible when there is knowledge without belief, when certainty and skepticism persist in tandem, each supporting but immune to the other? And, what does any answer to this question mean for aspirations to collective approaches to equity and justice?

Conspiracy Theory

Conspiracy theory is typically considered a vernacular discourse, one that speaks and thinks outside the official institutions of power about power's excess, about the crimes and obscenities hidden from and by power's public face. Critics fault conspiracy theorists for their amateurishness, considering them dabblers in a realm of expert knowledge, who try to know what they cannot know, what they should accept on faith. They dismiss conspiracy theorists as autodidacts unschooled in rules of evidence and rational argumentation. They deride conspiracy theorists for their extra-institutional position, their lack of conventional expertise. These critics emphasize as well the absence of the credentials necessary to speak in what is upheld as the public sphere. A language of infection tends to follow as the critic worries about the health of the public, the vitality of public reason. For critics, the overall unauthorized character of conspiracy theory signifies the illegitimacy of the theories produced by those who look for and find evidence of conspiracies. Thus, they treat conspiracy theorists in all their questions and suspicions, accumulations of facts and amassing of evidence, as extremists, as outside the norm, as deluded denizens of the lunatic fringe so alienated from general society that they are compelled to resort to the most outlandish explanations to make sense of the world and their lives in this world.

Some critics find conspiracy theorists to be so outside the mainstream, so beyond the pale or the norm of politics as usual, that they mar or insult true political memory. Accusing those involved in the 9/11 truth movement of insulting the police officers and firefighters who raced into the burning towers of the WTC (a strange insult, really, a displaced one, an insult that fails to grasp how the alternative explanations of September 11 hardly insult these workers but instead the government who allegedly caused their deaths and now covers its crimes in their heroism), Senator John McCain finds 9/11 conspiracy theories "a distraction from the proper lessons of 9/11, from what is truly important to this country" (Dunbar and Reagan 2006). McCain reiterates the accepted critique of conspiracy theories: "They ignore the methods of science, the protocols of investigation, and the dictates of logic. The conspiracy theorists chase any bit of information, no matter how flimsy, and use it to fit their preordained conclusions. They ascribe to the government, or to some secretive group, powers wholly out of proportion to what the evidence suggests. And they ignore the facts that are present in plain sight" (Dunbar and Reagan 2006).

The stigma attached to the "outsider-y-ness" of the conspiracy theorist enables the very term "conspiracy theorist" to be wielded so as to exclude or dismiss a view in advance. For example, *New York Times* columnist David Brooks (2006, A31) has dismissed Kevin Phillips' book, *American Theocracy*, as crude conspiracy mongering. The book is a critical account of the conservative coalition in American politics, a coalition that Phillips, as young Republican strategist, helped build. Similarly, Senator James Ihofe sought to discredit attributions of global warming to human factors as "the greatest hoax ever perpetrated on the American people" (Krugman 2006). In each case, the critic attempts to render a book or an issue as so outrageous, so beyond the pale, that no sensible person could possibly find it worth any serious attention.

The stigmatizing effect of labeling someone a conspiracy theorist is so great that allegations of conspiracy brought by governmental officials seem somehow not themselves to be conspiracy theories. Differently put, theorizing a conspiracy is not what makes someone a conspiracy theorist—thinking or positing something that mainstream common sense (what Lacan calls the big Other) deems paranoid nonsense is. Thus, we find ourselves in the weird situation where some conspiracy theories have a presumed legitimacy in part because they cannot be called conspiracy theories. Around the time that the Bush administration was asserting that a conspiring group of Islamic fundamentalists armed with boxcutters hijacked four planes, brought down the WTC, smashed through the west wall of the Pentagon, and crashed in a field in Pennsylvania, US government officials and the mainstream media publicized the proliferation of conspiracy theories in the Arab world, conspiracy theories that blamed the attacks on the WTC and the Pentagon on the Mossad or the US government itself. In a speech to the United Nations General Assembly on November 10, 2001, George W. Bush declared, "We must speak the truth about terror. Let us never tolerate outrageous conspiracy theories concerning the attacks of September the 11th; malicious lies that attempt to shift the blame away from the terrorists, themselves, away from the guilty" ("The Briefing Room" 2001).

As part of this effort not to tolerate conspiracy theories, the State Department has posted several articles "debunking" the top September 11 conspiracy theories on its website ("The Top September 11th Conspiracy Theories" 2006). Part of the problem with its debunking, however, is that it cites evidence that many in the 9/11 truth movement find suspect, evidence such as the video of a plane crashing into the Pentagon (many viewers, I among them, don't see a plane in this allegedly definitive proof) or tapes of Osama bin Laden taking responsibility for the attacks (some conspiracy theorists argue that the translation is wrong or that the tapes are fakes). The State Department site also refers to the *Popular Mechanics* book, *Debunking 9/11 Myths: Why Conspiracy Theories Can't Stand Up To The Facts* as well as the *9/11 Commission Report*, texts which the 9/11 truth movement has already heavily criticized. And, with respect to the *9/11 Commission Report*, the truth movement is not alone: immersed in controversy from the beginning—the Bush administration attempted to block the formation of a commission and, after it conceded, persistently failed to fund its work or supply it with the requested information—the Commission's Report was widely viewed as bland and disappointing at best. In the words of a *Harper's Magazine* article by Benjamin DeMott (2004, 35–45), the report is "a cheat and a fraud. It stands as a series of evasive maneuvers that infantilize the audience, transform candor into iniquity, and conceal realities that demand immediate inspection and confrontation."

Some self-proclaimed conspiracy theorists celebrate their outsider status, finding that it establishes the authenticity of their work: precisely because they have refused to be bought by the system, refused the privileges of the mainstream, they can be trusted. Their views are in no way compromised by the conflicts of interests typical of those working in the interstices of government—government- and corporate-funded science—and the universities (Firmage 2006, vol. 2). A frequent feature of conspiracy writings is the danger and hardship that the theorist encounters in his (nearly always his) endeavor to uncover the secret behind the lies.

Many conspiracy theorists prize their ability to cut through and reject the conceits and dissimulations inextricable from the discourse used by the government and the mainstream media. This rejection sometimes manifests itself aesthetically: conspiracy-oriented websites tend to be visually complicated and messy, crowded with links, facts, evidence, and information. The sites are often confusing, hard to navigate. One is never quite sure where one is. And, not surprisingly, they heavily interconnect, mutually citing and reinforcing each other even as they may disagree, furiously, over whether the WTC was taken down by planted explosives made of thermite or remote-controlled drones. Among conspiracy researchers, the vivid complexity of the images they use, the multiple fonts, the visual enactment of confusion and connection affirms their position as outsiders—their books, their sites, aren't slick, with slick denoting a mindset and aesthetic overattuned to the deceptions of the mainstream.

9/11 Truth

Two factors contributing to the production and circulation of alternative claims for what happened in the USA on September 11 distinguish the 9/11 Truth movement from other assemblages associated with conspiracy theories—one, the way that the ideas circulate on the internet as videos, and, two, the participation of a variety of highly reputable and regarded academics. These same factors also make 9/11 truth a central site for examining contemporary problems around credibility and certainty.

"Loose Change"

As I mentioned, most people who doubt the official story of the events of 9/11 get their information from the internet. Particularly interesting in this regard is the way 9/11 conspiracy theories circulate not simply through websites and blogs, but as full-length videos. I can compare this with alien abduction—in the 1990s, as accounts of alien abduction became more visible in American popular culture, those involved in the abduction community relied in part on email and websites (Dean 1998). Nevertheless, the circulation of knowledge of abduction took place primarily through books, conventions, and made for television investigative reports. The television specials—while exploiting the trash value of abduction—included heavy doses of skepticism; they gave a lot of airtime to debunkers. What's different with the 9/11 truth movement is that people make and distribute their own videos.

The most prominent video associated with 9/11 truth is "Loose Change," an 80 minute documentary made by Dylan Avery, a 22-year-old from Oneota, New York. It first appeared on the web in the summer of 2005. Since then it has had at least 10 million viewings. The magazine *Vanity Fair* calls "Loose Change" "the first internet blockbuster" (Sales 2006, 112–16).

The most striking aspect of the video is its production of certainty through repetition, intensity, and affect, in other words, the way it performs the shift from the questioning of the hysteric toward a certainty more characteristic of psychosis. Here is its version of "find out for yourself" in the film's final voiceover:

> I'll say it again: why are they hiding from us? What are they hiding from us? And what's it going to take until people in this country give a damn and do something about it? Now that the evidence has been presented, what will you do about it? Will you find comfort in the official version of events? Or will you go out and investigate for yourselves? Will you share this information or will you ignore it? Will you be at ground zero on September 11th? America has been hijacked. Is it more likely by Osama bin Laden and his ragtag group of Arabs with boxcutters or by a group of tyrants within

our own government, ready and willing to do whatever it takes to keep their stranglehold on this country? It's up to you. Ask questions. Demand answers.

To whom is this demand raised? To the tyrants, the all-powerful obscene tyrants supposed/produced through the operation of the theory. The same tyrants who allegedly committed the crime are here demanded to expose themselves, to admit to it, to come clean. There is thus a strangeness to this demand, an incompatibility between it and the crime and criminals it is raised to expose.

More interesting is the attitude of certainty: the viewer is enjoined to investigate. Yet, the film presents itself as already knowing what the subject will find out. It's certain and it manifests this certainty straightforwardly in the evidence presented, the information shared, the America hijacked. Even if "it's up to you" the film already knows what you will discover, as long, that is, as you are brave enough to leave the comfort of the official version of events. Overlaying the final credits is an austere hip-hop piece with a strong base line. The vocals begin: "we all know where you're goin,' we know that you're out there."

The effective and affective success of "Loose Change" stems from its use of music, from the way music provides the connections between different images, different screens, and different facts. A compelling drumbeat, strong base line, and repetitive samples bypass the mediation of argument to establish a feeling of certainty. The first eight minutes of the film, for example, feature images and a voice-over enumeration of a number of items: contradictory quotes from Condolezza Rice, Donald Rumsfeld, Ari Fleischer, and Richard Clarke; a description of Operation Northwoods, a 1962 plan involving a faked hijacking submitted by the head of the Joint Chiefs of Staff to the Secretary of Defense; the 1984 test of a remote-controlled Boeing Aircraft; and, so on up through news reports in early September 2001. The reports mention the significant increase in put options placed on United Airlines, Boeing, and American Airlines, Larry Silverstein's purchase of the WTC and the accompanying 3.5 billion dollar insurance policy, and Attorney General John Ashcroft's shift to traveling with private rather than commercial aircraft. The items are presented chronologically, events on a timeline leading up to September 11. Because the underlying music, particularly through its repetitions and driving base line, establishes continuity among the images, the viewer gets the sense that events are already connected to one another in the Real. Differently put, taking the connections between the events for granted, surrendering to the hypnotic rhythm, is easier than disrupting one's *jouissance* in the music.

The remainder of the film follows the pattern of voice-over, sampling from news media and interviews, and a sort of fort/da pattern wherein the ambient/chill/lounge samples reemerge. Most often, they reemerge at those moments when the voice-over is mentioning particularly telling facts, facts that need to be connected to other facts, facts when connected together produces the knowledge of a conspiracy within the US government. A segment on Hani Hanjour, the alleged pilot of American Airlines Flight 77, the one presumed to have crashed into the Pentagon, features an interview with a staff member from Hanjour's training school. The hypnotic beat and repetitive sampling come in just after the staff member finishes describing how inept Hanjour was as a pilot and the voice-over mentions that air traffic controllers at Dulles presumed the plane was flown by a military pilot.

The satisfying repetitions of the ambient/chill/lounge techno soundtracks also reinforce the pleasures of conspiracy theory. They provide the film with an edginess, a transgressive allure that reiterates, mirrors the transgressions the film purports to reveal. It's a soundtrack of revelation and disconcealment that invites viewers and hearers to share in the secret, the secret knowledge of political violence and obscenity. As mainstream a magazine as *Time* gets it. In a page one article from the September 11, 2006 issue, columnist Lev Grossman (2006) writes: "Watching *Loose Change*, you feel as if you are participating in the great American tradition of self-reliance and nonconformist, antiauthoritarian dissent. You're fighting the power. You're thinking different." We don't need to believe the Bush administration's lies when we can see the evidence and know what really happened.

One of the final clips featured in the film provides a bridge to the academics credentialing the larger 9/11 truth movement. The clip is from "Hannity and Colmes," a nightly program on the Fox News Channel. Hannity and Colmes are interviewing Kevin Barrett, the adjunct professor teaching an introductory course on Islam at the University of Wisconsin-Madison. Hannity attempts to browbeat and stigmatize Barrett as a crazed conspiracy theorist, asking about Barrett's opinion and whether he believes 9/11 was an inside job. Barrett responds that he knows, he doesn't believe, he knows. He has studied the evidence for two and a half years and he knows.

Scholars for 9/11 Truth

Barrett is a key point of overlap between the video and the second aspect of the 9/11 truth movement that distinguishes it from other conspiracy theories, the emergence of the group Scholars for 9/11 Truth. The group was founded on December 15, 2005 by James H. Fetzer (2006b), Distinguished McKnight Professor of Philosophy at the University of Minnesota, Duluth, and Steven E. Jones, Professor of Physics, at Brigham Young University. Affiliated with the group is the peer-reviewed *Journal of 9/11 Studies*. Fetzer is the author and editor of a number of books on the assassination of President John F. Kennedy, including *Murder in Dealey Plaza: What We Know Now That We Didn't Know Then*, *The Great Zapruder Film Hoax: Deceit and Deception in the Death of JFK*, and *Assassination Science: Experts Speak Out on the Death of JFK*. In November 2005, Jones posted a paper on the Web in which he argued that the WTC Center towers fell as a result of a controlled demolition (2006, vol. 3). As John Gravois (2006) notes in the *Chronicle of Higher Education*, "His paper—written by an actual professor who works at an actual research university—has made him a celebrity in the conspiracy universe." ABC News picked up an AP wire feature on Scholars for 9/11 Truth citing a Canadian chemist critical of Jones's account of the collapse of the twin towers. According to the chemist, members of the conspiracy community "practically worship the ground (Jones) walks on because he's seen as a scientist who's preaching to their side." So even as the ABC feature notes that few mainstream scientists will engage the work of Scholars for 9/11 Truth so as not to lend it "unwarranted credibility" it recognizes that the academic credentials of the groups "could do that anyway" (Pope 2006). And, perhaps more importantly, the feature alludes to a fundamental characteristic of the group: they already know that the official story of 9/11 is wrong; their effort is expended so as to prove it.

The 9/11 truth movement gained in momentum because of the involvement of credentialed academics. For those in the movement, these scholars provide the expert knowledge, the credibility, they need to fight their battle for truth in the public sphere. Among the most important and influential is David Ray Griffin, a well-established theology professor. Not only did Griffin synthesize in a clear, systematic study many of the criticisms of the official account circulating on the internet and published in European presses, but his book, *The New Pearl Harbor*, was endorsed by renowned history professor Howard Zinn and provided with a forward from Richard Falk, an emeritus professor of International Law at Princeton.

The combination of Scholars for 9/11 truth and the popularity of videos of videos like *Loose Change* make the 9/11 truth movement an interesting site for thinking about problems of credibility. For some in the movement, the slickness and popularity of *Loose Change* is propagandistic, and in effect make the film into an instrument for disinformation instead of for scientific inquiry into 9/11. Writing for the 9/11 Research website, Victoria Ashley, in an article praising the contribution of Steven Jones, criticizes *Loose Change*: "Propaganda techniques, such as repeating an emotionally charged scene over and over, or approaching the unanswered questions of 9/11 in the manner of a ghost story telling, keep viewers transfixed by the presentation without any involvement of a rational evaluation of evidence" (Ashely 2006). The very aspects of the film that make it powerful and popular thus seem, to some, to undermine the movement's efforts toward challenging the Bush administration's version, as well as that provided by the 9/11 Commission, and keeping inquiry open.

Additionally, the scholars whose work rejects the official story have had to fight to defend their academic freedom and their scholarly credentials. In October 2006, Brigham Young University announced Jones' retirement. This announcement followed a month after Jones had been relieved of his teaching responsibilities and placed on leave. Lawmakers have also challenged the academic integrity, not to mention the intellectual honesty and overall sanity of scholars working in the area of 9/11 truth. During the summer of 2006, Wisconsin legislators pressured the University of Wisconsin-Madison to fire Kevin Barrett for his view that September 11 was an inside job. The provost, Patrick Farrell, defended Barrett, although he warned him that should he continue to "illustrate an inability to control" his interest in garnering publicity for his ideals, he would have less confidence in Barrett's ability to teach the course (Twohey 2006). The same academic credentials providing credibility to the 9/11 truth movement are being called into question and, to some extent, revoked.

In yet a further twist, the challenges to scholars' credibility arise from within the ranks of those working on 9/11 truth. In late November 2006, Jones and others split from Scholars for 9/11 Truth. The following month, they formed a new group, Scholars for 9/11 Truth and Justice.

Some lamented the infighting among the Scholars, recognizing the link between this fighting and the larger struggle for credibility even as they displaced the fundamental problem. In the words of "Lividlarry" (n.d.): " I've been somewhat 'torn' on this infighting issue for quite some time and can see some truth in at least two positions with regard to what information is 'credible.' It comes as no surprise that disinformation agents are busy sowing confusing anywhere that they can when such a horrible reality is at stake." Aware of the problem of credibility, Lividlarry subsumes it under conviction and suspicion. A horrible reality is at stake, a certain horror and a certain reality. Confusion is thus a matter not of this reality but of disinformation, of those who want to cast doubt on what he, and others, already know for certain. In fact, Lividlarry is particularly skeptical regarding efforts to establish credibility. He continues, "when those interested in accumulating whatever information and/or insights are out there fall into the trap of determining 'credibility' based on their interpretation of plausibility there is a danger that a piece of the puzzle might go unnoticed." What happened on September 11 was incredible, implausible. To limit oneself to these terms, then, avoids encountering what is already certain.

Factions among the Scholars offered different explanations for the split. Fetzer claimed that Jones was blocking people from posting on the Scholars' website and trying to take over the group (2006a). He also charged Jones with attempting to keep controversial theories about 9/11 out of the public eye. The theories in question were proposed by Judy Wood, a former assistant professor at Clemson University with a Ph.D. in Materials Engineering Science, and Morgan Reynolds, Emeritus Professor of Economics at Texas A&M. Reynolds and Wood (2006a) had posted a number of critiques of Jones' work on the internet. Challenging Jones' claim that "nano-enhanced thermite or thermate" was used to bring down the WTC in a controlled demolition, they point out that Jones does not establish that thermite or thermate has ever been used to bring down large buildings much less pulverize them. They note as well that Jones doesn't account for how much thermite or thermate would need to have been used, where it would need to have been placed, and how it would have been ignited (Wood and Reynolds 2006a).

Additionally, Reynolds and Wood (2006b) accuse Jones of failing to credit the work of others on 9/11 truth, ignoring the fact that "no Boeing757 went into the Pentagon was proven years ago," and basically upholding too many components of the official government conspiracy theory. Wood suggests that space-based laser beams perhaps in connection with very large mirrors, brought down the WTC (2006b). Jones both rejects the "no planes hit the Towers" theory and charges Wood and Reynolds with engaging in *ad hominem* attacks, in part because they mention his previous work on cold fusion. In a January 2007 broadcast of Fetzer's radio show, "The Dynamic Duo," on which Reynolds and Wood appeared as guests, Fetzer, in what he claims is not an *ad hominem*, mentions a paper written by Jones wherein Jones uses archeological evidence to prove the Mormon claim that Jesus Christ visited the Americas (Fetzer 2007). For much of the remaining portion of the show, Fetzer, Jones, and Wood discuss problems in Jones' claims to follow the scientific method and suggest that his work has more in common with pseudo-science.

In yet a more fundamental critique, Gerard Holmgren, criticizes the entire community of Scholars for 9/11 Truth (including Fetzer and Jones by name) for plagiarizing the earlier work of internet researchers. In Holmgren's (2006) words: "The scholars make their presence in the media felt not through original research (they haven't done any), nor through quality of presentation (they make frequent factual errors—if indeed they are "errors"). They make their presence felt purely by swagger in parading that Jones and number of his associates are professors... Not only do the scholars plagiarize their "research" articles, but their press statements are calculated to reinforce the false notion that their work is original, that the revelations are new, and also to play the hero card by claiming personal risk in unveiling these shocking new revelations." On his website, Holmgren explains that the so-called 9/11 truth movement is actually controlled by the very people who perpetrated the crimes of September 11. This control relies on carefully placed disinformation and on the careerism and opportunism of those who want to profit from the 9/11 truth industry (Holmgren 2006). This disinformation keeps the myth that planes actually crashed into the Pentagon and WTC alive. Holmgren knows that these are fabrications. American Airlines flights 77 and 11 (the ones allegedly hitting the Pentagon and the North Tower) never existed. The well-known footage of the plane striking the South Tower is an animated cartoon. In sum, Holmgren is convinced that the events of 9/11 are like a giant snuff film consisting of real explosions and fake planes and hijackers.

Skepticism and Certainty

To sort through these layers of credibility, incredibility, and certainty, I turn to psychoanalysis, specifically, Zizek's account of the decline of symbolic efficiency, Santner's discussion of the crisis of investiture, and Lacan's teaching on psychosis. Together, these ideas help us understand the problem posed by 9/11 truth not as one of credibility but of its absence, more specifically, as the absence of conditions of possibility for something like belief or credibility.

I begin with Zizek. As I've mentioned, the decline of symbolic efficiency refers to a breakdown in signification: identities, arguments, or signs that are clear and compelling in some settings, carry little weight in others. One might imagine Britney Spears and Jürgen Habermas in an airport waiting area. Neither would recognize the other's symbolic weight or be able to assess the other's cultural capital.

That identities, arguments, and signs are limited in their power and range, that they fail to be thoroughly compelling in a variety of contexts, has repercussions for contemporary subjects. We are often skeptical about what we hear. To approach this from the other side, Zizek frequently describes symbolic efficiency with the question, "what do you believe, your eyes or my words?" The idea is that in a functioning symbolic order, we believe the words, no matter what our eyes tell us: we recognize that the judge is not just the man that we see but the office that he holds; we recognize that the doctor is more than the woman before us; she is also the trained, experienced, expert on whom we depend. These days, however, we don't believe their words. We believe our eyes. Contemporary subjects accept very little on face value. We don't believe what we hear. If a doctor gives us bad news, we'll get a second or third opinion and then reject Western medicine in favor of more authentic folk remedies. If the judge makes a ruling we reject, we suspect that he was paid off, corrupt, or invested in an opposing ideology. And, even when we concede that another is likely using his or her best judgment in as fair a way as possible, we find ourselves emphasizing the plurality of possible views: everyone has her own opinion; experts disagree.

So, we are skeptical. But, often our skepticism is combined with a kind of certainty or conviction. We don't challenge or reject everything all the time. To keep going, we have to keep some aspects of our lives stable and secure. We need base points from which to navigate. Skepticism toward the news media, then, is combined with an increased division between who watches what and who trusts whom. Some sources can be trusted. Republicans in the USA are more likely to watch Fox News and report that they trust what they hear on Fox. Vice President Dick Cheney has said that he only watches Fox. The notion of the decline of symbolic efficiency clicks on this fragmentation, on the inability of elements that flourish in one discursive habitat to take root and thrive in another.

As Zizek points out, Donald Davidson uses the notion of the principle of charity to designate the background assumption that everything another says is not completely wrong; it's a presumption of underlying agreement on which disagreement rests. Indeed, Davidson argues that "charity is not an option...charity is forced on us; whether we like it or not, if we want to understand others, we must count them right in most matters" (Zizek 2000, 114). The decline of symbolic efficiency points to the withering away of this principle of charity—less and less are people today forced to presume charity. There are strong material-technological explanations for this withering away: not only are communication technologies charitable in our stead, making connections with other machines, but the interconnecting of ever more people lets us find enough of those who share our convictions that we don't have to believe. In a previous age, we may have been isolated in our views, village idiots roaming the streets, madwomen in the attics, or psychotic judges driven to document our illness and our discoveries. Now we're part of a discourse, community, or movement.

I mention psychotic judges because Eric L. Santner's (1996) discussion of the memoirs of Judge Daniel Paul Schreber provides a second element useful for thinking about contemporary problems around credibility and certainty. Whereas Freud's reading of Schreber was central to his understanding of paranoia (particularly with regard to its presumed link with homosexuality), Santner underscores the similarity between the crises leading to Schreber's psychotic breakdown and those facing modernity more generally. He understands these crises as crises of symbolic investiture.

Symbolic investiture refers to the way a person becomes endowed with a new social status that informs his or her identity in the community (Santner 1996, xii). Examples might include the ordination of a priest, a marriage ceremony, graduation and the conferral of a degree, or winning a prestigious prize. In modernity, Santner argues, symbolic identities become ever more fragile, less able to "seize" the subject at the core of her self-understanding. Modern subjects, then, understand themselves as never fully occupying their identities; there is always more to the modern subject than her role. And this means that the roles themselves are less than they had been; they carry less meaning and weight; they are less impressive, less efficacious. In fact, fully aware of the distance between the person and her role, we are inclined to see the role as a sham, a ruse, a cover for corruption or abuse. We become aware, in other words, of the tautological character of symbolic roles and social institutions: the judge is a judge because we treat him as a judge; people become married in a marriage ceremony because that's what a marriage ceremony does.

The crisis of symbolic investiture impacting modernity thus reveals the violence and compulsion, the "vicious circularity," underlying social order [a point Santner (1996, 43) explores with reference to Walter Benjamin's "Critique of Violence"]. Typically, subjects forget or repress their knowledge of violence. This forgetting and repressing is necessary for the continued function of the social field and the credibility of symbolic identities. At points of crisis, however, knowledge of the dependence of the social function on coercion and repetition becomes difficult to repress (Santner 1996, 139). At these points, Santner (1996) tells us, "we are at the threshold of a psychotic universe where the subject has become unable to forget, unable (primordially) to repress the drive dimension of the symbolic function, which expands into a general state of rottenness and decay" (43).

Santner's crisis of symbolic investiture deepens and extends Zizek's account of the decline of symbolic efficiency insofar as it connects the crisis of symbolic investiture to paranoid psychosis. Santner (1996) argues that a central lesson of the Schreber case is that a generalized loss of symbolic power can generate feelings of overproximity, "loss of distance to some obscene and malevolent presence that appears to have a direct hold on one's inner parts" (xii). Confronted with the excessive proximity of authority, the subject can't continue to play the game of everyday life, a game that requires it to deny the "impasses and dilemmas of symbolic power and authority" (Santner 1996, 144). A challenge to or the traumatic loss of symbolic authority impacts the subject such that he feels this now missing authority to be all the more close, powerful, and intrusive, and confronts the underlying irrationality or violence underpinning authority per se—the tautological way we obey law because it is law and accept the judgments of a judge because she is the judge. Santner's psychotic, then, is not delusional because he accepts as certain what is necessarily false, but because he denies the falsity, the fiction, the lie necessary for the functioning of the symbolic order. The psychotic doesn't fall for the performative magic of utterances backed by symbolic authority; he focuses instead on the "rottenness and decay" that underlies them.

Before I turn to Lacan, I want to draw out the implications of Zizek's notion of the decline of symbolic efficiency and Santner's discussion of the crisis of symbolic investiture for thinking through the problems posed by the 9/11 truth movement. Zizek draws our attention to the movement's setting in a context of profound skepticism: contemporary subjects don't have to believe; they can find out. This skepticism is coupled, moreover, with a sense of certainty or confidence—not everything is called into question at the same time, and, some sources are more reliable than others. So, contemporary Americans might claim the media cannot be trusted and support that claim with evidence taken from media that they actually find trustworthy. Their trust, however, doesn't travel from one setting to another. What they find to be authoritative, to count as expert knowledge, is similarly limited.

I read Santner as extending Zizek's point in a more specific direction, one characterized by the loss of a powerful authority or of authorizing power. The subject responds to this loss by positing an all the more intrusive, invasive, and proximate power, by failing to believe the fiction of the symbolic order and suppress the sense in which it covers over arbitrary power. As a model for understanding some responses to 9/11, Santner's "crisis of symbolic investiture" suggests that those who see the event in terms of the USA's government's failure, its inability to secure its citizens and its territory, might respond to this loss by positing another power and by tracing the workings of this other power throughout the sociopolitical terrain. For them, the loss of US power is accompanied by a loss of signifying authority, an ability to provide meaning, and to authorize an explanation of the events of 9/11. They don't accept the authority of the administration's signification of the event; instead, they focus on the "rottenness and decay" underlying political and state power.

I turn now to Lacan so as to specify the discourse that arises at the site of this crisis of loss. In *Seminar III*, Lacan (1997, 74) distinguishes between the psychotic and the normal subject, writing:

> What characterizes a normal subject is precisely that he never takes seriously certain realities that he recognizes exist. You are surrounded by all sorts of realities about which you are in doubt, some of which are particularly threatening, but you don't take them fully seriously, for you think ... that *the worst is not always certain*, and maintain yourselves in an average, basic—in the sense of relation to the base—state of blissful uncertainty, which makes possible for you a sufficiently relaxed existence. Surely, certainty is the rarest of things for the normal subject.

The normal person has a lot of doubt, but he doesn't let these doubts get in the way of his everyday functioning. There are many things he doesn't know for sure, but this doesn't bother him. He doesn't worry about it.

In fact, his happy persistence requires him not to ask questions or look too closely at things. The normal subject carries on in an uncertain world where many things are unknown and lies are pervasive. Indeed, Lacan (1997, 76) says "the normal subject spontaneously rejects certainty," he may deny the truth that is right before his eyes just so he can keep on going.

In contrast, for the psychotic, Lacan (1997, 75) explains, "reality is not the issue," certainty is. What he is certain of may well be ambiguous, unclear, opaque. But, the psychotic is certain, nonetheless. And this certainty does not correspond directly with reality; reality isn't at stake; after all, normal subjects persist in a terrain of reality filled with uncertainty and falsity. The psychotic rejects this ambiguity, the ambiguity of the everyday, of language, replacing it with certainty. Further, Lacan notes that the psychotic's certainty is often expressed through writing. The paranoid write, they produce "sheets of paper covered with writing." Schreber, for example, published his writings on his psychosis, which raises the question for Lacan (1997, 78) of what the need for recognition might mean. Perhaps it might be a need for acknowledgment or community as a way of lessening the unbearable and direct confrontation with power alone; perhaps Schreber's desire for recognition is a desire for conversation and camaraderie, for others with whom he might discuss and compare his findings such that he might escape the isolation of his certainty. At any rate, networked communication technologies provide ways of meeting this need.

Lacan defines psychosis in terms of the foreclosure of the Name-of-the-Father and the hole this creates in the chain of significations. As he puts it, "something primordial regarding the subject's being does not enter into symbolization and is not repressed, but rejected" (Lacan 1997, 81). Because the Name-of-the-Father or Master signifier stabilizes and makes possible language and signification as such, in its absence there is chaos. The psychotic responds to this hole, this chaos, in various ways. He may affirm, emphatically, another Other. Most of us are familiar with paranoia as positing an Other behind the scenes, pulling the strings. Often, this Other remains mysterious, enigmatic (Lacan 1997, 194). This comes as no surprise given the absence of a way to hold the signifying chain together. The lack of such an anchoring point perpetually stimulates the effort to find meaning.

To compensate for the hole in the symbolic, the psychotic turns to the imaginary. Lacan (1997, 204) refers to a "captivating image." The psychotic fastens on this image, positioning himself in relation to it. Insofar as this relation remains at the level of the imaginary, it is not a symbolic relation capable of anchoring meaning or offering a clear degree of separation between the subject and the other. On the contrary, precisely because the relation is on the imaginary plane, it is characterized by fear, rivalry, and aggression (Lacan 1997, 205). He enters into a rivalrous game with the imaginary other, a game of deception and deceit that turns the subject's world into a kind of fantasmagoria, an uncertain terrain where nothing is as it seems and everything is permeated by meaning and significance (Lacan 1997, 69). The subject may try to mimic the conformist behaviors of those around him as he grapples with the intensity of his fears and of this rivalry. He may seek to avoid confronting his awareness of the power and aggression, but as his psychosis becomes more acute, he will be less able to deny the obscene intrusions of power that surround him.

Thus far I've emphasized several aspects of the Lacanian account of psychosis: that psychosis is a reaction to a hole or absence, that this reaction takes place on the level of the imaginary, and that it involves certainty, fear, distrust, and a sense of permeating meaning that may be expressed through writing and publication. I want to add one more aspect of Lacan's discussion, an aspect that returns us to the setting of psychosis. Lacan (1997, 63) writes:

> To be more or less captivated, captured, by a meaning is not the same thing as to express that meaning in a discourse designed to communicate it and reconcile it with other variously received meanings. In this term *received* lies the driving force of what makes discourse a common discourse, a commonly admitted discourse.

The hole to which the psychotic responds, the hole constitutive of psychosis, is a gap or absence in the "commonly admitted discourse." Normal subjects don't perceive the hole; for them, the symbolic order is intact and they ignore, as best they can, the ruptures of the Real. The psychotic perceives the hole and reacts to it, but he reacts in a way that he can't fully communicate. The image that covers over or takes the place of the hole doesn't function in the same way for normal subjects because for them its place is already occupied. Thus, they can't reconcile the psychotic's image, no matter how certain it may be, with the other meanings constitutive of reality. It is simply not part of a common discourse.

But, what if discourse is not common? What if our conditions are characterized by the decline of symbolic efficiency and the presence of a variety of differentiated discursive habitats? What, in other words, if the words of the government are already greeted with skepticism and doubt? Today, in part because of the internet and in part because of market-driven publishing, texts that might have once remained solitary, like Schreber's, can become part of a group, a scene, a genre, a movement, a community. Schreber's psychotic writings don't establish a social link; even as he narrates his experience, his writings remain an object within psychoanalytic discourse. Networked information and communication technologies end this isolation, allowing for the emergence of a discourse of the psychotic, a discourse that reacts to a hole with certainty, fear, distrust, and a permeating sense of meaning.

Because it is built around a hole, an absence, this discourse has trouble communicating its findings, its discoveries, to other discourses, to discourses that have already integrated a signifier in the place of the hole. So even as the psychotic discourse may adopt the patterns of other discourses, the hole which generates its investigations remains unrecognized, disallowed. What it finds meaningful cannot be reconciled in their terms.

As it tries to find acceptance, to be recognized, confirmed, as it tries to transmit its findings, the psychotic discourse tends to hold itself together by mimicking other discourses. It forms itself in their image, as their clone, attempting thereby to attract to itself their already established credibility. Particularly compelling in this psychotic attempt is its reliance on fundamental aspects of language and sociality. Psychotic discourse accentuates the truth that, as Lacan (1997, 115–116) says, "language entirely operates within ambiguity, and most of the time you know absolutely nothing about what you are saying." The psychotic confronts us with the lacks in languages, with indeterminacies that we normally overlook. And, more fundamentally, he reminds us of the violence and irrationality underlying the symbolic order, the way law "is sustained not by reason alone but also by the force/violence of a tautological enunciation, 'The law is the law,'" as Santner (1996, 11) explains. The psychotic discourse thus tries to prevent us from repressing what we already know, undermining thereby the conditions of possibility for credibility.

THE TRUTH OF 9/11

Having set out the idea of a psychotic discourse in terms of a hole around which a certainty, fear, distrust, and conviction of meaning circulate, I return now to September 11.

Both the official and the unofficial accounts of the events of 9/11 confront the specific horror of the disintegration of the social link, of the symbolic pact holding society together (Zizek 2006, 174). The official story emphasizes the incompetence of the US government, its failure to deliver on its trillion dollar defense budget and actually defend. In the face of this overwhelming display of the broken promise of security, Bush repeats, almost daily, his promise to protect the American people, to secure freedom and the American way of life. The repetition reminds us of the loss that compels it.

Part of what gives the administration's account of 9/11 its force is the way it hammers home a fact of which we are all secretly aware, namely, that of our underlying passivity, how we are "helplessly thrown around by forces out of our control" (Zizek 2006, 344). Rooted in this passivity, the logic of the incompetence theory is a drive for more power, more security, more surveillance. As it reiterates the meme of loss, the Bush administration seems almost to enjoy its own passivity, its own failure, finding therein a way to ask for, and get, more power.

Fortified by the efforts of the FBI, the CIA, the Department of Defense, and various foreign intelligence agencies, the Bush administration is certain it knows who did it and why. Initially, the administration didn't feel the need to back up its certainty with proof and was thus reluctant to provide evidence for its claims: the administration failed adequately to fund the 9/11 Commission, fought over the release of documents, and resisted testifying before the Commission; Bush and Cheney ultimately testified, but in the Oval Office and not under oath; any notes the Commissioners made during the meeting were confiscated. We should also note that even as the administration now claims to know who did it, it emphasizes that it did not know who was going to do it or when they were going to do it. They didn't have advance warning or information. Their incompetence is thereby rendered as their failure to function properly as a subject supposed to know. They didn't know, but now they do and they will continue to know. And, it doesn't matter if anyone believes them. Bush's conviction doesn't depend on polls, on what people think. He acts on what he knows—in his gut, a clear pervert in the Lacanian sense.

The 9/11 conspiracy theories follow a different circuit. Although certain, their certainty is not, like Bush's, that of the pervert who makes himself an instrument of the big Other. Rather, it is a psychotic certainty, a certainty that something horrible happened and that the evidence for this horror is clearly before us, if we only know how to see it. They know that some in the administration are not victims but criminals, powerful, wicked, evil criminals able to carry out a conspiracy that took the lives of nearly 3000 Americans, sent the economy into a tailspin, and led to two wars. Countering the official story of passivity, here the government acts, ruthlessly. It's organized, efficient, able to execute its plans without a hitch. Those arguing that 9/11 was an inside job challenge the Bush administration's efforts to reinforce its power by drawing attention to the already excessive, obscene power on which the administration rests. It can already do whatever it wants, whenever it wants, and get away with it. It has the means, the capability, and, most of all, the will. The underlying conviction affect that this view generates, then, lies from its expression of our fundamental unfreedom—an unfreedom awareness of which we normally repress.

One might wonder why, if the government or a subgroup within it already has this sort of power, would it go to the trouble of taking down the WTC, particularly in the redoubled fashion that appears in emphases on both controlled demolition and airplanes. If the Bush administration, Cheney, or some secret cabal wanted war, and some advocates of alternative explanations point out that plans to invade Afghanistan were already in play as early as June of 2001, why would they orchestrate an elaborate attack on US office buildings rather than just going to war? If Bush and Cheney are so powerful do they really need permission, consent, legitimation? Or, if they wanted to attack Iraq, why not blame the Iraqis for the destruction of the WTC directly, why not have Iraqi hijackers rather than Saudi and Yemeni hijackers, particularly given the close relationship between the Bush family and the House of Saud? Or why not just attack Iraq on trumped up intelligence of an imminent nuclear threat? Given power's demonstrable excess—which is what the 9/11 conspiracy theories demonstrate, what they can't repress—why would power need to display this excess? For whom is it staged?

In the psychotic discourse of 9/11 truth, power is staged for itself. It's the way that power is trying to produce itself as new world order, a new big Other at the site of loss. The 9/11, in other words, was power's attempt to found a world through the massive expenditure of *jouissance* and institution of the Law. From the standpoint of the conspiracy theories, 9/11 is the founding obscenity or crime that initiates a new order. For those involved with 9/11 truth the primary political task is dissolving this order. Yet, at this point, they come up against the passivity underlying their fundamental fantasy: the subjects or, in their words, "sheeple" who fail to share their certainty. And, here they overlap with the official discourse on 9/11.

I think of the problem posed by this passivity in two ways. First, the excess of obscene power is so overwhelming that one is rendered powerless in its presence. In the official discourse, this appears in the impossibility of being able to prevent another attack, in guaranteeing safety—measures like taking off our shoes and belts and putting liquids in tiny bottles in clear plastic bags accentuate this pervasive helplessness. Anything could happen. Everything is dangerous. In the psychotic discourse of 9/11 truth, passivity before power appears in the way that, if the government or a secret cabal of insiders could carry out so effectively the incredible conspiracy of 9/11, then it can do anything. We can do nothing to stop it. Its control is everywhere, an octopus with eye-covered tentacles. Second, insofar as the psychotic certainty displaces belief, it comes under the pressure of its own drive. On one hand, its knowledge persists despite disproof of certain claims—as David Ray Griffin argues, the knowledge of 9/11 is cumulative, not deductive. On the other, such certainty tends to demand uniformity—we can't necessarily believe those in our own movement. Thus, already members of the 9/11 truth movement accuse one another of spreading disinformation or of producing unreliable and unverifiable studies. We know government is all powerful—and if it's all powerful, how can we trust anything we know? How do I know I'm not being manipulated?

This is where the conflict over the truth of September 11 comes up against the hard rock of the Real. And, not surprisingly, this doesn't provide us with a way out, with a way through the radically incommensurable perspectives on 9/11 that we see in the official and unofficial theories. The gap between the official and unofficial accounts of events can't be filled in with a set of facts. It's more fundamental, an indication of the larger disintegration of symbolic efficiency, diminution of the conditions of credibility, and change in the status of knowing and knowledge. Indeed, as an event that can be signified, it's "never fully verified precisely because ... there is no external limit to it" (Zizek 2006, 167). The official and unofficial accounts thus perpetually circle around a void that cannot be filled, deriving their enjoyment from the circuit of drive.

Psychotic Media?

What is the role of alternative or progressive media in this environment? My discussion of 9/11 truth shows that new media can be vitally and virally effective. It helps build movements and communities. It provides alternative sources of knowledge and information. The counterknowledge it produces enables the emergence, and the flourishing, of epistemologically differentiated spaces. Networked communications—particularly in their continued entanglements with the mainstream media—format the terrain of battle between competing conceptions of the Real.

Of course, the subjects navigating these spaces cannot be understood as modernity's typical rational individuals. It's not the case that they simply evaluate the available alternatives, choosing among them on the basis of the best evidence. Far from it—they have no basis for evaluation, particularly insofar as they confront competing alternatives daily, alternatives about which some are certain, others skeptical, and few actually believe, precisely because of the persistent undermining of belief under conditions of the decline of symbolic efficiency.

The proliferation of contents and voices, sources and alternatives, links and possibilities so vital a counter to corporate media's investments in and support of global capitalism—particularly in its neoliberal form—creates conditions amenable to the flourishing of psychotic discourses. Does it make sense to try to learn from them? Is it possible that endless confrontation with skepticism combined with an inability to repress our knowledge of power's obscene underpinnings could potentially release people from acceptance of the status quo, from the law, from the powers that be? Or does constituent anxiety render us passive, fearful, vulnerable to the lure of the more powerful, the more authoritative? Is the Left somehow doomed to a false choice between the embrace of unlimited possible truths and the singular truth of right-wing dogmatism?

While I am pessimistic with regard to the potential of progressive media, seeing it as trapped within and furthering the very suppositions it attempts to combat, my wager is nonetheless for the possibility of breaking out of deadlock around 9/11 that so constrains contemporary Left politics in the USA. Confronting our desire for 9/11 is a crucial step in this direction. I don't mean that collectively some group called the American people longed for the destruction of the WTC or hoped for an attack on the Pentagon. Rather, the USA produced the situation within the disintegrated spectacle of communicative capitalism. It desired shock, horror, rupture, some kind of break with the neoliberal confidence, dot-com euphoria, and consumer-oriented cultivation of unique identities characteristic of the Clinton years. Perhaps it is more accurate to say that the events, meanings, and affects linked together and captured by the term "9/11" were an object of intense (and productive) desire.

The Bush administration's appropriation of 9/11 puts this desire to work. Rather than presenting the events of September 11 in their complexity—with regard, say, to Europe's past decades of terrorism, the global economic and geopolitical position of the USA, the history of American foreign policy in the Middle East, the repercussions of the Soviet war in Afghanistan and covert US participation in this war, the worldwide market in arms and munitions—the administration locks 9/11 into a simple binary: good versus evil. And, for all its preoccupations with the details of the design of the WTC, the training of the 9/11 pilots, the exercises and war games of the US military planned for September 11, the truth movement accepts and intensifies this binary. Even as it may seem to deny this desire, projecting it instead onto a malevolent government or faction therein, 9/11 conspiracy theories embrace it; the event is the irrational nugget holding it together, a symptom (or, in Lacanese, *sinthome*) invested with violence and obscenity—rockets, missiles, bombs, explosives, planes filled with passengers taken to secret locations and executed. In each case, the seduction of the opposition between good and evil tells people who they are, it gives them a place in the world, one larger than the ever fragile and mutable imaginary identities hawked in communicative capitalism.

Without our desire for 9/11, the Bush administration would not have been able to mobilize support for its version of the event. Even as the work of the truth movement raises doubts about the administration's account and even as support for Bush and his so-called war on terror plummets to new depths, most continue to speak in hushed tones about 9/11, to sacralize it, to retain not just respect for the dead but a kind of awe before the event. Even among Leftists, this awe seems to condition and constrain action, making many wary of being labeled un-American or anti-patriotic. At the same time, however, for many of us on the Left, the years subsequent to the attacks on the WTC and Pentagon have been invigorating. Just as right-wing righteousness drives what is for all intents and purposes a religious war, a crusade against Islam, so is Left outrage so much more satisfying than during the cultural wars. But, for all the hatred of Bush and his wars, for all the protests and petitions, for all the energy our anger provides, we remain unable or unwilling to take the next steps of imagining, organizing, and creating another world. We have a moral concept, an ethical sense. But we lack a coherent politics, primarily because we remain attached to our present values.

Bibliography

Americans Question Bush on 9/11 Intelligence. 2006. *Angus Reid Global Monitor*. http://www.angus-reid.com/admin/collateral/pdfs/polls/NYT_October2k6.pdf. Last modified 14 Oct 2006.

Ashley, Victoria. 2006. Steven E. Jones: A Physics Professor Speaks Out on 9/11; Reason, Publicity, and Reaction. 9-11 Research.com. January 14. http://911research.wtc7.net/essays/jones/StevenJones.html

Briefing room. 2001. *White House.gov*. http://www.whitehouse.gov/news/releases/2001/11/20011110-3.html

Brooks, David. 2006. The Paranoid Style. *New York Times*, May 4.

Dean, Jodi. 1998. *Aliens in America: Conspiracy Cultures from Outerspace to Cyberpace*. Ithaca: Cornell University Press.

———. 2002. *Publicity's Secret: How Technoculture Capitalizes on Democracy*. Ithaca: Cornell University Press.

DeMott, Benjamin. 2004. Whitewash as Public Service. *Harper's Magazine*, October, 35–45.

Dundar, David, and Brad Reagan, eds. 2006. *Debunking 9/11 Myths: Why Conspiracy Theories Can't Stand Up to the Facts*. New York: Hearst Books.

Fetzer, James H. 2006a. An Open Letter About Steve Jones. November 19. http://www.911scholars.org/OpenLetterToJones.html

——— 2006b. Scholars on its First Anniversary. November 25. http://www.911scholars.org/ScholarsAnniversary.html

Fetzer, Jim. 2007. The Dynamic Duo Transcript. January 2. http://www.911scholars.org/070102_transcript.html

Firmage, Joseph P. 2006. Intersecting Facts and Theories on 9/11. *Journal of 9/11 Studies* 2. http://www.journalof911studies.com/

Gravois, John. 2006. Professors of Paranoia? *Chronicle of Higher Education*, June 23. http://chronicle.com/free/v52/i42/42a01001.html

Grossman, Lev. 2006. Why the 9/11 Conspiracies Won't Go Away. *Time*, September 11. http://www.time.com/time/magazine/article/0,9171,1531304-1,00.html

Half of New Yorkers Believe U.S. Leaders Had Foreknowledge of Impending 9/11 attacks and Consciously Failed to Act, 66% Call for New Probe of Unanswered Questions by congress of New York's Attorney General, New Zogby International Polls Reveals. 2004. *Zogby International*. http://www.zogby.com/search/ReadNews.dbm?ID=855. Last modified 30 Aug 2004.

Hargrove, Thomas, and Guido H. Stemple III . 2006. Anti-Government Anger Spurs 9/11 Conspiracy Beliefs. *Scripps Howard News Service*, August 2. http://newspolls.org/story.php?story_id=55

Holmgren, Gerald. 2006. Scholars for 9/11 Plagiarism and Disinformation. February 6. http://members.iinet.net.au/~holmgren/scholars.html

Jones, Steven E. (2006). Why Indeed did the World Trade Center Buildings Completely Collapse? *Journal of 9/11 Studies* 3. http://www.journalof911studies.com/

Krugman, Paul. 2006. Who's Crazy Now? *New York Times*, May 8.

Lacan, Jacques. 1997. *The Psychoses 1955–1956. The Seminar of Jacques Lacan Book III*, ed. Jacques-Alain Miller, trans. Russell Gregg. New York: W.W. Norton.

Lividlarry. n.d. I've been somewhat torn.... *Alaska Free Press*. http://www.alaskafreepress.com/msgboard/board/10.

Pope, Justin. 2006. 9/11 Conspiracy Theorists Thriving. *ABC News*, August 6. http://abcnews.go.com/US/wireStory?id=2279963&page=1

Sales, Nancy Jo. 2006. Click Here for Conspiracy. *Vanity Fair*, August: 112–116.

Santner, Eric L. 1996. *My Own Private Germany*. Princeton: Princeton University Press.

The Top September 11th Conspiracy Theories. 2006. *America.gov*. http://usinfo.state.gov/xarchives/display.html?p=pubsenglish&y=2006&m=August&x=20060828133846esnamfuaK0.2676355. Last modified 25 Oct 2006

Twohey, Megan. 2006. UW lecturer's 9-11 media blitz is rapped. *Milwaukee Journal Sentinel*, August 4. http://www.findarticles.com/p/articles/mi_qn4196/is_20060804/ai_n16661953

Wood Judy, and Morgan Reynolds. 2006a. The Scientific Method Applied to the Thermite Hypothesis. *The Journal of 9/11 Research and 9/11 Issues*, December 14. http://drjudywood.com

———. 2006b. Why Did Indeed the WTC Buildings Disintegrate? *No More Games.Net*, October. http://nomoregames.net

Zizek, Slavoj. 2000. *The Fragile Absolute*. London: Verso.

———. 2006. *The Parallax View*. Cambridge: MIT Press.

Computational Culture and the New Platonism in Neoliberal Rhetoric

Gerald Voorhees

From this author's standpoint, we can thank Plato for two contributions to the study of rhetoric. For one, there is Plato's position, articulated in *The Phaedrus* and championed in the Modern era by Richard Weaver's (1955) *The Ethics of Rhetoric,* that rhetoric is only good when it communicates something that is always already true. For another, in response to Plato, Aristotle developed his Art of Rhetoric, introducing a notion of rhetoric centrally concerned with probabilistic proofs.

It is with no small irony that despite the increasingly un-Platonic, postmodern rationality underwriting contemporary North American rhetorical criticism, the rhetorical practices that fill the everyday lives of North Americans are more and more Platonic. To wit, an increasingly common rhetorical strategy is the enthymematic appeal that is premised in the presumption that there is only one possible, correct solution to moral, social, and political problems, the very types of questions that Aristotle distinguished from philosophy and placed firmly within the domain of rhetoric. In the midst of the preliminaries of the 2016 election, these sorts of claims pervade mediated, American publics. The treatment of practical judgments as incontrovertible truths betrays a New Platonism and reveals invaluable

---

G. Voorhees (✉)
Department of Speech Communication, University of Waterloo,
Waterloo, ON, USA

insights about the neoliberal character of contemporary rhetoric, particularly how enthymemes and *doxa* are employed in everyday argument. Of course, I am not suggesting that North Americans are reading Plato—in fact more and more they are reading less and less (Stephen 2014)—but rather that a cultural logic readily identified as Platonic is resurgent as a result of the contemporary social and material conditions.

This chapter will proceed by first discussing the circumstances that constitute the context of this New Platonism, the prevalence of computational culture and neoliberal governmentality. It is no coincidence that during the same decades that computational systems became so ubiquitous that they are now banal, neoliberal economic policies and rationalities of everyday life also became so pervasive. I turn, in the second part of this chapter, to discuss how rhetorical studies have conceptualized the relationship between enthymemes and doxa. Because enthymematic arguments rely on appeals to doxa, examining enthymemes can tell us, as my analysis will show, what interlocutors take for granted as truths. Finally, I will examine this New Platonism as it manifests in the enthusiast communities that have organized around digital games in order to make the case for its prevalence in computational culture generally and, even more broadly, in public culture.

At the Nexus of Neoliberalism and Computational Culture

Computers and neoliberalism are inescapable elements of the contemporary rhetorical situation. These facets of everyday life do not simply determine the resources available for addressing situations that demand response (Bitzer 1968) but also inform how subjects will define what constitutes a demand and a viable response (Vatz 1973). More accurately, neoliberalism and the ubiquity of computers are integral aspects of the lifeworld that constitutes subjects and the terrain upon which those subjects decide what circumstances demand rhetorical response. As such, they are integral components of an interaction that crystalizes in the rhetorical event, "an incident that produces and reproduces the identities of subjects and constructs and reconstructs linkages between them" (Biesecker 1989, 126). Rather than belabor the artful and extensive discussion of neoliberalism offered in this volume's introduction, I only briefly discuss neoliberalism and its relation to governmentality and, instead, focus on the dimensions of neoliberalism most salient to this paper: population, security and their interrelation in calculative, economic rationality. Similarly, I cannot hope to provide a thorough explication of the genealogy, ontology, and morphology of computational culture. In lieu of a comprehensive examination of the matter, I focus on the dimensions of computational culture that are most relevant to contemporary neoliberalism.

Eschewing a technological determinist position maintaining that computational technologies have reshaped social and cultural formations, I am cognizant of the mutually constitutive relationships between human actors and technological objects in the configuration of computational culture (Friedman 2005, 3). For instance, Friedman recounts how the researchers developing the first digital computers in the 1940s designed them to not only celebrate but also reinforce the speed, precision, and objectivity valued by an increasingly "scientific and military culture," a deliberate move away from the analytical engines of the early twentieth century which were designed to emboldened the user's creative application of knowledge in tandem with the machine (41). Nevertheless, I strategically center the computer as the cipher that makes legible the contours of what I term computational culture. It is the computer, after all, that has become a fulcrum for cultural change. In little more than five decades, the computer has (d)evolved in the North American cultural imaginary from a *subject* whose power bordered on magic to an utterly banal and commonplace *object*.

Computational media has been integral to this process. For instance, Lev Manovich comes to his description of computational culture through a circuitous route after examining the five qualities he ascribes to digital media: numerical representation, modularity, variability, automation, and transcoding. "Because new media is created on computers, distributed via computers, and stored and archived on computers," Manovich says, "the logic of a computer can be expected to significantly influence the traditional cultural logic of media" (2002, 46). As if the echo of Marshall McLuhan was not already reverberating through the assertion that the five characteristics defining the computational nature of the medium effect its cultural impact, Manovich expands on the notion of transcoding by arguing, "The computerization of culture gradually accomplishes similar transcoding... That is, cultural categories and concepts are substituted... by new ones that derive from the computer's ontology, epistemology and pragmatics" (47). Manovich grounds these sweeping claims about the nature of computational media in a series of comparative analyses that distinguish the cultural logics embodied in books and film with those of games and websites. Similarly entelechial arguments, in which the ontology of the medium is said to determine its cultural impact, have emerged in other fields of inquiry germane to digital media.

To this end, there is a relatively small but rich current of research that looks to digital games as an exemplary, even generative, form of computational culture. Indeed, Bob Rehak (2008) argues that digital games were the "killer app," the must have piece of software that hastened the widespread adoption of personal computers in the home (78). That said, consensus among scholars is that digital games are primarily a reflection of contemporary culture and only secondarily participate in its reproduction. Ted Freidman (1999), for instance, argues that players form a "symbiotic circuit" with games, identifying not with particular roles but rather with the very processes that underwrite games. In other words, games teach players how to relate to computers, imparting distinct "structures of thought" by requiring player to "internaliz[e] the logic of the program" in order to succeed in the game. This premise is developed into a programmatic line of inquiry by Manovich (2002), who refigures it as a form of transcoding, Alexander Galloway (2006), who describes digital games as allegorithmic to the extent that they are "direct synchronization[s] with the political realities of the information age" (91) and McKenzie Wark (2007), who brings Manovich's five qualities of computational media full circle by arguing that allegorithms shift the traditional allegory's relation of sign to sign to a relation of sign to number and one number to another (par. 41).

Of course, the technology itself is hardly the actor in the shift Wark describes, much less the shift to computational culture. Rather, various social and intellectual and mo(ve)ments that have historically attempted to define human experience through the conceptual lens of computation have reasserted themselves in the context of nearly ubiquitous computing. The logic grounding these efforts adhere to the maxim that "mathematical calculation can be made to stand for propositions that are not themselves mathematical" (Golumbia 2009, 14). In this regard, that is to say, from the perspective of the discursive construction of the social, computational culture is integrally linked to both the economic and governmental dimensions of neoliberalism. Jonathan Crary (2014) makes this connection between computational culture and the increasing ubiquity of neoliberalism, arguing that the patterns of lived experience constituted by neoliberal global capitalism parallel the automated processes of the digital technologies upon which they are founded.

In Michel Foucault's theorization, neoliberalism extends the line of economic theory that stretches from Adam Smith's concept of the laissez-faire to the Chicago School (the origin of neoliberal economics) into the multifaceted arenas of everyday life. To wit, neoliberalism is a "massive expansion of the field and scope of economics" into "[e]verything for which human beings attempt to realize their ends, from marriage, to crime, to expenditures on children, [which] can be understood 'economically' according to a particular calculation of cost for benefit" (Read 2009, 28). Government "becomes a sort of enterprise whose task is to universalize competition and invent market-shaped systems of action for individuals, groups and institutions" (Lemke 2001, 197). In this neoliberal condition, the boundary between society and government, in the political-juridical sense, becomes porous as both domains are reconfigured by the influence of economic rationality and in this way subject to neoliberal governmentality, a concept Foucault deploys in order to explain "The ensemble formed by the institutions, procedures, analyses and reflections, the calculations and tactics that allow the exercise of this very specific albeit complex form of power, which has as its target *population*, as its principal form of knowledge *political economy*, and as its essential technical means apparatuses of *security*" (emphasis added, Foucault 1991, 192).

A crucial but little examined concept in Foucault's later work, *population* is grounded in the emphasis of a "common abstract essence" that allows each person to be thought of as equivalent to every other (Curtis 2002). A population allows for statistical analyses of patterns, trends, and rates. In this way population is both a "mass" of beings and a "purchase for concerted interventions (through laws, but also through changes of attitude, of ways of acting and living that may be achieved by 'campaigns')" (Foucault 1997, 70). In other words, population is the entry point of *economy*, the management of the "imbrication of men and things," into government (Foucault 1991, 92). It is this conjunction of population and economy that enables the rationalization of the relations between persons, goods, and resources that is essential to the "science of government" and the operation of apparatuses of security (Foucault 1991, 99). In contrast to the individual focus of disciplinary apparatuses, *security* is concerned with the employment of tactics that exploit the relations between things in order to create a milieu capable of generating a set of desired effects. An apparatus of security endeavors to apply economic principles, by undertaking the "rationalization of chance and probabilities," to manage and cajole the regularities of a population and suppress the aleatory (Foucault 2009, 59). Neoliberal governmentality, then, operates at a distance. With a thorough knowledge of the relevant objects and their relations to one another and the population, governmentality is concerned not with direct intervention, but rather with establishing the conditions capable of regulating the economy of a system—economic, political, cultural, and so on.

Studies of governmentality have tended in one of two directions—on the one hand the examination of purposeful actions on the part of the state and social institutions, and on the other hand the diffusion of neoliberal rationality throughout everyday life, which turns culture into a form of government (from an analytical standpoint). This necessarily entails an understanding of culture as discursive, or even rhetorical, rather than material. As "a distinctive set of knowledges, expertise, techniques and apparatuses which—through the roles they play as technologies of sign systems connected to technologies of power and working through the technologies of the self—act on, and are aligned to, the social in distinctive ways," culture is a "grid of intelligibility" (Biesecker 1995, 354). This is to say that people act in accordance to what makes sense in a particular situation given what they know and how they understand the probable effectivity of their possible actions. In this way, power governs; disciplinary technologies and technologies of the self, "which permit individuals to effect by their own means or with the help of others a certain number of operations on their own bodies and souls, thoughts, conduct, and way of being," operate in and according to the same neoliberal cultural logic (Foucault 1988, 19).

It is not my intention to suggest a causal relationship between the emergence of neoliberalism and the near ubiquity of computing and computational logic in the West. Nevertheless, these two cultural forces are integral components of any contemporary rhetorical situation, and constitutive of the subjects who would define it. And presumptions of causality aside, it would be naïve to disregard how neoliberalism and computational culture intersect and feed into one another. Indeed, David Golumbia's (2009) formulation of the cultural logic of computation as the belief that "something like *rational calculation* might account for every part of the material world, and especially the mental and social world" (1) is more than eerily similar to neoliberalism's mandate that economic logics encompass everything for which human beings attempt to realize their ends.

The Enthymeme and *Doxa*

Scant attention has been paid, in rhetorical studies, to the relationship between the enthymeme and *doxa*, even though the interworking of the two concepts is quite consequential. Indeed, the success of an argument from enthymeme is predicated on an appropriate reference to *doxa*. Within a constitutive theory of rhetoric premised on a logic of articulation (Biesecker 1989; Greene 1998), a successful argument from enthymeme signals that the discourse has either effectively constituted an audience or contributed to the entrenchment of a doxastic truth by appealing to its authority. This much is intimated in Michael McGee's (1975) article announcing the constitutive turn in rhetorical studies, in which he suggests a periodization of constitutive rhetorics that includes a phase in which the discourse becomes the uncontested basis for judgment and action. In this section, I offer an extremely condensed explication of the enthymeme, as it has been understood in rhetorical theory and criticism. I also discuss *doxa*, a term that has experienced a resurgence of interest in rhetorical studies over the past 30 years, (even though most of the writing on the topic took place in the 1990s). The concept of *doxa*, as I understand it, is vital to contemporary theorizations of rhetorical criticism and practice that attend to the materialization of subjects and the affective grounds of public identity.

I would be remiss to begin discussing the enthymeme with any text other than Aristotle's *Rhetoric* (1950). As James Allen (2001) explains, for the Sophists and even Aristotle's contemporary, Isocrates, the word enthymeme does not have the specific denotation that Aristotle ascribes to the term. In its most general sense, Isocrates uses the term to refer to a "consideration" and in its closest approximation to the Aristotelian construct, Isocrates describes a stylistically effective expression of thought (46). Aristotle, however, describes enthymemes as the "body of proof," and in deriding how others teach the non-essentials, asserts that enthymemes are the substance of persuasion and essence of rhetoric (I.I.3–4). Contrasting them to examples, which proceed by drawing a conclusion from a number of cases, Aristotle describes enthymemes as "rhetorical syllogisms," a form of deductive reasoning wherein a certain proposition being true dictates a second proposition must also be true in consequence (I.II.9).

These truths, however, are not necessary but contingent. That is to say, enthymemes do not deal with the necessary truths of science and logic but rather with the probabilistic truths of moral and political judgments. As G. Thomas Goodnight (1982) explains, rhetorical argument can only exist in spaces characterized by uncertainty. These are, furthermore, social rather than individual truths. "Rhetoric will not consider what seems probable in each individual case," Aristotle writes, "but that which seems probable to this or that class of persons" (I.II.11).

There is a wide consensus among rhetorical scholars, though not universally accepted (Conley 1984), that enthymematic arguments are not simply rhetorical syllogisms but also truncated syllogisms. Aristotle provides the basis for this thinking in writing: "The enthymeme [is] a kind of syllogism, and deduced from few premises, often from fewer than the regular syllogism; for if any one of these is well known, there is no need to mention it, for the hearer can add it himself [sic]" (I.II.14). Contemporary rhetoricians now take for granted, thanks to Lloyd Bitzer's (1959) work, that the truncation of the syllogism is in fact a co-construction between the speaker and audience. However, the extent to which this involves the audience is not settled. Aristotle provides the basis for a fairly conservative explanation of the audience's involvement: "[O]ne must not argue from all possible opinions, but only from such as are definite and admitted, for instance, either by the judges themselves or by those of whose judgment they approve" (II.XXII.3). This does not deter Jeffrey Walker (1994) from suggesting that the audience has a significant impact on the rhetorical interaction. He locates that influence in the invention, in what he describes as a "dialogic relationship between the writer and audience… requiring the writer to include the audience's thinking in the invention process rather than merely 'adapting' the discourse to the audience after the fact" (46–7). The truncation of enthymematic syllogisms, then, presupposes the audience's ability to supply the missing premise.

This, in turn, suggests that *doxa* is implicated in successful enthymemes. Like many terms in the rhetoricians' lexicon, *doxa* comes from the Greeks. Indeed, *doxa* is a term both employed by the sophists, Plato, Aristotle, and Isocrates, among others, but also disputed. Plato's (n.d./1927) reference to *doxa* as "mere opinion" in the *Gorgias* established the prevailing conception of the term in rhetorical studies. James Jasinski (2001) summarizes this conceptualization: "*doxa* refers to the realm of appearance, ambiguity, fluctuation, becoming, and (most importantly) opinion… *doxa* is commonly contrasted to the realm of episteme, a realm that emphasizes truth, knowledge, science, certainty and a fixed reality" (183). Rhetorical studies has endured a long infatuation with episteme, from early modes of criticism concerned with the truthfulness of address (c.f. Weaver 1953 and Campbell 1972) to the long debate inaugurated by and organized around

Scott's (1967) claim that "rhetoric is epistemic," which saw some scholars argue in favor of the epistemological proposition that rhetoric is a way of knowing (Cherwitz and Hikens 1982, 1983) and others for the abandonment of epistemic preoccupations altogether (Brummett 1990; Whitson and Poulakos 1993).

However, it was only at the tail end of the "rhetoric as epistemic" debate that rhetoricians began working in earnest to recover and rehabilitate *doxa*, focusing both on classical rhetorical conceptions of *doxa* and on the concept's utility for postmodern rhetoric.

The conceptualization of *doxa* that is most readily articulated to the enthymeme is the one deployed by Pierre Bourdieu and put forward by Raymie McKerrow. Bourdieu (1977), differentiating *doxa* from opinion, defines it as "that which is beyond question and which each agent tacitly accords by the mere fact of acting in accord with social conventions" (169). As McKerrow (1989) rightly notes, this implies a sense of concealment, and so he contrasts *doxa* not with episteme but *alethiea* (revealing). Thus, when McKerrow argues that a critical rhetoric "constitutes doxastic rather than epistemic knowledge" (103) he explicitly argues for rhetorical critics to do the work of making *doxa* into *aletheia* by "bringing the 'undiscussed' or concealed to the forefront" (105). This notion of *doxa* is readily connected to the enthymeme; it presumes a hidden idea or set of ideas that can act as an undisclosed premise for an argument.

Unfortunately, this formulation of *doxa* is trapped within a logic of representation and, as Robert Hariman (1991) argues, neglects the performed, lived dimension of *doxa*. Like Bourdieu and McKerrow, Marcel Detienne's (1999) study of the Archaic Greeks poets who preceded the Sophists leads him to an understanding of *doxa* as distinct from truths revealed through religious rites, *aletheia*. However, in contrast to Bourdieu and McKerrow, Detienne conceived of *doxa* as the active belief in something, as opposed to the passive acceptance of some reality decreed by a priestly authority (109). Takis Poulakos (2001) further develops this conception, arguing that Isocrates employed *doxa* not to pander to existing opinions but so as to constitute audiences and their identities. Isocrates' goal, Poulakos argues, is to bring *doxa* in line with *kairos* so that general cultural truths could be made relevant to arguments pertaining to specific situations (62). To wit, Detienne and Poulakos provide a basis from which we might draw an understanding of *doxa* as socially constructed truths that, as they become implicated in rhetorical address, do not simply reflect but also constitute their audiences' identity and culture.

This understanding of a mutually constitutive relationship between enthymemes and *doxa* is compatible with a logic of articulation. In this formulation, the "audience participation" an enthymeme requires (Jamieson et al. 1999, 13) does not simply draw upon preexisting doxastic truths but also repeats, (re)iterates and thus reaffirms a commitment to a certain cultural knowledge. Furthermore, the extent to which an enthymematic appeal "inscribes consensus" (Scenters-Zapico 1994, 71) is coterminous with its ability to (re)constitute a set of contingent relationships between subjects.

What then, is the status of enthymemes, and the *doxa* implicated in them, in the contemporary rhetorical context characterized by computational culture and neoliberalism? As indicated in the opening of this chapter, I have termed this situation a New Platonism. In the next section, I discuss New Platonism in greater detail, both explaining its relation to neoliberalism and computational culture and discussing how it exploits the typical relationship between enthymemes and *doxa*.

THE NEW PLATONISM IN THE RHETORICS OF DIGITAL GAMES

In this section, I illustrate how New Platonism operates in the discourses of communities organized around digital game play. My hope is that demonstrating the pervasiveness of this trope in this one area of digital culture will illuminate how it works in others. By starting from the discourses prevalent in game culture, I hope to be able to outline a vivid, grounded definition of New Platonism as a rhetorical form that derives the effectivity of its special enthymematic appeal to *doxa* from computational culture and neoliberalism.

The emergence of digital games from the basement (where a home console could literally be tucked away from sight and from the everyday life of a family, and where they had been metaphorically relegated as a geeky, juvenile pastime) in the mid-2000s was accompanied by a revaluation of game culture. In contrast to the figure of the alienated, overweight, and maladjusted gamer that dominated post-Columbine rhetoric, there emerged the figure of the gamer as intrinsically motivated problem solvers and high achievers (Beck and Wade 2004; Johnson 2006). Both of these discourses, however, made the critical error of treating games and game cultures as something radically distinct from mainstream culture. In fact, as Adrienne Shaw (2010) and Andrea Braithwaite (2014) have argued, it is vital that we understand game culture as imbricated in everyday life. To wit, I treat digital games as an exemplary site where the discourses and practices of neoliberalism and computational culture intersect, and which highlight the operation of NeoPlatonic rhetoric within the computational cultural milieu of neoliberalism.

Unsurprisingly, scholars studying game cultures have somewhat naively noted this pattern of discourse for some time, despite neglecting to examine its significance as a rhetorical form. Notably, I previously encountered this in my own analyses of the "rationalization" of play in turn-based strategy games (Voorhees 2008). In a paper examining *Sid Meier's Civilization* series I noted the tendency of players to study the rules of the game so as to minimize the expenditure of game resources and maximize the return of in-game rewards. As Soren Johnson (2006), lead designer for *Civilization III* and *Civilization IV*, explains: "The fun in *Civilization* often comes from imagining a plan, executing it, and then reaping the rewards. At every step, the fun works because the player understands what his and her choices are as well as their ramifications. Randomness just tends to muddy this process." Johnson's description of *Civilization* suggests that players derive pleasure not from the game *per se* but from how the game enables players to analyze every aspect of the game and discern how each aspect is related to and effects every other. Just as Wark describes a relation of sign to number and one number to another, "Postings on Apolyton.net and civfantatics.com outline detailed roadmaps for civilization building that… resemble a math problem" (Voorhees 2008, 267). This is not only the internalization of the logic of the program that Freidman writes about and which characterizes computational culture; this is also the condition of possibility for the rationalization of play.

However, this is necessary but not sufficient to the rationalization of play which is only accomplished through the discursive construction of the community of players. On websites and forums where people who play *Civilization* gather to discuss strategies, the discourse is predicated on analysis of the game and the relationships between various game elements. Chris Paul's work has closely examined this discourse in communities of players organized around *World of Warcraft*. Paul's analysis is grounded in the "explosion in the use of statistical analysis to facilitate understanding" of a variety of social phenomena and his discussion of the emergence of statistical analysis in baseball and other sports as a precursor to what he calls "theorycraft" in games. Describing theorycraft as a practice of "optimization," Paul traces its origins in digital games to communities of *Starcraft* players who would debate optimal strategies to playing and winning. At the heart of theorycraft is the analysis of the game rules and mechanics that enable a systemic understanding of the game and the relations between units within the game. But theorycraft goes further than analysis and embraces a neoliberal rationality by thinking those relationships through an economic logic in order to produce and optimal approach to play. That is, this information is mobilized to make claims about the 'correct' way to play, where correct is the outcome of the calculation of what is the most efficient and effective means to victory.

The "Strategies" page of the *Civilization* wiki hosted by wikia.com is exemplary not only for the *Civilization* community but for this discourse that is widespread in game cultures. Similar to other contemporary genres of digital rhetoric such as the listicle or the news feed, this wiki page presents its claims in a fairly straightforward manner, with little embellishment. In the first part of the document is the claim: "In the early game its [sic] most important for your city to grow." This claim, however, is premised on the unstated proposition that the player is motivated by the desire to minimize the expenditure of and maximize the return of resources. Another notable example comes from further down the page, from the section on "Basic Tech Order and Building." The wiki instructs readers:

> First thing you need to do is get Writing so you can construct Libraries in your cities. Then you head towards Philosophy so you can complete the National College in the city that's best suited for science (usually your capital [sic] or and expansion that's next to a lot of jungle tiles and a mountain). After that you have to get to Education to build Universities. After that, go for Acoustics to reach the Renaissance Era early and rush the Sistine Chapel.

These claims are not invalid. Rather, they simply fail, once again, to make plain all of the premises of the argument. These are the steps that will most quickly and effectively enable the player to gain the positon to dominate opposing civilizations both militarily and economically. In other words, these instructions presume that the reader is interested in economizing their gameplay.

In gaming and game cultures, this neoliberal attitude is enshrined by the most prominent communities of players, professional gamers, and power gamers. The hundreds who compete in professional e-sports, the thousands who play in online qualifiers, and the millions more who have embraced a sportive style of digital gameplay instantiate neoliberal rationality. The work of T.L. Taylor (2013) and Nick Taylor (2011, 2012) provide rich, deep ethnographic accounts of professional gaming, in which tactical thinking and skilled improvisation are integral elements of a competent player's judgment and action. By virtue of their practice regimens and long, studied engagement with the games played on the competition circuit, professional players know how to react to situations in ways that maximize their chances, however slim, of winning. As T.L. Taylor describes, players run scrimmage matches to not only refine existing skills but also to develop new skills. In these practice games, different possible responses, or counters, to effective strategies employed by the professional community, or even specific teams, are explored in order to research their effectivity. "Elite play," Taylor claims, "is interwoven with opening moves, set and known tactics, and a high dose of improvisation" which consists of employing learned skills to "maneuver dynamically based on the actual play situation at hand."

Elsewhere, in the context of massively multiplayer online role-playing games (MMORPGs), T.L. Taylor (2007) analyzed the neoliberal mentality in the instrumental play practiced in the community of power gamers. Unlike the engaged but unexamined gameplay of a casual player (Juul 2010), instrumental play is rationalized to achieve the most efficient return upon an action and is the product of a great deal of study of game footage, databases containing game data, and discussion forums. Though instrumental players and professional players are easily distinguished by whether or not they make a living from gaming and their degree of expertise and proficiency, they play many of the same games and apply the same economizing rationality in order to optimize the effectivity of their gameplay. Indeed, this mentality that games should be played and won as quickly and efficiently as possible is widespread in game cultures.

This is not an incontrovertible truth of gaming, however; it is a doxastic truth of certain communities of players. The instrumental style of play enabled by theorycrafting may be very common but many players play for fun. That is, people play games not simply to win, and sometimes not even to win at all. Within communities of griefers, people who play with the intent of disrupting the typical flow of a game, the pleasure of playing is not derived from winning but from artfully upsetting conventions (Snider et al. 2012). Players who migrated from the game *Uru* to other online games, the Uru diaspora, play in an improvisational manner, primarily to maintain their connections to one another and the sense of community that entails (Pearce 2009). Other communities of players are organized around their own equally idiosyncratic pleasures: creating challenges for each other within extant games; having aesthetically pleasing experiences; modifying games by adding new art, stories, and mechanics; or making machinima or other digital media using games.

What does this brief analysis of the discourses that pervades game culture illustrate? How do these claims about how to play, how to act, exemplify a New Platonism? They make plain that New Platonism is characterized by two qualities.

First is the presumption that there is only one possible correct outcome to ethical or political dilemmas that are typically open to deliberation. From a lay perspective, the question of how to interact with the game is either not a practical judgment or one with less weight than most political or ethical dilemmas, but from another perspective, one that takes seriously the discursive construction of reality and the act as an inauguration of identity, it is of no small importance. And in the example above and numerous other wikis and strategy guides, these practical decisions are treated as foregone conclusions. Likewise in digital culture more broadly, in countless posts on Facebook, Twitter, Reddit, and YouTube—the social media spaces that we turn to hoping to resuscitate the public sphere (Kushin and Kitchener 2009; Valtysson 2012)—and in the increasingly ubiquitous web tabloids like Buzzfeed, Gawker, Upworthy, and BoingBoing. Rather than a *dissoi logoi*, much less multiple possible ways of thinking through a situation and generating possible responses to it, the New Platonism admits only one logical outcome.

In this way, New Platonism is a topoi, however fallacious, in which a doxastic truth is treated as episteme. Despite the inherent uncertainty of all matters rhetorical, these claims are presented as if they were matters of fact. I argue that this is not simply a matter of the writers failing to recognize that they are making claims (as opposed to stating facts); rather, it is a matter of refusing to countenance that any other position might be valid. One need look no further than to those who support Donald Trump's presidential bid, best exemplified by Susan DeLemus's notorious performance during a CNN focus group in which she claimed that there are "people in positions of power who I know for a fact are liars... my President comes on the TV and he lies to me, I know he's lying. He lies all the time." Trump, she says, "is resonating with the people... he is speaking our minds." There is no room for difference of opinion between interlocutors in this New Platonism, just a centered subject and all those liars.

Second, only the logic of neoliberalism is an acceptable means of arriving at the truth. That is, the one possibility that is treated as a necessary truth is derived from an economizing calculation. In this way, the *doxa* implicated in a Neo-Platonic claim is not a subject-matter specific truth but rather is the trueness of a particular rationality. In game communities, this is the outcome of theorycraft: analysis produces understanding of the distinct units with the game and how they relate, which enables the formulation of an optimal pattern of play. In social media, this can be discerned retroactively. Like, shares, retweets, up votes, or comments generated, depending on the social network, provide a quantitative measure of truth. Meanwhile, a million "lifehacks" fill online tabloids, instructing readers how to do almost anything—from getting ready for work in the morning to cleaning a house to preparing low-calorie snacks—efficiently. Elegance, beauty, quality, personal growth, and any other value that interferes with speed and effectivity are bracketed for the sake of quantitative improvements in performance.

The application of neoliberal rationality to everyday life is possible because computational culture has created the conditions where any and everything can be quantified, where, as Wark reminds us, the relations between things can be converted to relations between signs and numbers, and from one number to another. The quality of a batch of cookies can be substituted for the quantity of cookies produced or the aesthetic pleasure of a delicious cup of coffee can be exchanged for minutes and seconds saved. Of course, someone must make the subjective decisions that give shape to the allegorithm. That is, someone or some group of people must do the work of theorycrafting, or in other contexts, of deciding how to measure and by what formulas to calculate the cost benefit analysis. And it's the work of making these subjective processes seem objective that computational culture accomplishes.

Conclusion

The New Platonism is everything that contemporary rhetorical theory is not. Neither artful, nor prudential nor civic minded; New Platonism has no model for how to practice rhetoric, but only an explanation of how it already, unfortunately, is. Instead of imagining what rhetoric should be, it is an effort to understand what rhetoric, as it is practiced in everyday life, actually is. And it is self-righteous and conceited. A wholly Cartesian practice, it entails arrogation of the speaker's *doxa* to *episteme*. And quite ironically, it is trusting. A naively decentered practice, it requires the presumption that the situation in which it is situated is necessary, even natural (in other words, a recentering of the subject).

More plainly, the New Platonism has two features: the unwavering faith in both a single right way forward and neoliberal rationality as the means to discover the truth. In the same year that the internet became a commercial communication medium, Walker argued that "since it is the epistemology/ideology of an audience that is in question" when an enthymeme appeals to *doxa*, "this approach then leads to some form of cultural criticism or to something like the ancient sophists' skeptical mode of inquiry into conventional belief" (47). In my analysis, this is decidedly lacking and, in fact, appeals to *doxa* are treated as statements of fact. Moreover, this New Platonism is uniquely enabled by the confluence of neoliberal governmentality and computational culture. Whereas neoliberalism provides the impetus to economize every decision, computational culture provides the pretense that everything can be quantified and submitted to calculation.

What do we have to look forward to in this era of New Platonism? Arrogance, unsubstantiated claims, and righteousness: a formula for divisiveness. And in this, perhaps, some glimmer of hope. New Platonism may be the communication style that fuels the operation of what Jodi Dean (2003) terms "neodemocracies." Looking for alternatives to the failure of the public sphere, Dean identifies "neodemocratic networks [as] contestatory networks," that "accept that democracy is animated by a split: they thrive on this split" and unlike the public sphere "[focus] on contestation instead of consensus" (109). A political model premised on the idea that not all viewpoints are equal and that acknowledges that the struggle is not for consensus but for hegemony, neodemocracy sounds like a relatively accurate description of civic life in democratic societies, "neo" only in its frank acceptance that this is the case. Perhaps it is best left for another paper to explore in full, but Dean's conceptualization of neodemocracy may also be a suitable description for the terrain upon which New Platonism is practiced.

References

Allen, James. 2001. *Inference from Signs: Ancient Debates about the Nature of Evidence.* Oxford, UK: Oxford University Press.

Aristotle. (n.d.)/1950. *The "Art" of Rhetoric*, trans. John Henry Freese. Cambridge, MA: Harvard University Press.

Biesecker, Barbara. 1989. Rethinking the Rhetorical Situation from within the Thematic of Difference. *Philosophy and Rhetoric* 22: 110–130.

———. 1995. Michel Foucault and the Question of Rhetoric. *Philosophy and Rhetoric* 2: 351–364.

Bitzer, Lloyd. 1959. Aristotle's Enthymeme Revisited. *Quarterly Journal of Speech* 45: 399–408.

Beck, John, and Mitchell Wade. 2004. *Want 'Tude With That?: How Gamers' Values and Skills Shape Their Professional Performance*. Cambridge, MA: Harvard Business Publishing.

———. 1968. The Rhetorical Situation. *Philosophy and Rhetoric* 1: 1–14.

Bourdieu, Pierre. 1977. *Outline of a Theory of Practice*. Cambridge, UK: Cambridge University Press.

Braithwaite, Andrea. 2014. 'Seriously, Get Out': Feminists on the Forums and the War(craft) on Women. *New Media & Society* 16(5): 703–718.

Brummett, Barry. 1990. A Eulogy for Epistemic Rhetoric. *Quarterly Journal of Speech* 76: 69–72.

Campbell, Karolyn K. 1972. Conventional Wisdom—Traditional Form: A Rejoinder. *Quarterly Journal of Speech* 58: 451–454.

Cherwitz, Richard, and James W. Hikins. 1982. Toward a Rhetorical Epistemology. *Southern States Speech Journal* 47: 135–162.

———. 1983. Rhetorical Perspectivism. *Quarterly Journal of Speech* 69: 249–266.

Conley, Thomas M. 1984. The Enthymeme in Perspective. *Quarterly Journal of Speech* 70: 168–187.

Crary, Jonathan. 2014. *24/7: Late Capitalism and the Ends of Sleep*. New York City, NY: Verso.

Curtis, Bruce. 2002. Foucault on Governmentality and Population: The Impossible Discovery. *Canadian Journal of Sociology* 27(4): 505–533. http://www.cjsonline.ca/articles/foucault.html. Accessed 30 Dec 2015.

Dean, Jodi. 2003. Why the Net is Not a Public Sphere. *Constellations* 10(1): 95–112.

Detienne, Marcel. 1999. *The Masters of Truth in Archaic Greece*. New York City, NY: Zone Books.

Foucault, Michel. 1988. Technologies of the Self. In *Technologies of the Self: A Seminar with Michel Foucault*, eds. Martin Luther, Huck Guttman, and Patrick Hutton Amherts, 16–49. Amherst, MA: University of Massachusetts Press.

———. 1991. Governmentality. In *The Foucault Effect: Studies in Governmentality*, eds. Graham Burchell, Colin Gordon, and Peter Miller, 87–104. Chicago, IL: University of Chicago Press.

———. 1997. Security, Territory and Population. In *The Essential Works of Foucault, 1954–1984*, vol I, ed. Paul Rabinow, 67–72. New York City, NY: The New Press.

———. 2009. *Security, Territory, Population: Lectures at the Collège de France 1977—1978*, ed. Michael Senellart, trans. Graham Buirchell. New York City, NY: Palgrave McMillan.

Friedman, Ted. 1999. The Semiotics of SimCity. *First Monday* 4. http://firstmonday.org/ojs/index.php/fm/article/view/660/575. Accessed 30 Dec 2105.

———. 2005. *Electric Dreams: Computers in American Culture*. New York City, NY: New York University Press.

Galloway, Alexander. 2006. *Gaming: Essays on Algorithmic Culture*. Minneapolis, MN: University of Minnesota Press.

Golumbia, David. 2009. *The Cultural Logic of Computation*. Cambridge, MA: Harvard University Press.

Goodnight, G. Thomas. 1982. The Personal, Technical, and Public Spheres of Argument: A Speculative Inquiry into the Art of Public Deliberation. *Journal of the American Forensic Association* 18: 214–227.

Greene, Ronald. 1998. The Aesthetic Turn and the Rhetorical Perspective on Argumentation. *Argumentation and Advocacy* 35: 19–29.

Hariman, Robert. 1991. Critical Rhetoric and Postmodern Theory. *Quarterly Journal of Speech* 71: 67–70.

Jamieson, Kathleen H., Erika Falk, and Susan Sherr. 1999. The Enthymeme Gap in the 1996 Presidential Campaign. *PS: Political Science & Politic* 32: 12–16.

Jasinski, James. 2001. Doxa. In *Sourcebook on Rhetoric: Key Concepts in Contemporary Rhetorical Studies*, 183–187. Thousand Oaks, CA: Sage.

Johnson, Steven. 2006. Everything Bad is Good For You. New York, NY: Riverhead Books.

Juul, Jesper. 2010. *The Casual Revolution: Reinventing Videogames and Their Players*. Cambridge, MA: MIT Press.

Kushin, Matthew, and Kelin Kitchener. 2009. Getting Political on Social Network Sites: Exploring Online Political Discourse on Facebook. *First Monday* 14(11). http://firstmonday.org/article/view/2645/2350

Lemke, Thomas. 2001. 'The Birth of Bio-politics': Michel Foucault's Lecture at the College de France on Neo-liberal Governmentality. *Economy and Society* 30(2): 190–207.

Manovich, Lev. 2002. *The Language of New Media*. Cambridge, MA: MIT Press.

McGee, Michael Calvin. 1975. In Search of 'the People': A Rhetorical Alternative. *Quarterly Journal of Speech* 61: 235–248.

McKerrow, Raymie. 1989. Critical Rhetoric: Theory and Practice. *Communication Monographs* 56: 91–111.

Pearce, Celia. 2009. *Communities of Play: Emergent Cultures in MultiplayerGames and Virtual Worlds*. Cambridge, MA: MIT Press.

Plato. (n.d.)/1927. Gorgias. In *Lysias. Symposium. Gorgias*, trans. W.R.M. Lamb, 247–533. Cambridge, MA: Harvard University Press.

Poulakos, Takis. 2001. Isocrates' Use of *Doxa*. *Philosophy and Rhetoric* 34: 61–78.

Read, Jason. 2009. A Genealogy of Homo-Economicus: Neoliberalism and the Production of Subjectivity. *Foucault Studies* 6: 25–36.

Rehak, Bob. 2008. The Rise of the Home Computer. In *The Video Game Explosion: A History from PONG to Playstation and Beyond*, ed. Mark J.P. Wolf, 75–80. Westport, CT: Greenwood Press.

Scenters-Zapico, J. 1994. The Social Construct of Enthymematic Understanding. *Rhetoric Society Quarterly* 24: 71–87.

Scott, Robert. 1967. On Viewing Rhetoric as Epistemic. *Central States Speech Journal* 27: 9–17.

Shaw, Adrienne. 2010. What Is Video Game Culture? Cultural Studies and Game Studies. *Games and Culture* 5(4): 403–424.

Snider, Evan, Tim Lockridge, and Dan Lawson. 2012. Challenging the Rules and Roles of Gaming: Griefing as Rhetorical Tactic. In *Guns, Grenades and Grunts: First-Person Shooter Games*, eds. Gerald Voorhees, Josh Call, and Katie Whitlock, 277–298. New York City, NY: Continuum.

Stephen, Bijan. 2014. You Won't Believe How Little Americans Read. *Time*, June 22. http://time.com/2909743/americans-reading/. Accessed 30 Dec.

Taylor, T.L. 2007. *Play Between Worlds: Exploring Online Game Culture*. Cambridge, MA: MIT Press.

Taylor, Nick. 2011. Play Globally, Act Locally: The Standardization of Pro *Halo 3* Gaming. *International Journal of Gender, Science and Technology* 3(1): 229–242.

———. 2012. 'A Silent Team is a Dead Team': Communicative Norms in Competitive FPS Play. In *Guns, Grenades and Grunts: The First-Person Shooter*, eds. Gerald Voorhees, Joshua Call, and Katie Whitlock, 251–275. New York City, NY: Continuum.

Taylor, T.L. 2013. *Raising the Stakes: E-sports and the Professionalization of Computer Gaming*. Cambridge, MA: MIT Press.

Valtysson, Bjarki. 2012. Facebook as Digital Public Sphere: Processes of Colonization and Emancipation. *Triple C: Journal of a Global Sustainable Information Society* 10(1): 77–91. http://www.triple-c.at/index.php/tripleC/article/view/312

Vatz, Richard. 1973. The Myth of the Rhetorical Situation. *Philosophy and Rhetoric* 6: 154–156.

Walker, Jeffrey. 1994. The Body of Persuasion: A Theory of the Enthymeme. *College English* 56: 46–65.

Wark, McKenzie. 2007. *Gamer Theory*. Cambridge, MA: Harvard University Press.

Weaver, Richard. (1953/1985). *The Ethics of Rhetoric*. Hermagoras Press, Davis, CA.

Weaver, Richard. 1955. *The Ethics of Rhetoric*. Hermagoras Press. Davis, CA.

Whitson, Steve, and John Poulakos. 1993. Nietzsche and the Aesthetics of Rhetoric. *Quarterly Journal of Speech* 79: 131–145.

Afterword

Bradford Vivian

Neoliberalism remains, at the time of this writing, a weirdly mundane yet occasionally shocking economic and political phenomenon that transects multiple registers of contemporary society. Neoliberalism constitutes, on the one hand, the relatively normal (and oftentimes unchallenged) economic and political ensemble responsible for: the current state of international monetary policy; excesses of corporate capitalism and increasingly unregulated financial markets; constant cycles of exorbitant political fundraising; the aggressive use of professional lobbyists wedded to private sector interests in order to influence all manner of public policy debates; the persistent degradation of labor unions; strategically instituted obstacles to social and environmental justice in numerous domains; systematic depredations to existing federal provisions for everything from the protection of minority rights to public education; and numerous other developments. A host of influential academics, economists, politicians, and scholars have promoted neoliberal programs for decades, thus rendering them now-ordinary features of contemporary social, economic, and political life.[1] Many of the chapters in this volume address significant aspects or entailments of such neoliberal programs, from questions of political power,

---

B. Vivian
Department of Communication Arts and Sciences
Pennsylvania State University
University Park, PA, USA

© The Editor(s) (if applicable) and The Author(s) 2017
K. Hong Nguyen (ed.), *Rhetoric in Neoliberalism*,
DOI 10.1007/978-3-319-39850-1

education, and humanitarianism to those of citizenship, technology, and consumerism.

Yet the broad and deep lineaments of neoliberalism occasionally produce, on the other hand, allegedly shocking (even destabilizing) outcomes. These outcomes appear all the more disturbing in light of the fact that neoliberalism is relatively uncontested by the public at large, despite its exacerbations of economic inequality and private-sector coopting of local, state, and national governance. Such allegedly unpredictable and shocking effects reveal, in turn, the dangerous threats to civil society and political stability that forms of neoliberalism engender. Many journalists and established politicians reacted to the 2016 presidential campaign of real estate mogul and television personality Donald Trump as if his frontrunner status throughout the Republican Party primaries represented a shocking, disturbing deviation from contemporary electoral conditions and populist sentiments, which no one allegedly could have foreseen (Applebaum 2016; Guo 2015; Kurtzleben 2015; Sherlock 2015; Singleton 2015). Such widespread professions of political and journalistic surprise belied the fact that Trump's candidacy—including the simmering anger, xenophobia, and anxiety among sizable voting demographics from which it fed—was enabled precisely by neoliberal values and agendas that the Republican Party (in addition to large sectors of US society) had aggressively promoted for a generation or more (Balz 2016; Barro 2016). Such values and agendas include radical distrust of federal government, uninhibited corporate financing of political campaigns, vilification of state regulations in favor of free market economic policies, and an institutional embrace of paranoias prevalent in specific voting demographics (especially among white male middle-class voters). Trump's candidacy was a quintessential, and entirely predictable, manifestation of intensifying trends that characterize neoliberal economic and political culture writ large in the early twenty-first-century USA. The financial collapse that led to the Great Recession of 2008, which many pundits, politicians, and economic experts also failed to predict, likewise dramatized the extreme potentialities of inherent flaws in neoliberal policies in the form of complex structural conditions rather than electoral politics.

One may observe the workings of neoliberalism, therefore, in mundane economic and political processes as well as in ostensibly irregular and disconcerting upheavals within established structures of power or influence. Hence the value of the present volume: the logic of neoliberalism has already reshaped the form and function of authoritative financial, governmental, and even moral institutions to an appreciable degree, thus acquiring a quasi-hegemonic ethos in various arenas of power; but neoliberalism also remains, in important ways, an emergent force within those institutions, rife with ideological or rhetorical inconsistencies and therefore eminently contestable. Rhetorical dynamics of neoliberalism do not apply to any one social, economic, or political sphere; rather, they coordinate and transect numerous financial, legislative, and judicial processes.

This afterword uses the incisive contributions in this volume as a justification for considering how rhetorical scholarship may help us to further identify, examine, and critique sundry forms of neoliberal economic and political discourse as well as their myriad social, legislative, and judicial entailments. Doing so requires a twofold inquiry into the rhetorical production or promotion of neoliberalism as well as the extent to which facets of neoliberalism oblige rhetoricians to amend existing frameworks of rhetorical theory and criticism. The following remarks suggest three especially productive thematics according to which one might pursue or extend that twofold inquiry, as prompted by the chapters in this volume: the changeable rhetorical dimensions of neoliberalism; the waning fortunes of the *res publica* in the era of neoliberal governance; and the emergent question of pluralism, or the *demos*, intrinsic to the prospect of political organization in the time of neoliberal power.

The fact that neoliberalism operates according to a wide spectrum of both consciously promoted as well as tacitly accepted economic or political conditions obliges rhetoricians to reflexively consider conventional methodological principles in their aim to study the rhetorical catalysts of neoliberal phenomena. The chapters in this volume provide valuable rationales and resources for assessing the degree to which the conventional tools of rhetorical theory and criticism are equipped to account for the rhetoric *of* neoliberalism as well as the rhetorical forms and functions *in which* neoliberalism consists. This distinction amounts to accounting for discourses *about* neoliberal policies as well as the discursive formations that *produce* neoliberal ideologies and material realities. Neoliberalism poses interpretive challenges for rhetorical scholars insofar as the forms of speech and symbolic action that promote it, and those forms of speech and symbolic action that neoliberalism inspires in turn, resist analytic reduction to conventional sources or media. Neoliberalism traverses formal political ideologies, class positions, national identities, religious or secular values, and social agendas. Rhetorical dimensions of neoliberalism may appear in either public controversies or institutional deliberations over school vouchers, gun control policy, political fundraising legislation, tax codes, environmental regulation, judicial nominees, hydraulic fracking, K-12 curricula, immigration reform, consumer protection laws, civil rights, commercial journalism, and more. The social, economic, political, and moral agents of neoliberalism—whether individual or collective—are therefore diverse; neoliberalism operates as a distributed network with multiple loci of power and influence—a confederacy of alternately coordinated and uncoordinated agendas, intersecting with and dependent upon multiple human as well as non-human forces (Chaput 2010; Connolly 2013; Greene 2004). The analyses of Phillip Goodwin et al. (Chapter "Accountable to Whom? The Rhetorical Circulation of Neoliberal Discourse and its Ambient Effects on Higher Education"), David Seitz and Amanda Tennant (Chapter "Constitutive Rhetoric in the Age of Neoliberalism"), and Jodi Dean (Chapter "The Psychotic Discourse of 9/11 Truth") all offer especially clear variations on this theme. No single type of debate, persuasive campaign, strategic argument, or rhetorical agent is responsible for neoliberalism, however much it encompasses many disparate debates, persuasive campaigns, strategic arguments, and rhetorical agents.

Neoliberal economic policies, political agendas, and sociocultural norms are the product of both conscious rhetorical appeals and regimes of discourse that often appear to unfold of their own accord. Where and how forms of rhetoric are implicated in the quasi-hegemonic status or further consolidation of neoliberal agendas is therefore a complicated question. Adherents to neoliberal philosophy, on the one hand, aggressively promote dramatic changes in institutions of governance, finance, law, and more. Rhetoric functions, in such circumstances, according to a logic of representation, or a conception of rhetoric in which power, ideology, and subjectivity, and the like are mediated through conscious linguistic strategies.[2] Prominent economist Friedrich Hayek, to cite one example, recognized that the cultivation and normalization of neoliberal market conditions required the promotion of neoliberal ideology in explicit terms (1976, 58).[3] Rhetorical critics may easily identify numerous and diverse spokespersons for various expressions of neoliberal thought and policy, whether in the form of notable public figures or ideological organizations. Mark Meister and Carrie Anne Platt (Chapter "Warren Buffett's Celebrity, Epideictic Ethos, and Neoliberal Humanitarianism") and Samuel Jay (Chapter "The Capable American: Ethos, Pathos, and the Governance of Education") incisively illustrate how such figures and organizations strategically promote neoliberal thought and policy according to the respective examples of Warren Buffet and the Obama administration. The rhetoric of relevant individuals and groups is explicitly available, as these authors illustrate, for critique according to principles of persuasion, argumentation, and the like. One may say that their statements fulfill representational roles for rhetoric insofar as rhetoric here denotes the instrumental use of language to shape institutional judgment, collective thought, belief, or behavior, and ideological patterns in general. A logic of representation is therefore fundamental to the many modes of rhetorical influence that have led to current neoliberal realities and which continue to enlarge their scope or intensify their effects.

But the aforementioned complexity of self-organizing neoliberal processes, which disrupt conventional role performances and stable ideological positions, shows that a representational logic of rhetorical influence fails to account in full for the myriad forms and effects of rhetoric ingredient to neoliberalism writ large. Advocates of, or spokespersons for, patently neoliberal agendas abound; such agendas are conceptually unified under the broad umbrella of neoliberalism because of shared investments in the dream of rationally self-organizing markets unimpeded by government regulations. But iterations of neoliberal thought and policy traverse formal role performances or conventional subject positions: Democrats and Republicans alike promote so-called neoliberal policies; various presentations of neoliberal values appeal to the wealthiest as well as the working classes and poor; the formative dimensions of neoliberal hegemony originate and circulate from within the private and public sectors alike; and faith in free market solutions at the cost of legislated non-interference with those markets spans a wide variety of nation-state borders, economic systems, and governmental apparatuses. Neoliberal hegemony, to the degree that it has taken root, is not the product of a unified social or economic movement, structural mode of production, or political mandate. Definitions of neoliberal priorities or concepts vary among its intellectual originators. Ideological proponents of policies and values that one may describe as neoliberal in character can operate in vastly different (if not disconnected) national, state, or local arenas.

Neoliberalism therefore offers a wide variety of rhetorical fronts for examination, which the full spectrum of chapters in this volume amply demonstrates. These rhetorical sites span strategic logics of influence as well as aleatory or autopoetic modes of articulation. Various economic and political configurations of neoliberalism evince a diversity of both human and non-human loci of agency, including forms of rhetorical agency, ranging from influential spokespersons or proponents for particular neoliberal policies to the allegedly apodictic discourses of rational markets and private-sector solutions to complex problems in lieu of pluralist deliberation. Neoliberal political or economic arrangements therefore challenge rhetoricians to remain self-reflexive about the specific probity and representativeness of claims that they make concerning the rhetorical production and elaboration of such widely varying arrangements. The putative rhetoric of neoliberalism, the preceding chapters demonstrate, is comprised of something like self-perpetuating and impersonal forces or dynamics (those of the allegedly rational market, of global capitalism, of corporate media) as well as consciously crafted suasory or argumentative campaigns. Jennifer Wingard's analysis (Chapter "Branding Citizens: The Logic(s) of A Few Bad Apples") of rhetorical assemblages that allow individuals to be placed in states of legal and political exception offers an especially evocative example of the former emphasis on self-perpetuating and impersonal forces or dynamics. The sum of the authors' contributions to this volume in general reflect the fact that rhetorical critiques of neoliberal economic and political formations may require different forms of reasoning and evidence, or require strategically circumscribed (if not qualified) claims about neoliberalism writ large, as compared to rhetorical critiques of economic and political orders more strictly delineated according to class ideologies, formal political affiliations, or established hierarchies of power.

If the putative rhetorical substance of neoliberalism is given to shifting sources, appearances, and degrees of personal or impersonal agency, then the political realm—or the *res publica* as such—is equally questionable in the era of neoliberal economic and political power. Neoliberalism functions notably according to patterns of deterritorialization and reterritorialization. Constant cycles of corporate fundraising significantly steer political elections; the political agendas of powerful ideological groups funded by wealthy private sector interests increasingly impact state and local legislative processes; omnipresent digital as well as consumer networks ensure that feedback loops abound between widely dispersed suburban, exurban, or rural spaces and massive urban centers, international markets, and the global information economy. Neoliberalism consists, to an impressive degree, in complexly organizing movements of deterritorialization and reterritorialization by which forces and logics of so-called free or rational markets and private-sector ideological interests reorganize public and political space.[4]

The public realm, as a space of pluralist speech and action, is not given to appear easily amid the ongoing deterritorializations and reterritorializations ingredient to neoliberal political and economic formations. Michael Hardt and Antonio Negri's analysis of so-called free markets indicates that neoliberal policies effectively confuse conventional distinctions between public and private domains as nation-state political systems become increasingly wedded to the fortunes of particular market configurations (2004, 167–168). "In the social," they explain, "the tendency is to make everything public and thus open to government surveillance and control; and in the economic, to make everything private and subject to property rights" (203). Hence, neoliberal forms of order diminish the public realm as a forum of speech and action to the degree that they render explicitly public arenas of political life subordinate to priorities of "government surveillance and control" while simultaneously recoding questions of rights according to economic calculi (as in now-familiar attributions of personhood and thus rights to corporations or in the use of corporate wealth and branding techniques to promote awareness of particular sociopolitical causes).

The concerns enumerated to this point rely on a definition of the political realm as a forum of speech and action. Portions of the present volume have demonstrated how neoliberalism functions according to the biopolitical management of societies or populations; one may contrast neoliberal biopolitics as such, which depends upon the disarticulation of pluralist speech and the active management of economic and political superstructures, with Hannah Arendt's account of the classical Greek (and especially Aristotelian) formulation of the *bios politikos*—the form of political life that fused speech with action in the person, in the very being, of the political actor as such. One may extrapolate a heuristic principle for assessing patently neoliberal separations of speech from action in Arendt's observation that, throughout the classical *polis*, "[t]o be political, to live in a *polis*, meant that everything was decided through words and persuasion and not through force and violence" (1998, 26). The force and violence that sublimates speech in neoliberal economic and political orders is both literal and metaphorical, diverse and distributed: applications of vast military power abroad intended to protect and enlarge interinvolved economic and political hegemonies; skillful manipulations of public opinion data through the professional media, and powerful lobbying techniques intended to create the appearance of deliberative support for such actions; technocratic managements of capital markets, global information networks, and legislative processes; expansions of corporate influence, in lieu of representative politics, over environmental policies, health and safety regulations, state and federal judiciaries, and public information; and dramatic enhancements of public surveillance as well as military-style police forces in the name of state security. The premise that neoliberal economic and political practices function biopolitically to denude *bios politikos* itself—to deterritorialize and reterritorialize iterations of the political realm as a forum in which "words and persuasion" rather than "force and violence" dictate action—suggests the severity with which neoliberal uses of power undermine the ideal of the *res publica*.

This claim regarding the diminution of the political realm, and of *bios politikos*, in the era of neoliberal power therefore holds acute significance for such rhetorical scholars invested in the critique of neoliberalism as those collected in this volume. Their combined efforts to document and delineate various manifestations of rhetoric amid neoliberal economic and political orders—whether those manifestations adhere to a logic of influence or of articulation, from the rhetoric *of* neoliberalism to the rhetorical forms *in which* neoliberalism consists—offer critical diagnostic resources. Such studies indicate the precise degree to which specific neoliberal formations indeed contribution to erosions of the political realm and, with it, political subjectivity (or the *bios politikos*). Gerald Voorhees' perception of a "New Platonism" in neoliberal milieus (Chapter "Computational Culture and the New Platonism in Neoliberal Rhetoric") speaks to such concerns. Many dimensions of neoliberalism are inherently talky. Pundits, technocrats, and economists debate the workings and allegedly supreme importance of financial markets on cable television ad nauseam; contemporary politicians' daily activities consist significantly in executing various communications strategies, much of it intended to support constant cycles of fundraising; corporations craft and market their goods and services according to the symbolism of consumer freedom, traditional moral values, and responsiveness to public concerns; and digital consumers daily use corporate-owned and administered social media for myriad and motley forms of grassroots advocacy. Talk, and a lot of it, is fundamental to neoliberal political and economic processes. The pressing rhetorical question is which forms of speech translate into action, of whose "words and persuasion" trump "force and violence," by Arendt's definition—or even, to extend the point, whether the words and persuasion of some (especially those who promote allegedly rational self-organizing markets and radical government deregulation) amount to a mode of force and violence that diminishes patently political speech.

Neoliberalism consequently poses the critical question, for rhetorical scholars especially, of how the political realm may be said to appear as a sphere of effective speech and action. Economic and political forms of neoliberalism appropriate and neutralize, or deterritorialize and reterritorialize, potent ideals, argument claims, and symbolic resources historically associated with petitions for individual equality and minority protections—from corporate sponsorship of civil rights commemorations and commercial appropriations of revolutionary history to definitions of corporations as persons with equal rights and invocations of religious freedom as a justification for state-endorsed discrimination against minorities. Neoliberal processes thus demonstrate with especial effectivity the Nietzschean principle that one may not effectively contest the harms and injustices that those processes engender by transcending them or by returning to some classical political and economic order; instead, tensions inherent to neoliberal dynamics of economic and political power can be profitably *intensified*, sped up or slowed down from within, repeated in ways that introduce destabilizing differences or lines of flight beyond. Connolly speaks to such themes of intensity and speed when considering how Nietzsche's cosmology provides principles of advocacy in the era of global neoliberal policies: "Given the more rapid minoritization of the world and the globalization of fragility since the time of Nietzsche, it is now even more urgent to forge a positive ethos of engagement between diverse and contending creeds" (2013, 174). Thus, the central rhetorical and political question of neoliberalism is also an *aesthetic* question to the extent that it requires one to reflect on how *the demos* may be said to appear in creative and destabilizing forms—and not as a symbolic iteration of the people, populist advocacy, or individual freedom instrumental to dominant logics of neoliberalism (such as the people understood as polling blocs, populist anger stoked by wealthy corporate interests, and freedom in the forms of consumer choices or rights of discrimination). "The *demos*," Jacques Ranciére posits, "is not the population, the majority, the political body or the lower classes. It is the surplus community made up of those who have no qualification to rule, which means at once everybody and anyone at all" (2010, 61). The *demos* is a political community in waiting, a virtual image radical democracy to come, the irreducible supplementary status of which invokes moments of *dissensus*, or forces of destabilization, within the ostensibly consensual, rational, and self-evident goods of neoliberal rule. It appears, by Ranciere's formulation, "only as a rupture within the logic of the *arkhê*" (41). The rhetorical and political emergence of the *demos* is an aesthetic question, in other words, because such emergence consists in the cultivation of new modes of political communication, collective symbolic expression, and democratic advocacy less susceptible to the ingeniously totalizing logics of neoliberal economic and political formations.

The notion here of the *demos*, as a political entity wedded to a commensurate vision of speech and action, signifies an emergent or virtual collective force. Neoliberal social, economic, and political discourses are steeped in traditional idioms or symbolic ideals of democratic values and individual freedoms; yet such discourses invert the original sense of those idioms and ideals in using them to support the alleged rationality of free market systems and expansive governmental deregulation of the private sector. This recognition—combined with the aforementioned fact that many varieties of rhetoric (ranging from instrumental logics of influence to self-organizing modes of articulation) support neoliberal economic and political processes—presupposes that the *demos* may not appear in the midst of those processes as an outcome of conventional efforts at public persuasion, ideological demystification, or grassroots advocacy alone. The contributors to this volume suggest how rhetorical scholars may further identity those discursive or symbolic conditions according to which the *demos* may emerge as an effective collective agent across multiple sites and according to multiple modes of rhetorical intervention. This premise is central to Robert Danisch's compelling reflections on the fortunes of rhetorical agency in the time of neoliberal power (Chapter "Rhetorical Agency in a Neoliberal Age: Foucault, Power, Agency and Ethos"). In the current era, Connolly maintains, "the drive to significant change must today be mobilized by a large, pluralist assemblage rather than by a single class or other core constituency" (2013, 188) precisely because of the intrinsic dexterity with which hegemonic neoliberal interests deterritorialize and reterritorialize potentially countervailing forces of reform, resistance, and destabilization. "Such an assemblage," Connolly continues, "must be primed and loaded by several constituencies at many sites. Role experimentations and the shape of a pluralist assemblage thus inflect one another" (188). A primary value of the contributions to this volume therefore consists in their collective capacity to help identify sources of pluripotentiality within diverse neoliberal economic and political formations—to diagnose conditions of potentially effective pluralist speech and action between and across myriad constituencies, material sites, and political arenas. Doing so may well help to identify rhetorical strategies that allow the *demos* to appear amid neoliberal orders of power, oriented according to a distributed vision of the *res publica* no longer beholden to the political model of the nation-state or classical *polis*. Such a distributed vision of the *res publica* would be but rooted, instead, in emergent questions of governance reflected in the activities of international markets rather than state agencies; in unceasing military interventions or police actions rather than democratic deliberation and electoral politics; and in the political potential of consumer practices rather than traditional union organizing alone. The preceding remarks, as well as the analyses collected in this volume, prove that neoliberal political and economic formations offer rhetorical scholars ample opportunities for searching out such potentially transformative sites and strategies.

Notes

1. Background works on neoliberalism (or financial and economic phenomenon relevant to it) include Aune (2001), Chaput (2010), Greene (2004), Hanan and Hayward (2014), Vivian (2006), and Wingard (2013). Relevant interdisciplinary scholarship includes Baldwin (1993), Campbell and Pedersen (2001), Comaroff and Comaroff (2001), Dardot and Laval (2013), Dean (2009), Duggan (2004), and McChesney (1999).
2. Greene (1998) helpfully synopsizes how the logic of influence continues to operate in rhetorical theories of materialism relevant to the *topoi* addressed in this volume.
3. Not all proponents of neoliberalism, however, shared Hayek's premise in this regard. Milton Friedman, most notably, was less sensitive to the need for ideological translation of the strict market principles that he advocated [see, for instance, Friedman (1993)].
4. Chaput (2010), DeLanda (2006), Greene (2004), Hanan and Hayward (2014), and Hardt and Negri (2000, 2004) offer analyses compatible with this claim.

REFERENCES

Applebaum, Yoni. 2016. Trump's Popular Appeal. *The Atlantic*, March 10. http://www.theatlantic.com/politics/archive/2016/03/republican-debate-miami/473307/. Accessed 12 Apr 2016.

Arendt, Hannah. 1998. *The Human Condition*, 2nd edn. Chicago: University of Chicago Press.

Aune, James Arnt. 2001. *Selling the Free Market: The Rhetoric of Economic Correctness*. New York: Guilford Press.

Baldwin, David, ed. 1993. *Neorealism and Neoliberalism: The Contemporary Debate*. New York: Columbia University Press.

Balz, Dan. 2016. How the Republican Party Created Donald Trump. *Washington Post*, March 5. https://www.washingtonpost.com/politics/behind-the-rise-of-trump-long-standing-grievances-among-left-out-voters/2016/03/05/7996bca2-e253-11e5-9c36-e1902f6b6571_story.html. Accessed 12 Apr 2016.

Barro, John. 2016. The Republican 'Establishment' Made Donald Trump's Nomination Possible. *Business Insider*, March 7. http://www.businessinsider.com/gop-establishment-created-trump-2016-3. Accessed 12 Apr 2016.

Campbell, John L., and Ove K. Pedersen, eds. 2001. *The Rise of Neoliberalism and Institutional Analysis*. Princeton, NJ: Princeton University Press.

Chaput, Catherine. 2010. Rhetorical Circulation in Late Capitalism: Neoliberalism and the Overdetermination of Affective Energy. *Philosophy and Rhetoric* 43: 1–25.

Comaroff, Jean, and John L. Comaroff, eds. 2001. *Millennial Capitalism and the Culture of Neoliberalism*. Durham, NC: Duke University Press.

Connolly, William E. 2013. *The Fragility of Things: Self-Organizing Processes, Neoliberal Fantasies, and Democratic Activism.* Durham, NC: Duke University Press.

Dardot, Pierre, and Christian Laval. 2013. *The New Way of the World: On Neoliberal Society,* trans. Gregory Elliot. Brooklyn, OH: Verso.

Dean, Jodi. 2009. *Democracy and Other Neoliberal Fantasies: Communicative Capitalism and Leftist Politics.* Durham, NC: Duke University Press.

DeLanda, Miguel. 2006. *A New Philosophy of Society: Assemblage Theory and Social Complexity.* London: Continuum.

Duggan, Lisa. 2004. *The Twilight of Equality?: Neoliberalism, Cultural Politics, and the Attack on Democracy.* Boston, MA: Beacon Press.

Friedman, Milton. 1993. *Why Government Is the Problem.* Stanford, CA: Hoover Institution of War, Revolution, and Peace.

Greene, Ronald Walter. 1998. Another Materialist Rhetoric. *Critical Studies in Mass Communication* 15: 21–41.

———. 2004. Rhetoric and Capitalism: Rhetorical Agency as Communicative Labor. *Philosophy and Rhetoric* 37: 188–206.

Guo, Jeff. 2015. The Real Reason's Trump's So Popular—For People Totally Confused by It. *Washington Post,* December 15. https://www.washingtonpost.com/news/wonk/wp/2015/12/12/the-four-basic-reasons-that-explain-why-donald-trump-actually-is-so-popular/. Accessed 12 Apr 2016.

Hanan, Joshua S., and Mark Hayward. 2014. *Communication and the Economy: History, Value, and Agency.* New York: Peter Lang.

Hardt, Michael, and Antonio Negri. 2000. *Empire.* Cambridge: Harvard University Press.

———. 2004. *Multitude: War and Democracy in the Age of Empire.* New York: Penguin.

Hayek, Friedrich A. von. 1976. *Rules and Order, vol. 1 of Law, Legislation and Liberty: A New Statement of the Liberal Principles of Justice and Political Economy.* Chicago: University of Chicago Press.

Kurtzleben. 2015. Surprised about Trump's Popularity? You Shouldn't Be. National Public Radio 10 December 2015. http://www.npr.org/2015/12/10/459207587/surprised-about-donald-trumps-popularity-you-shouldnt-be

McChesney, Robert W. 1999. *Rich Media, Poor Democracy: Communication Politics in Dubious Times.* Urbana, IL: University of Illinois Press.

Ranciére, Jacques. 2010. *Dissensus: On Politics and Aesthetics,* trans. Steven Corcoran. New York: Continuum.

Sherlock, Ruth. 2015. Why Is Trump So Popular? *The Telegraph,* December 9. http://www.telegraph.co.uk/news/worldnews/us-politics/12042218/Why-is-Donald-Trump-so-popular.html. Accessed 12 Apr 2016.

Singleton, Shermichael. 2015. Why Is Trump So Popular? *The Hill*, August 20. http://thehill.com/blogs/congress-blog/presidential-campaign/251463-why-is-trump-so-popular. Accessed 12 Apr 2016.

Vivian, Bradford. 2006. Neoliberal Epideictic: Rhetorical Form and Commemorative Politics on September 11, 2002. *Quarterly Journal of Speech* 92: 1–26.

Wingard, Jennifer. 2013. *Branded Bodies, Rhetoric, and the Neoliberal Nation-State*. Lanham, MD: Lexington Books.

Index[1]

NUMBERS AND SYMBOLS
9/11 attacks, 6
　truth, psychotic discourse of, 157–86

A
Abbot, J., 135–6
accountability, 17
　education, 18–25
　funneling, 30
　No Child Left Behind Act, 34n6
　statistics, 27
　transparency and, 10
Achbar, M., 135–6
affect, 56, 136
　assembling brands, 152n3
　branding, 143
　investments of, 141
　jouissance, 162
affective identification, 137, 139–40, 142, 144
affective labor, 8

Afghan civilians, 2, 148–50, 151n2
Agamben, G., 150
agency, 9, 33
　market, 29
　professional, 27
　rhetorical agency, 7–9, 11, 40, 42, 56, 57, 63–85, 93
aletheia, 197
Alexander, L., 23
Allen, J., 195
ambient rhetoric, 10, 16, 24
　from neoliberalism to common, reconstitution of, 31–3
　power of, 17
American economy, 6, 95
American neoliberal democracy, 84
American neoliberalism, 16
American "New Deal" liberalism, 92
American Recovery and Reinvestment Act (ARRA), 94, 95
American tax code, 41
American Theocracy (Phillips), 164
anti-neoliberal political theory, 110

---
[1] Note: Page numbers followed by 'n' refer to notes.

© The Editor(s) (if applicable) and The Author(s) 2017
K. Hong Nguyen (ed.), *Rhetoric in Neoliberalism*,
DOI 10.1007/978-3-319-39850-1

anxiety, 102, 140, 162, 163, 184
Apple, "Think Different," 120
Aristotle, 43, 77–81, 111, 189, 195–6
    definition of, 65–9
    dynamis and *techne*, 72, 75
    notion of rhetoric, 76
ARRA. *See* American Recovery and Reinvestment Act (ARRA)
Arvidsson, A., 140, 141
Ashcroft, J., 24, 168
Ashley, V., 171
assembling brands, 152n3
Athenian, 43, 79, 81
    democracy, 111, 113
    ideals and virtues, 112
Aune, J., 6, 7, 34n3
autonomous citizen/subject, 4, 12, 81
Avery, D., 167

B

Bales, R., 11, 137–9, 141, 143, 148–51
Banet-Weiser, S., 125
bare life, 115, 150–1
Barker, M., 41, 45, 59
Barrett, K., 169–71
Battle Hymn of a Tiger Mom, 3
Beaumont, P., 149
Bell, T., 21
Benjamin, W., 176
Bennett, W.J., 21–2, 34n5
Bentham, J., 64, 70, 159
"Big-T Truth," 111
Bill & Melinda Gates Foundation, 52–3
bin Laden, O., 165, 167
biopolitical, 8, 23, 28
    health of university, 10, 30
    labor, 7
    metrics, 26, 29, 33
    neoliberalism, 16
    production of life, 4
    rhetoric, 31
biopolitics, 17, 27, 31, 32. *See also* biopolitical
    Foucauldian analysis of, 16, 18
    Foucault's theory of, 56
    market statistics of, 25
Bitzer, L., 196
Bosanek, D., 40
Bourdieu, P., 197
Bower, J., 41
Braddock, case of, 121–7
Braddock Redux, 122, 124, 127
Braithwaite, A., 199
brand, 11, 59, 110, 121, 124–6
    citizens, 135–54
    of George Zimmerman as "bad apple," 143–6
Brooks, D., 164
Brown, M., 153n7
Brown, W., 4
Buba, T., 124
Buffett, W., 10, 39–59
Burke/Burkean identification, 31–2, 68, 112, 127n1
Bush, G.W., 2, 6, 24, 94, 100, 157, 158, 161, 163, 165, 166, 169, 171, 181, 182, 185
Butler, J., 17, 26

C

California Association of Teachers, 26
California State University (CSU), 10
    Board of Trustees Committee on Educational Policy, 25
    English Council, 26
    Mandatory Early Start Program (MESP), 18, 25–31
capital, 4, 39, 55, 56, 58, 140, 174
capitalism, 193

INDEX 227

acceptance and adoption of, 4
  communicative, 2, 12, 159–61, 163, 184, 185
  free-market version of, 41
  modern-day, 8
  subject of, 6, 7
The Care of the Self, 73, 74, 79
Carnegie, A., 41, 121
cartographic methodology, 10, 17
Castle Doctrine, 146
celebrity, 39–59
celebrity wealth, 47–9, 56, 57
Chaput, C., 6–8, 10, 42, 56, 57, 93, 95, 99
Cheney, D., 174, 181, 182
Chomsky, N., 40
Civilization (Johnson), 199–200
Clarke, R., 168
classical Aristotelian concept, 64
Clinton, H., 49
Cloud, D., 2, 45
commercial equality, 116, 128n9
communication, 77, 79, 93, 94, 99, 118, 175, 178, 180
communicative capitalism, 2, 12, 159–61, 163, 184, 185
communicative labor, 7, 8, 32, 93
computational culture, 12
  New Platonism in neoliberal rhetoric, 189–94
computational media, 191, 192
computers, 24, 190–2
"conduct of conduct," 92, 94
conspiracy theory, 163–6, 169
constitutive rhetoric, 195
  in age of neoliberalism, 109–30
  Braddock/Levi's case, 121–7
  neoliberalism's challenge, 113–15
  Rancièrian constitutive rhetoric, 115–21, 127, 129n15
  through ages, 111–13
consubstantiality, 47, 54–5, 68

contemporary rhetoricians, 196
cool hunting, 120
cooperative labor, 33
corporate behavior, 135, 136
  legality/ethics of, 42
The Corporation, 2, 135, 136
count, 11, 115, 118, 175, 177
Crary, J., 192
criminal justice system, 141
Crowley, S., 1
culture, 1, 23, 46, 53, 73, 164, 194, 197–202

D
Danisch, R., 10, 11
Dardot, P., 4, 113
Davidson, D., 175
Dean, J., 2, 11, 33, 93, 140, 142, 204
Dean, M., 91
decision-making processes, 8, 83
"Declaration of Independence," 81, 161
"Declaration of the Occupation of New York City" in 2011, 80, 81, 84
"Declaration of the Occupation of Wall Street," 81
de France, C., 91
DeLanda, M., 152n3
DeLemus, S., 202
democracy, 9, 43, 59, 81, 82, 84, 87, 159–61, 204. *See also* democratic politics
  neodemocracies, 204
democratic politics, 110, 113
democrats, 19, 89, 161
demos, 111–12
DeMott, B., 166
Depew, D., 12n1
Detienne, M., 197
Dewey, J., 79

digital games, 190, 192
    New Platonism in rhetorics of, 198–203
Dingo, R., 141, 152n3
Discipline and Punish (Foucault), 63, 69–71
dissensus, 115, 117–21, 123, 125, 127, 128–9n11, 128n5, 128n10, 159
dissoi logoi, 202
Dorell, O., 149
doxa, 190, 203, 204
    enthymeme and, 195–8
drive, 4, 42, 65, 68, 122, 160–3, 176, 181, 183
Duggan, L., 141
Duncan, A., 87, 88, 91, 96, 97, 99–103
dynamis, 43, 44, 64–9, 72, 75, 78, 79

E
ECIA. *See* Education Consolidation and Improvement Act (ECIA)
economic inequality, 20, 140, 142
economic philosophy, 6, 110
economic rationality, 191, 193
economic subject, 5, 6, 11, 12
economization of speech, 2
educational accountability, 18–25
Educational Testing Service (ETS), 24
Education Consolidation and Improvement Act (ECIA), 21, 24
Elementary and Secondary Education Act (ESEA), 18
Emergency Economic Stabilization Act of 2008, 94
English Placement Test, 25
enthymeme, 43, 190, 195–8, 204
Entrance Level Mathematics exam, 25
epideictic ethos, 10, 39–59

epideictic rhetoric, 42–5, 56
equality, 9, 18, 81, 110, 114–19, 128n4, 128n7, 129n12, 129n13
ESEA. *See* Elementary and Secondary Education Act (ESEA)
The Ethics of Rhetoric (Weaver), 189
ethos, 63–85, 87–104, 122, 124, 136, 137, 139, 143, 145, 147, 151
    epideictic, 10, 39–59
ETS. *See* Educational Testing Service (ETS)
Executive Order 1048, 25, 27

F
Falk, R., 171
Farrell, P., 171
Fetterman, J., 122–4, 126, 127, 130n19, 130n20
Fetzer, J., 161, 170, 172, 173
"financially distressed municipality," 122
Fleischer, A., 168
Foley, M., 2
Foucault, M., 5, 7, 8, 27, 28, 32, 64, 79–80, 89–92, 193
    and Aristotle, 80
    governmentality concept, 91
    homo economicus, 4
    neoliberalism, 16
    notion of governmentality, 76–7
    The Order of Things, 63
    on power and subjectivity, 69–76
    rhetoric, 10
    theory of biopolitics, 16, 56
    theory of power, 11
Frank, T., 152n4
free speech zones, 117
Freidman, T., 191, 192, 199
Friedman, M., 6, 20–3, 191
funneling accountability, 30

G

Galloway, A., 192, 203
game cultures, 198–202
gaming, 200, 201
Garn–St. Germain Depository Institutions Act (1982), 95
Gates, B., 49, 52, 54, 56
Gill, C., 68–9
Goodnight, G.T., 89, 90, 195
Goodwin, P., 10
governmentality, 4, 10, 74, 75, 91–3, 135, 190, 194
   characteristics of, 92
   Foucault's notion of, 76
   neoliberalism, 2, 6, 9, 11, 64, 67, 78, 79, 136, 139, 143, 190, 193, 194, 204
Gravois, J., 170
Great Recession, 87, 94, 97, 102, 110, 121–2, 125
Great Society, 18–25
Greene, R.W., 7, 8, 15, 17, 93, 99
Griffin, D.R., 170, 183
Grimaldi, W., 66

H

Habermas, J., 114, 174
Habermasian model of communication, 118
Hanan, J., 6, 7, 95
Harding, F., 48
Hardt, M., 8, 10, 32, 33
Hariman, R., 197
Hawhee, D., 1
Hawkins-Stafford Amendments, 24
Hayek, F., 6
Hayward, M.V., 47
health of university, biopolitical, 10, 30
Henderson, A., 34n4
Hesford, W., 139
Hicks, D., 93

high-quality education, 87
high school Early Start Assessment Program, 25
Hirschman, A.O., 34n3
The History of Sexuality, 63, 72, 73
Holmgren, G., 173
homicide rates, 154n10
homo economicus, 4, 9

I

identification, 32, 43, 45, 46, 52, 57, 58, 71, 110, 112, 114, 125, 128n2, 143
   affective, 137, 139, 142, 144
   Burke/Burkean, 68, 112, 127n1 (*see also* (consubstantiality))
ideographs, 11, 111
imaginary identities
   fluidity and adaptability of, 140
   fragile and mutable, 185
irony bribe, 2
Isocrates, 67, 111, 112, 195–7

J

Jamieson, K.H., 1
Jasinski, J., 196
Jay, S., 11
Johnson, L.B., 18–20, 33
Johnson, S., 199
Jones, S.E., 170–3
Jordan, S., 52
jouissance, 162, 169, 182
Jung, R., 34n4
justifiable homicides, 147

K

K-12 initiatives, 24, 26
Kennedy, J.F., 158, 170
Keynesian, 18, 141

"killer app," 192
King, M.L., Jr., 113
Kirn, W., 40, 42, 53
Korczynski, M., 48

L
labor, 7, 75, 142
  affective, 8
  communicative, 7, 8, 32, 93
  cooperative, 33
Lacan, J., 160, 162, 163, 173, 176–80
laissez-faire concept, 123, 193
Lauer, I., 43, 44
Lauren, R., 56
Laval, C., 4, 113
Levi Strauss, 110
  case, 121–7
liberal governmentality, 139
logic of articulation, 195, 198
logic of representation, 197
logos, 67, 91, 114, 116, 117
Loomis, C.J., 50, 57
"Loose Change," 167–9, 171
Lowenstein, R., 46, 53–5
Lyon, A., 127n1

M
made-it-happen-on-purpose (MIHOP), 158
Magna Carta, 113
Mandatory Early Start Program (MESP), 18, 25–31
Manovich, L., 191, 192
market agency, 29
marketing strategy, 141, 142
Martin, T., 2, 137–9, 141–8, 150, 151, 153n7, 153n9
Marx, K., 48. *See also* Marxist
Marxist, 7, 126

massively multiplayer online role-playing games (MMORPGs), 201
McArdle, M., 53
McCain, J., 164
McChesney, R., 40
McCloskey, D., 6, 7
McGee, M.C., 112, 195
McKerrow, R., 197
McLuhan M., 191
McNay, L., 4
Meister, M., 10
Michaels, J., 149
MIHOP. *See* made-it-happen-on-purpose (MIHOP)
Miller, K., 10
Miller, P., 91
Miller, T., 75, 77, 98, 102, 103
MMORPGs. *See* massively multiplayer online role-playing games (MMORPGs)
modern communicative technologies, 93–4
modern-day capitalism, 8
multimedia ad campaign, 110, 121
the multitude, 32

N
NAEP. *See* National Assessment of Educational Progress (NAEP)
Naqvi, J., 27
National Assessment of Educational Progress (NAEP), 22–4
National Council of Teachers of English (NCTE), 26
National Institute of Education (NIE), 19
A Nation at Risk, 22–4
NCTE. *See* National Council of Teachers of English (NCTE)
Negri, A., 8, 10, 32, 33
neodemocracies, 204

neoliberal age, rhetorical agency in, 63–85
neoliberal discourse, rhetorical circulation of, 15–35
neoliberal economic policies, 50, 190
neoliberal epideictic, 10
neoliberal governance, 11, 89, 91, 96, 97, 103, 104
neoliberal governmentality, 2, 6, 9, 11, 64, 67, 75, 78, 79, 136, 139, 143, 190, 193, 194, 204
neoliberal ideology, 47, 57, 109–10, 152n5
neoliberalism, 16, 17, 26–8, 30–3, 40–2, 55, 58, 59, 65, 77, 79, 89, 90, 92–5, 97, 99
  and computational culture, 190–4
  challenge of, 113–15
  constitutive rhetoric in age of, 109–30
  logic of, 15
  political economy of, 16
  rhetoric in, 1–12, 56
  techne in, 7
neoliberal marketplace, 18–25, 28, 32
neoliberal milieu, 25–31
neoliberal models, 32
neoliberal rationality, 6, 194, 200–1, 203–4
NeoPlatonic rhetoric, 199
networked communications, 12, 178, 184
Newman, K.M., 126
Newman, R., 47, 54
The New Pearl Harbor (Griffin), 170
New Platonism, 12, 189–204
  in rhetorics of digital games, 198–203
NIE. *See* National Institute of Education (NIE)

Nixon, R., 19
No Child Left Behind Act, 24, 34n6, 100
North American rhetorical criticism, 189

O

Obama, B., 11, 41, 87–8, 90–1, 94–103
Occupy Wall Street (OWS), 2, 10, 11, 79–85
Olbrechts-Tyteca, L., 44, 45
Omnibus Act, 21
Omnibus Reconciliation Act of 1981, 19
Ong, A., 153n6
Ong, W., 1
Open Society Foundation, 148
Open SUNY, 29
"Oracle of Omaha," 40
Oravec, C., 44
OWS. *See* Occupy Wall Street (OWS)

P

partisan educational policy, 88–9
pathos, 67, 87–104, 149
Paul, C., 199–200
Pear, R., 34n5
Pearson, J., 124
the people, 20, 32, 113, 117, 121, 125, 147, 159
Perelman, C., 44, 45
personal responsibility rhetoric, 141
The Phaedrus (Plato), 189
pharmakon, 136
Phillips, K., 164–5
Plato, 2, 111, 189–90, 196
Platonic, 189, 190
Platt, C.A., 10

police, 115–17, 119, 125, 127, 128–9n11, 128n7, 128n8, 137, 138, 143–5, 153n7, 164
police order, 115–21, 123
political economy of neoliberalism, 16
political identity, 114, 119, 123, 124
political moment, 119
political theory, 11, 75, 114, 121, 127
  anti-neoliberal, 110
  of Jacques Rancière, 11, 110, 114, 121, 127
population, 3, 9, 18, 21, 23, 24, 27–30, 74, 75, 92, 113, 140, 150, 191, 193–4
post-modern rationality, 189
Poulakos, T., 197
power, 7–9, 16, 17, 20–1, 48, 63–85, 92–5, 98, 109–12, 149, 150, 159–60, 162–4, 169, 171, 174, 176–9, 181–4, 191, 193, 194
  of biopolitical regulation, 28
  capitalism, 4
  of constitutive rhetoric, 123
  decentralized, 32
  disciplinary, 27
  negotiation, 6
  society and, 115
  theory of, 11
The Power of SUNY, 28, 30
Pratt, J., 43
Precarious Life (Butler), 17
Pritchett, H., 34n1
problematization, 91, 92, 94, 97
professional agency, 27
psychotic discourse, of 9/11 Truth, 157–86
psychotic media, 184–6
PTSD, 149
Puar, J., 151n1
public funds, 3

R

Race to the Top program, 87–92, 95, 96, 99, 103
Rancière, J., 11, 110, 114–23, 125, 127, 128n4, 128n5, 128n7–128n10, 129n12, 129n13, 129n15
rationality of governance, 92
"Ready to Work" campaign, 129n18
Reagan, R., 19–22, 95
Reed, C., 25, 27
Rehak, B., 192
Reichard, G.W., 25
relationality, 10, 65, 79–85
revitalization project, Braddock, 122
Reynolds, M., 172, 173
Rhetoric (Aristotle), 43, 65, 66, 69, 76, 189, 195, 196
rhetorical agency, 9, 11, 40, 42, 56, 57, 93
  communicative labor, 8
  in neoliberal age, 63–85
  rigid models of, 7
rhetorical assemblage, 11, 137, 138
rhetorical circulation, 8, 10–12. See also cartographic methodology
  of neoliberal discourse, 15–35
rhetorical power, 65–9, 75, 78–80
rhetorical scholars, 7, 8, 44, 93, 94, 98, 127, 196
The Rhetoric of Motives, 68
rhetoric scholarship, 93
Rice, C., 162, 168
Rickert, T., 16, 31
Robles, F., 137, 145
Rose, N., 91, 98
Rousseau, J.-J., 5
Rumsfeld, D., 168

S

Sandberg, S., 3
Santner, E., 160, 163, 173, 175–7, 180

SAT, 22
Schmitt, C., 159
Schreber, D.P., 175, 176, 178, 180
Schroeder, A., 46–8, 51, 54, 55
scientific and military culture, 191
Scott, R., 197
Scripps Survey Research Center-Ohio University, 157
Scythians, 119–20
Seamless Transfer, 25–31
security, 98, 162, 181, 191, 193
Seitz, D., 11
self-disciplined, 113
self-governance, 4, 89, 90, 102
sense-making structure, 90
shared value system, 109
shareholders, 42, 50, 136
Shaw, A., 3, 199
Sheard, C.M., 43–4
Shirazi, N., 148
Shoot First law. *See* Stand Your ground law
Silverstein, L., 168
skepticism, 158, 162, 163, 167, 173–80, 184
Smith, A., 6, 12n1, 193
social body, 115
social media, 5, 126, 202, 203
Sophists, 109, 111, 195–7, 204
Soros, G., 52, 58
Spears, B., 174
Spellings Report, 24
Stand Your ground law, 138, 144, 146–8, 154
State University of New York (SUNY), 18, 25–31, 34n2, 35n8
Strategic Plan, 18, 28–30
statistical accountability, 27
statistical analysis, 199
statistics, 1, 18, 27, 75. *See also* statistical analysis
market, 25, 32

Steele, J., 49
Stewart, M., 56
subject
of capitalism, 6, 7
classical, 64, 68, 69, 76, 80
of neoliberalism, 5, 6, 12 (*see also* (autonomous citizen/subject; economic subject; *homo economicus*))
psychotic, 163, 176
of right, 5
"subject-centered" concept, 68, 69
subjective anxiety, 140
subjectivity, 63–5, 68–78, 80–2, 84, 85
Sullivan, D.L., 42–7, 50, 52, 54
SUNY Council of Writing (SUNY CoW), 29, 30
symbolic efficiency theory, decline of, 140, 173–6, 179, 184

T
Tashjian, M., 34n4
The Task Force on College Quality, 24
Taylor, N., 201
Taylor, S., 3
Taylor, T.L., 201
techne, 66, 72, 75
in neoliberalism, 7
of rhetoric, 67–9, 76, 78, 79, 111
Tennant, A., 11
"terministic screens," 112
A Test of Leadership, 24
Order of Things (Foucault), 63
theorycraft, 199–201, 203
theory of biopolitics, 16, 56
theory of identification, 112
theory of power, 11
totalitarianism, 150
traditional rhetorical scholars, 8
transparency, 11, 33
and accountability, 10

tribal communities, 120
Trump, D., 26, 42, 202
Turner, T., 52

U
The Use of Pleasure, 72–4, 79
US exceptional protectionism, 136, 138
  collateral damage of, 148–50

V
violent events, 137
Vivian, B., 1, 44, 45, 65
Voorhees, G., 12

W
Walker, J., 196, 204
Wark, M., 192, 199, 203
"Warren Watch," 52–4
Washington Redskins', "Original
  Americans Foundation," 120
"We Are All Workers"
  multimedia ad campaign, 110
  slogan, 126
Weaver, R., 189, 196
The Well-Termpered Self (Miller), 77
Williams, R., 16
Winfrey, O., 52
Wingard, J., 11
Wood, J., 172, 173
Wynn, S., 56

Z
Zelikow, P., 162
Zimmerman, G., 11, 137–9, 141,
  143–51, 153n8, 153n9
Zimphor, N., 28, 29
Zinn, H., 170
Žižek, S., 140, 160–2, 173–7